The English Language:

A HISTORICAL READER

The English Language:

A HISTORICAL READER

A. G. RIGG

University of Toronto

Editor

New York: Appleton-Century-Crofts

Division of Meredith Corporation

ACKNOWLEDGMENTS

The Council of the Early English Text Society granted permission to reprint passages from *The Old English Heptateuch*, ed. S. J. Crawford, EETS 160, and Reginald Pecock's *Reule of Crysten Religioun*, ed. W. C. Greet, EETS 171.

The modern American translations of the Old Testament are reprinted from *The Bible: An American Translation*, by J. M. Powis Smith by permission of The University of Chicago Press. Copyright 1923, 1927, 1948 by The University of Chicago. All rights reserved. Published 1939. Fifteenth impression 1951. Composed and printed by The University of Chicago Press, Chicago, Illinois, U.S.A.

The Old English verse psalm and Boethius meter are printed from *The Paris Psalter and the Meters of Boethius*, ed. G. P. Krapp, Anglo-Saxon Poetic Records V (New York, 1932), pp. 72–73, 161–163, by kind permission of the Columbia University Press.

The modern versions of the psalms are from *The Psalms: A New Translation*. Published in the U.S.A. by The Westminster Press, 1965. © The Grail (England), 1963. Used by permission. These psalms are also printed by permission of Collins Publishers (London) and The Grail, and the Paulist Press, Glen Rock, N.J.

The extracts from Tyndale are printed from the *New Testament translated by William Tyndale*, ed. N. Hardy Wallis, by kind permission of the Cambridge University Press.

The modern versions of the New Testament are from: *The New English Bible: New Testament*. © The Delegates of the Oxford University Press and the Syndics of the Cambridge University Press, 1961. Reprinted by permission.

The extract from John Walton's translation of Boethius is from *English Verse between Chaucer and Surrey*, ed. E. P. Hammond, by kind permission of the editor and Duke University Press.

The modern versions of Boethius are from *Boethius: The Consolation of Philosophy*, translated by Richard Green, copyright ©, 1962, by The Bobbs-Merrill Company, Inc., reprinted by permission of the Liberal Arts Press Division.

The modern translation of Bede is from *Bede: A History of the English Church and People*, translated by Leo Sherley-Price, published by Penguin Books, Ltd. It is reprinted by kind permission of the publishers.

The following passages are reprinted by permission of the Clarendon Press, Oxford: *Selections from Gavin Douglas*, ed. D. F. C. Coldwell; *Earle of Surrey: Poems*, ed. Emrys Jones; *The Works of John Dryden*, ed. J. Kinsley; *The Homilies of Wulfstan*, ed. Dorothy Bethurum; *Paston Letters*, ed. Norman Davis; *Early Middle English Verse and Prose*, ed. J. A. W. Bennett and G. V. Smithers, with a Glossary by Norman Davis; *The Works of Sir Thomas Malory*, ed. E. Vinaver.

Passages are taken from *The Aeneid of Virgil*, translated by C. Day Lewis. Copyright 1952 by C. Day Lewis. Reprinted by permission of the Harold Matson Company, Inc. Also reprinted by kind permission of C. Day Lewis and the Hogarth Press, Ltd. (London).

The passage from *The Parker Chronicle*, ed. A. H. Smith, is reprinted by kind permission of Methuen & Co., Ltd.

To My Mother and Father

Preface

This book is the result of several years teaching the history of the English language, formerly in Oxford and more recently in Stanford. I have often found that students, having worked only from general histories, have lacked a firsthand acquaintance with the evidence on which the histories are based. My aim has been to provide texts that illustrate the general developments of English (particularly in the form of parallel versions of the same original), in the hope that students will be enabled to support their general observations with a full knowledge of the linguistic facts. The book is to some extent experimental. I shall be glad to receive criticisms and suggestions for any alterations or improvements designed to make it more useful to students of the history of the language.

I have to thank Professors Martin Evans and V. A. Kolve of Stanford for their painstaking reading of the Introduction, and for their many helpful suggestions. I am grateful to my students, past and present, for their intelligent curiosity and their enthusiasm for the subject. My wife, in this as in all else, has been a constant encouragement.

A. G. R.

ABBREVIATIONS

Abbreviations for parts of speech follow normally accepted practice: *n.* noun; *perf.* perfect; *pers.* person; *pl.* plural; *pr.* or *pres.* present; *prep.* preposition; *pt.* past or preterite; *sg.* singular; *subj.* subjunctive; *vb.* verb; etc.

EETS	Early English Text Society
KJ	King James *Authorized Version* of the Bible (1611)
ME	Middle English
MnE	Modern English
MS(S)	Manuscript(s)
NEB	New English Bible (1961)
OE	Old English
OED	Oxford English Dictionary
OF	Old French
ON	Old Norse
Vulgate	Jerome's Latin Bible (fourth century)
WS	West Saxon
>	becomes
<	comes from
*	an unrecorded but historically expected or predictable form

PHONETIC SYMBOLS

Only a few consonants and the basic vowels are given here. As it is impossible to find illustrations of sounds which will satisfy every speaker of the English language, I have tried to produce a list acceptable to most American students.

[æ]	*the vowel of* hat
[a]	*the vowel of* yacht (*general American pronunciation*)
[a:]	*the vowel of* father
[ɛ]	*the vowel of* bed
[e:]	*the vowel of* take
[ɛ:]	*the vowel of* stair
[ɪ]	*the vowel of* tip

[i:]   *the vowel of* lead (*vb.*)
[ɔ]   *the vowel of* off (*many American speakers do not have this vowel*)
[o:]   *the vowel of* dome
[ɔ:]   *the vowel of* awe
[u]   *the vowel of* bull
[ʌ]   *the vowel of* hut
[u:]   *the vowel of* moon
[ai]   *the vowel of* eye
[ɔi]   *the vowel of* oil
[au]   *the vowel of* house
[ə]   *the final syllable of* china
[tʃ]   *the consonant of* church
[ʃ]   *the initial consonant of* shall
[dž]   *the consonant of* edge
[θ]   *the initial consonant of* thin
[ð]   *the initial consonant of* then

OLD ENGLISH LETTERS

The OE letters þ and ð may both be used for either [θ] or [ð]; the letter æ has the sound [æ]. OE vowels may be short or long; the long vowels are printed with a "macron" (e.g., hāt). The letter ȝ in ME may correspond to MnE *y* (e.g., ȝelde 'yield') or *gh* (e.g., nyȝt 'night'). For a fuller account, see p. 19.

Contents

INTRODUCTION

PART ONE

PART TWO

Passages of original writing in Old and Middle English,
accompanied by modern versions

INTRODUCTION

Ye knowe ek, that in forme of speche is chaunge
Withinne a thousand yeer, and wordes tho
That hadden pris, now wonder nyce and straunge
Us thinketh hem, and yit thei spake hem so,
And spedde as wel in love as men now do.

Chaucer, *Troilus* II, 22–26

This collection of texts is the result of several years experience of teaching the history of the English language to undergraduates and graduates. I have found that students, although they read many general histories of the language, often fail to grasp the essential developments, and confess to feeling that they are working in a vacuum. I hope this present volume of illustratory texts will enable the student to observe for himself the constant changes to which the English language has been subject. In order to show how the book can be used, I have given a set of parallel translations of the Bible, plus a specimen analysis of the sort a student should aim to be able to make by the end of his course. Naturally, no one could expect to make so complete an analysis right at the start. The student should begin by studying one specific area of linguistic interest (e.g., vocabulary) in a general history, and should then apply this knowledge by making the kind of analysis given below. In teaching such courses, I find it convenient, because of the initially limited linguistic background of most students, to begin with an outline of the principal spelling differences between earlier and later English, and then to proceed immediately to vocabulary, a topic easily grasped without previous experience; after this, the study can move on to morphology (the modification of words by inflexion, vowel alterations, etc.), syntax, and word order. Phonology (the sounds of the language), if studied at all, should be taken last.

Although most sets of texts in this collection begin with a passage of Old English, a knowledge of Old English, or even of Middle English, is not necessary to make use of this book. The student with no previous experience of any early English (e.g., not even of Chaucer) may find it best, however, to confine himself at first to comparing the later versions and to omit the Old English, or even the Middle English. At the same time, by casting an eye back to the passages of early English, he should eventually

1

find that the Old and Middle English becomes less strange and difficult. I have provided at the end of this Introduction (pp. 34-35) a few aids to the reading of Old English, and at the foot of the pages of the text I have given a glossary of most of the Old English words.

The main purpose of this collection is to present texts that illustrate the changing possibilities of expression within the language, by showing how writers of widely differing periods coped with the same texts. The first section, I through XXI, consists of parallel passages, in which a common original lies behind each of the English translations. In some cases the originals may have differed slightly. For instance, in the passages from the Bible, the Old and Middle English translators used the Latin Vulgate of Jerome, whereas the Hebrew of the Old Testament and the Greek of the New Testament were used for the King James version of 1611 and the *New English Bible* of 1961. Essentially the same needs of expression had nevertheless to be met. The notes after each set of texts point out the main differences in source. The second section, XXII through XXXIV, consists of passages of Old and Middle English, from the ninth to the fifteenth century, all of which were written without any dependence on a text to be translated. These passages are accompanied by modern versions that have been written as idiomatically as possible in order to facilitate the same kind of comparison possible in the first section.

These texts are best used in conjunction with a more general history of the language, and with reference to the various grammars and specialized studies. It has not always been possible in this Introduction or in the Notes to explain the technical terms of linguistic study, or to go into any details on general topics. General histories of the language include: A. C. Baugh, *A History of the English Language*, 2nd ed. (New York: Appleton-Century-Crofts, 1957); T. Pyles, *Origins and Development of the English Language* (New York: Harcourt, Brace & World, 1964);[1] Simeon Potter, *Our Language* (Harmondsworth: Penguin, 1950). There are many other excellent histories of the same kind.

For the Old English period the standard grammar is by A. Campbell, *Old English Grammar* (Oxford: Clarendon Press, 1959). Introductory grammars for beginners include: N. Davis, *Sweet's Anglo-Saxon Primer* (Oxford: Clarendon Press, 1953); R. Quirk and C. L. Wrenn, *An Old English Grammar* (London: Methuen, 1955); G. L. Brook, *An Introduction to Old English* (Manchester: Manchester University Press, 1955). All these grammars give information on word formation, loan words, etc., as well as the standard grammatical material on inflexions and sound changes. The fullest

---

[1] The companion volume, J. Algeo and T. Pyles, *Problems in the Origins and Development of the English Language* (New York: Harcourt, Brace & World, 1966), provides many useful texts and interesting problems for students.

account of Old English word order and syntax is to be found in B. Mitchell, *A Guide to Old English* (Oxford: Blackwell, 1964), pp. 58–117, a book that is also very useful to the student who is working on his own.

The standard grammars of Middle English are in German. A book that covers both Old and Middle English is J. W. Clark, *Early English* (New York: Norton, 1964; first published by the Oxford University Press, 1957). Useful introductory grammars include F. Mossé, *Handbook of Middle English*, translated by J. A. Walker (Baltimore: Johns Hopkins, 1952); E. E. Wardale, *Introduction to Middle English Grammar* (London: Kegan Paul, 1937). Two very useful accounts of Middle English grammar in the early and later periods are to be found in J. A. W. Bennett and G. V. Smithers, *Early Middle English Verse and Prose*, with a Glossary by Norman Davis (Oxford: Clarendon Press, 1966), pp. xviii-lviii, an invaluable account of the early developments of Middle English, and K. Sisam, *Fourteenth Century Verse and Prose* (Oxford: Clarendon Press, 1921), pp. 265–292. The student of Middle English is very fortunate in having a really thorough work on syntax, which has relevance for the English language at all periods, T. F. Mustanoja, *A Middle English Syntax*, Part I "Parts of Speech" (Helsinki: Société Néophilologique, 1960).

The phonology of the early Modern English period is thoroughly treated by E. J. Dobson, *English Pronunciation 1500–1700*, 2 vols. (Oxford: Clarendon Press, 1957).

The following deal with specific topics: R. W. Chambers, *On the Continuity of English Prose* (EETS o.s. 191a, 1932); Norman Davis, "Styles in English Prose of the Late Middle and Early Modern Period," in *Les Congrès et Colloques de l'Université de Liège*, 21 (1961), 165–184, which answers many of the suggestions made by Chambers; M. S. Serjeantson, *A History of Foreign Words in English* (London: Kegan Paul, 1935); S. Ullmann, *Semantics: an Introduction to the Science of Meaning* (Oxford: Blackwell, 1962); G. H. Vallins, *The Pattern of English* (Harmondsworth: Penguin, 1957).

Constant reference should be made to the *Oxford English Dictionary* (OED). It is not only indispensable for any study of the history of words, but also provides useful information on syntactic problems (under words like *would, should,* etc.). It records all the spelling forms of any word as well as all morphological forms, and so may be used for reference on almost any point in the history of the language. On the etymology of modern English, the standard work is C. T. Onions, *The Oxford Dictionary of English Etymology* (Oxford: Clarendon Press, 1966). The standard dictionary of Old English is that generally referred to as "Bosworth-Toller." J. R. Clark Hall, *A Concise Anglo-Saxon Dictionary*, 4th ed., with Supplement by H. D. Meritt (Cambridge: Cambridge University Press, 1960), is adequate for most purposes. The new *Middle English Dictionary*, edited by H. Kurath, S. M. Kuhn, and J. Reidy (Ann Arbor, Mich.: The University of Michigan Press, 1956–) is still in progress.

HOW TO USE THIS BOOK

The purpose of this Introduction is not to replace in any way the full-length treatments in the books mentioned in the last paragraph, but to demonstrate how the book may be used, what particular points the student should look for, and how the information may be related to further generalizations about the development of the language as a whole. Below are printed four versions of Matthew 2: 1–15 on the attendance of the Magi at the Nativity;[2] they are taken from the Old English version of ca. A.D. 1000, the "Wycliffite" translation by John Purvey (late fourteenth century), the King James *Authorized Version* of 1611 (KJ), and the *New English Bible* of 1961 (NEB).[3] The *New English Bible* aimed at a translation "in which an attempt should be made consistently to use the idiom of contemporary English to convey the meaning of the Greek" (pp. viii-ix).

The passages are followed by a detailed comparison and analysis of their language; at the same time it has been necessary to indicate certain other features in the history of the language which, although they do not appear in these particular passages, may turn up in other selections. The analysis is divided into: Orthography, Vocabulary, Morphology, Syntax, and Word order — these terms and their applications are discussed fully below. All of these linguistic features need not be analyzed thoroughly for every set of texts in the book. The student may indeed wish to analyze some for their vocabulary, others for their morphology, and so on. Consequently, the length of the texts in the book has been varied for this purpose. On the other hand, one aspect of the language cannot always be isolated quite so easily; for instance, how can one consider syntax as completely apart from the inflexional system, or word order from syntax or morphology? At other times, a linguistic area can be subdivided conveniently for investigation; for example, morphology into the forms of pronouns, verbal endings, resolved verbs, and so on.

A few general observations need to be made about each of the topics.

---

[2] Other books on the history of the language have used a set of parallel texts such as this in order to illustrate the development of English: Algeo and Pyles, pp. 12–13, 77–78; Clark, pp. 15–29 (with analysis); Vallins, pp. 40–51 (on word order); C. Laird and R. M. Gorrell, *English as Language* (New York: Harcourt, Brace & World, 1961), pp. 55–62; see also R. Kaiser, *Medieval English: an Old English and Middle English Anthology*, revised (Berlin: Rolf Kaiser, 1961).

[3] For bibliographical details of these translations, see below, pp. 39-40, 75.

ORTHOGRAPHY[4]

The English spelling system is in origin phonetic; that is, it attempts to reproduce in spelling the actual sounds heard in speech. It does not, for instance, like some languages, use pictograms to represent meaning.[5] Late Old English[6] spelling became increasingly divorced, however, from pronunciation, and does not indicate certain sound changes known to have taken place within the Old English period. After the Norman Conquest, the Old English spelling system was radically modified by Norman scribes, with the result that it sometimes regained a degree of phonetic accuracy, though only in rare cases did scribes consciously devise a phonetic spelling. The variety of dialects[7] and the absence of any kind of "Standard English" throughout the Middle English period kept the spelling very fluid, and only in the fifteenth century did a widely accepted spelling system come into use. Even then the writing of one man might vary a great deal. The social importance of London and the invention of printing, however, helped to produce a degree of standardization. This newly "fixed" spelling reflected the pronunciation of English before several important sound changes, notably the Great Vowel Shift. The spelling of Modern English, therefore, bears an illusory resemblance to that of late Middle English, although the pronunciation is in fact quite different. The length of time since the "hardening" of the spelling system has meant that although the alphabet was originally phonetic, present-day spelling is in many respects far removed from any kind of phonetic "reality."

Texts can be used to illustrate this development, with the aid of a grammar that gives the sounds of English at any period. It is possible to isolate a single word, or set of words, which retain essentially the same spelling throughout English, and then to see how the pronunciation has changed. Conversely, sometimes the symbol representing a sound has changed, even though the sound has remained the same: the [ʃ] in MnE *shall* has been represented in OE by *sc*, *sce*, and in ME by *sch*, *sh*, *ss*, etc. Also of interest is the gradual disappearance from written English of certain letters (such as OE ð, þ, ƿ, Ð) and the emergence of others (such as *k*, which was rare in OE, and *z*).[8]

---

[4] The term "orthography" is generally used to include both spelling and the actual forms of letters.

[5] On the development of writing, see Pyles, Chapter II, pp. 21–49.

[6] On early and late Old English, see below, p. 11.

[7] See below, pp. 11-12.

[8] This book does not reproduce the OE flat-topped ȝ or the rune *"wynn"*; see below, p. 19.

VOCABULARY[9]

Many OE words have disappeared from our vocabulary, many of them by the time of ME. Some of them may have been lost because the things they denoted changed or vanished, others because they were pushed out by newer words. Most evident of all is the influence of other languages on the native vocabulary. First of all the Danish invasions and settlements of the ninth, tenth, and eleventh centuries contributed a large number of Norse words to the English lexicon, particularly in Northern dialects, from which many of them eventually entered Standard English.[10] The Norman Conquest of 1066 brought into English many words of Romance origin, first of all in a Norman form, and later from Central French[11] (the latter often from literary sources as well as from the spoken language). The consequent flexibility of English made it easy for it to adopt and to adapt many words directly from Latin, and ultimately from Greek, particularly in the language of science. All these influences on the vocabulary can be seen by comparing passages in a tabular fashion, as below. The emergence in ME of "phrasal" verbs, formed by verb + adverb (*set out, get up*, etc.)[12] is also of great importance.

In any analysis of the vocabulary one should use a dictionary of etymology and the OED, to see where a word came from, when it is first recorded (and in what sort of context), and what kind of vogue it enjoyed. In addition to the loss of old words (obsolescence) and the appearance of new ones (innovation, either from other languages, or by word formation), one should also note change of meaning (semantics), for words may become specialized in significance, or generalized, or simply changed, etc., and so become unavailable in their old senses.[13]

A writer or speaker is not, of course, limited solely to *words* he has seen or heard before. He has available (the extent depending on the linguistic conservatism of the period) a number of devices of word formation, such as the addition of suffixes (*-ly, -ness, -wise*, etc.) or prefixes (*un-, pre-*, etc.), or the making of compounds (e.g., *weekend, highball*). The language has always had such devices, though their nature has varied from time to time. OE, for instance, made abstract nouns by the addition of the suffix *-iþū,*

---

[9] It is normal for books on the history of the language to have full sections on the origins of the English vocabulary (e.g., Baugh, pp. 83–126, 200–227, 257–282; Pyles, pp. 323–352); the fullest treatment of the subject is by Serjeantson.

[10] See below, pp. 11-12.

[11] The distinction between the early borrowings from the French of Normandy, and the later borrowings from Paris, is not one of date alone: it accounts for such pairs as *catch – chase* (the *ca-* form from Norman French), and *war* beside French *guerre*. Forms in *oy* are a mark of late borrowing (as in *loyal* beside earlier *leal*, or *royal* beside *Real Tennis*). See Serjeantson.

[12] See particularly Bennett and Smithers, Introduction, pp. xxix–xxxi.

[13] See Ullmann, *passim*; Potter, pp. 104–116; Pyles, pp. 301–322. Almost all books on language have sections on semantics. Constant reference should be made to the OED.

and MnE has even used acronyms (*NATO, ANZUS*) as a source of new vocabulary. The student should be aware of these opportunities to writers of different periods.[14]

MORPHOLOGY[15]

By morphology is meant the study of those elements of the language which are used to extend or limit the meaning of a word, or to define its relation to other parts of a sentence. By the addition of the suffix -*s* to a noun we denote that it is plural (*dogs*) or possessive (*dog's*); the suffix -*ing* on a verb indicates the present participle or the verbal noun, the dental sound spelt -*t* or -*ed* shows that a verb is in the past tense (*walk–walked*); in OE the prefix *ge*-, later *y*-, was often used with the past participle. Such suffixes and prefixes are known as inflexions. The morphology of English also includes the declension of the pronouns (*he–him–his*, etc.). The distinction between strong and weak verbs is important. In Germanic languages, weak verbs are those that form their past tense by the addition of a dental suffix (*kiss–kissed*); the weak verbs also include many that now appear "irregular," such as *bring–brought, teach–taught, send–sent.* Germanic strong verbs form their tenses by variation of the root vowel ("ablaut, vowel gradation"); surviving examples in English include *ride–rode–ridden, choose–chose, swim–swam–swum, take–took–taken, grow–grew–grown.* The student with no knowledge of either OE or modern German, which is often a great help in the study of early English, is advised to consult a dictionary to find out whether a verb was originally strong or weak. Other topics covered by morphology will become clear in the following remarks and in the analysis below.

The contrast between OE and MnE is often expressed as that between a "synthetic" language, one that uses inflexions, vowel gradation, etc., and an "analytic" language, one that uses prepositions, auxiliary verbs, and a fairly rigid word order instead of inflexions. For instance, *Jack's dog* (synthesis) can be expressed by *the dog of Jack* (analysis); OE has no future tense distinct from the present, whereas MnE uses *shall, will*, etc.; the subjunctive is often expressed in MnE by auxiliary verbs such as *would, should, might.* In Latin the relationship of the words in *canis hominem mordet* is indicated only by the inflexions, whereas in MnE *dog bites man* depends on the word order. To push the contrast too far, however, is misleading. MnE does have many inflexions, and OE certainly made use of prepositions and some auxiliary verbs. OE also had its own conventions in word order, as we shall see. The contrast is simply one of degree.

---

[14] On the OE period, see Mitchell, pp. 52–57 — most OE Grammars have a similar section; on MnE, see Pyles, pp. 262–300.

[15] A concise account of OE and ME morphology is given by Clark, but all histories of the language give more or less full descriptions.

Features to which special attention should be given include loss of endings of various cases, loss of adjectival endings, disappearance of the declension of the definite article, disappearance of all verbal endings in the present, except for the present third person singular. The process of analogy can be seen in operation at all periods of English, since words whose declensions or conjugations are unusual tend to be assimilated to the pattern of the majority. For example, nearly all the distinctive noun declensions of OE eventually fell into the pattern of the -s plural type. Many strong verbs became weak: OE *wēpan* 'weep' was originally strong (past *wēop*), but even in the OE period began to acquire the dental suffix of a weak verb (MnE *wept*). The process of analogy was resisted only by words that were very common: e.g., *man, mouse, goose* (with their "mutated" plurals *men, mice, geese*), irregular verbs like *be*, the common auxiliaries like *can, will, may*, and common strong verbs (*sing*, etc.). The OE distinction between the singular and plural in the past tense of strong verbs (and in the present tense of a few verbs which conjugated like strong ones) also disappeared during the ME and late ME period. For instance, OE distinguished *hē rād* 'he rode' from *wē ridon* 'we "rid" '.

The development of some of the personal pronouns is very notable: the emergence of the form *she* (OE *hēo*), the eventual triumph of the Northern (originally Norse) *th*- forms of the third person plural pronoun *they, them, their* (OE *hīe, him, hira*, ME *hi* or *they, hem, here* or *hire*, etc.); the gradually increasing use of the second person plural pronoun *ye* for singular *thou* (the "plural of polite address"), and the replacement of *ye* by the originally objective form *you*.[16]

In considering "resolved" forms (i.e., those that employ prepositions instead of case endings, and make full use of auxiliary verbs), an attempt should be made, with the aid of the OED, to see how and why the resolving element came to be used; for instance, how *of* came to serve as a possessive, or how verbs like *will* and *shall* became future auxiliaries (originally they implied volition and obligation respectively), and how *would, should, might* developed as auxiliaries to form the subjunctive.

SYNTAX

It is more profitable to list eight topics that may be considered under syntax, than to attempt to give a definition.

1. The loss of grammatical gender, and its replacement by "natural" gender; for instance, OE *wīf* 'woman' is neuter. After the OE period, because of the disappearance of the declension of the definite article, gender can only be observed when a noun is referred to by a pronoun.[17]

---

[16] See Pyles, pp. 186–187, and the valuable set of illustrative examples of the *thou – ye – you* distinctions in Algeo and Pyles, pp. 190–194.

2. The use of originally interrogative pronouns (*who, which,* etc.) as relative pronouns, beside *that.* Attention should be paid to the possibility of omitting the object relative pronoun (e.g., *Have you lost the book I gave you?*) or, in ME only, the subject relative pronoun (e.g., *to bye hym a perle watȝ mascelleȝ* 'to buy himself a pearl [which] was spotless'[18]).

3. Analysis of adverbial clauses, particularly those of time, involves the opposition between parataxis (parallel clauses, as in *he came and he conquered,* or *Now you see it, now you don't*) and syntaxis (subordination, *when he came, he conquered*). The habit of subordinating elements of the sentence is not necessarily a MnE one — for example, in the passages below the subordinated construction of the King James is replaced in the New English Bible with a perfectly idiomatic parataxis. Attention should also be paid to the conjunctions that introduce adverbial clauses. An important feature of OE syntax is the use of "correlative" conjunction-adverb pairs, such as *þā . . . þā . . .* 'when . . . then . . . '

4. The complexities of conditional clauses include the way the *if*-clause (the "protasis") is introduced, which is sometimes by *if, and,* etc., sometimes by inversion (*had I known*), sometimes by a participle or verbal noun (*going there would be foolish*), or sometimes suppressed (e.g., *I wouldn't do it for a thousand bucks,* meaning, even if anyone offered me a thousand bucks); the use of the subjunctive, according to the degree of likelihood of fulfillment (e.g., *if you go there, you will see her,* beside *if you went there, you would see her*); negative conditionals (*unless-, although-* clauses, etc.).

5. Reported speech includes indirect statements, indirect questions, etc. The tense of the verb in the dependent clause should be observed. In OE the verb in the dependent clause is sometimes in the subjunctive. On the other hand, modern editors often doubt whether an OE or ME text intends direct or indirect speech. The end of XXII offers an example of where such hesitation has been felt.

6. One of the most marked features of MnE, from a historical point of view, is the use of the auxiliary verb *do* in the formation of questions and negative sentences: e.g., *do you think so?* for the earlier *think you?,* and *they did not go* for the earlier *they went not.* The emergence of this syntactical feature should be noted carefully and compared with earlier methods of expression. Its origin was in ME, where *do* was widely used with the infinitive in all types of sentences, particularly as an auxiliary to form the past tense (*he did go*), sometimes perhaps for emphasis, but often redundantly.

7. The change in meaning of certain prepositions is probably to be regarded as an aspect of syntax: e.g., OE *on* where MnE would use *in.* The

---

[17] The fullest account of the change from grammatical to natural gender is by Mustanoja, pp. 42–52.
[18] Example from Mustanoja, p. 205.

change in application of prepositions is remarkably great, and may be observed easily.

8. A feature of the language which is difficult to define is the use of introductory adverbs and conjunctions. Modern colloquial English, for instance, commonly uses *however* as a resumptive adverb (often with the sense "to get back to what I was saying"). English has used various adverbs in this way at different periods (e.g., *now*). OE often uses *sōþlīce* and *witodlīce* (literally, 'truly, definitely') in this more or less colorless way. The literalness of the ME (Purvey) version of the Bible makes it difficult to use for this purpose, in that it frequently renders literally the connectives *autem* and *vero*. The nonbiblical ME texts and the freely written passages are more fruitful in this connection. Modern literary English is very sparing in its use of such connective adverbs, but colloquial English has many.

WORD ORDER[19]

To say that OE has no fixed word order is incorrect; many combinations of words, such as the placing of the negative *ne* at the end of the sentence, to take an extreme example, were impossible. It was certainly more flexible, however, than that of later English; the gradual fixing of the word order in its MnE pattern should be noted. Some word orders were normal in OE, but later ceased to be acceptable. For example, the predominance of the order subject-verb-object was strong enough to make the regular OE order verb-subject after an adverb or adverbial clause, or the placing of the verb near the end of a dependent clause, unusual in later times. These two circumstances should be watched for in all versions. The early OE tendency to place "pronoun clusters" before the verb is also important. The placing of the negative changes from OE, where *ne* precedes the verb, to MnE, in which *not* always follows the verb or auxiliary verb. The reason for this is that *not* was originally an emphatic adverb which reinforced a preceding *ne*. OE was very prone to multiple negatives.

Some sequences have become firmly fixed in MnE for no immediately apparent reason. For example, we say *give John the book* or *give the book to John*, but never *give the book John*. The establishment of such "natural" orders should be noted. Other aspects of word order have already been discussed insofar as they concern inflexions, the use of resolved phrases with auxiliary verbs, and prepositions. In OE the word order can often be used to tell us which clause is dependent (with the verb near the end of the clause), but this is rarely the case in ME or MnE, except for rare phenomena such as the reversal of subject and verb to indicate a conditional clause, as in *had I known*. An established verb-subject order in MnE, of course, is in direct questions.

---

[19] See Vallins, *passim*, and, for OE word order, Mitchell, pp. 60–63.

Before we proceed to an analysis of the specimen texts, a few other points relevant to the history of the language need to be mentioned briefly.

EARLY AND LATE OLD ENGLISH

English prose had a long and continuous history throughout the Old English period. A distinction is regularly made between early Old English, that written before and during the Alfredian period (late ninth century), and late Old English, the most productive period of which is associated with the writing of Ælfric and Wulfstan (late tenth and early eleventh centuries). In this text XIII through XVII and XXII through XXV are "early," and the remainder, I through XII and XXVI, "late." Only XXIV, however, is written in a MS of Alfred's time, and the spelling of the other Alfredian pieces is therefore liable to show late Old English features. The distinction between early and late is necessary because of certain linguistic developments during the OE period. The word order became in some respects more like that of MnE. For instance, direct or indirect object pronouns often moved from their position before the verb to follow it. Because the spelling system throughout the OE period was conservative, many sound changes known to have taken place are not recorded in the spelling. Some short vowels, for example, were lengthened in OE before certain consonant groups, but this change is not shown in spelling until the ME period (e.g., OE *hund* 'dog,' lengthened and spelt *hound, hownd* in ME). Most important of all, vowels in unstressed syllables, particularly in inflexions, were weakened and reduced to an indeterminate [ə] sound; this weakening is illustrated by the occasional inconsistency or "error" in the spelling of an inflexion (e.g., dative plural in *-on* for expected *-um*, or present plural subjunctive in *-on* for expected *-en*). This loss of distinctive endings was made possible by the increased use of prepositions and the gradual fixing of the word order, both of which performed the grammatical function originally served by inflexions.

ENGLISH DIALECTS

All the Old English texts in this book are written in the West Saxon dialect, the language of the southwestern part of the country, that is, of the counties of Somerset, Dorset, Wiltshire, and Hampshire. In the ME period the political importance of Wessex was superseded by that of London and the surrounding counties, an area that in OE times had been partly Mercian, partly East Saxon, and partly Kentish. There is, therefore, no direct geographical linguistic continuity between the OE and ME texts in this collection. Fortunately for our purposes the dialect differences of OE, at any rate between West Saxon and non-West Saxon, were not very great (at any rate, in writing),[20] and the linguistic development of English

[20] The principal differences involve WS *ǽ* from Germanic *ā* (non-WS *ē*), and WS *ea* before *l* + consonant (non-WS *a*). MnE *old* comes from non-WS *ald*, not WS *eald*.

can be studied without an overwhelming fear that West Saxon is "irrelevant" to the later history of the language.

The widely divergent dialects of ME affect the use of this book in a somewhat different way.[21] The dialect boundaries of the country did not remain static; features of the language that were originally northern gradually moved southward, and many of them affected the dialect of London, the geographical ancestor of Standard English. When looking for the origins of modern Standard English, we must therefore consider not only geographical area, but also date. For instance, the two psalms by Richard Rolle (V and VI) contain features that are now part of Standard English, present third person singular in -s and third person plural pronouns *they–them–their*, whereas the Wycliffite Bible has present third person singular in -(*e*)*th* and *h*-forms for the genitive and objective cases of the pronoun. Some vocabulary also moved in the same direction, notably words of ON origin (e.g., *take*, which replaced OE *niman*, and *egg*, which replaced the OE form *æg*, ME *ey*).

This selection, although not intended as a sampling of English dialects, does include some texts that played no part in the linguistic or geographical continuum of the language, and therefore require some comment. XXVII was written at Peterborough in Norfolk, but its orthography has been greatly influenced by the OE (i.e., West Saxon) sections of the *Chronicle* which precede it. The *Sawles Warde* (XXVIII) was written in the West Midlands, and is an excellent example of the way in which OE developed in a more or less isolated area. We have already commented on the North Yorkshire dialect of Richard Rolle; even more northern, though later in date, is the Middle Scots of Gavin Douglas (XVIII through XXI). John Trevisa (XVI, XVII, and XXIX) was a Cornishman, but his language does not show any extreme southwestern dialect characteristics, and may be described as "southern." The Pastons (XXXII) were a Norfolk family, but the language of the letters tends to vary according to the education and ability of the writer — in this particular case, of the scribe who wrote Margaret Paston's letter for her.

INFLUENCE OF PRESCRIPTIVE GRAMMAR[22]

Until the eighteenth century the only grammatical restraints on a writer or speaker of English were those imposed by the usage of his own

---

[21] Brief accounts are given by Baugh, pp. 227–231, Clark, pp. 126–135.

[22] The most thorough account of the subject is by S. A. Leonard, *The Doctrine of Correctness in English Usage, 1700–1800* (Madison: University of Wisconsin Studies in Language and Literature, No. 25, 1929). See also Baugh, pp. 306–355; Pyles, pp. 190–194. There is an interesting collection of pronouncements by seventeenth and eighteenth century literary and linguistic scholars in Susie I. Tucker, *English Examined* (London: Cambridge University Press, 1961).

linguistic community (i.e., the people he wished to communicate with) or of writers whom he wished to emulate. In the eighteenth century, however, the study of philology flourished, and knowledge of, or interest in, linguistic subjects increased remarkably. This combined with the spread of education in the vernacular to produce a great number of grammatical textbooks for use in schools. The rules set forth by most of these grammars were based on a priori notions of how a language should behave; they attempted to prescribe rules of "good English" and to condemn what they regarded as "bad grammar." Frequently the rules of these textbooks were made according to linguistically irrelevant criteria, such as analogy with Latin, or Reason, which usually meant consistency, or etyomlogy. Modern philologists tend to reject all such rules of correctness,[23] and prefer to speak of "socially acceptable" rather than "correct" grammar. The rules of the eighteenth-century grammarians, however, had a tremendous vogue — many of them are still taught today — and must therefore be regarded as an important formative influence on the development of English. Even in their condemnation of prescriptive rules of grammar, modern scholars are bound by education and "educated usage" to follow many of the rules.

By a few examples we may illustrate these rules, which, along with some formulated later than the eighteenth century, illustrate the tendency towards linguistic prescription. Should we follow usage and say *It is me*, or grammar (i.e., Latin grammar) and say *It is I*? Common usage accepts, but prescriptive grammar condemns, the nominative case after a preposition in *between you and I*. A perennial problem is the "correct" case after *than* or *as*, in *He is bigger than I (me), He is as big as I (me)* — it is only ex post facto reasoning that argues either that *as* and *than* are prepositions or that we must understand *am* after *I*. Analogy with Latin argues that we should always use *whom* when it is governed by a preposition or is the object of the verb, but *who* is heard more often than *whom* in *Tell me who(m) you were with last night*. Associated with the last example, and perhaps arising from it, is the rule that forbids the placing of a preposition at the end of the sentence, a rule which gave rise to Sir Winston Churchill's well-known *reductio ad absurdum*, "This is the sort of English up with which I will not put."[24]

A totally unfounded distinction, still apparently being taught in some schools, was made between the use of *shall* (first person) and *will* (second and third person). One rule, based on an appeal to Reason, was totally successful for written English. It condemned the double negative (*We didn't go nowhere*) as a usage that "rationally" produced a positive (= *We*

---

[23] For a thorough discussion of the problem, see O. Jespersen, *Mankind, Nation and Individual from a Linguistic Point of View* (first published 1946; Bloomington, Ind.: Indiana University Press, 1964), Chapters V and VI.
[24] Cited by Sir Ernest Gowers, *The Complete Plain Words* (London: Her Majesty's Stationery Office, 1954), p. 139.

went somewhere). Modern British (but not American) English generally avoids split infinitives (*to quickly go),* despite the fact that they are often found in ME.

Many modern literary habits derive not from grammatical assumptions, but simply from a desire to avoid colloquialisms. These include the avoidance of abbreviated forms (*I'll, didn't, won't),* scrupulous care over consistency in verbal tense and number, the shunning of slang or dialect words however generally understood, etc. Linguistic parochialism in England often results in the disapproval of "Americanisms."[25]

SPECIMEN TEXTS

Matthew 2: 1-15[26]

Old English

Truly   when the Saviour   born   was   in   Jewish   Bethlehem,   in   the
1 Eornustlīce þā sē Hǣlend ācenned wæs on Iūdēiscre Bethleem, on þæs

king's   days   Herod's,   then   came   the   astronomers   from   East-part   to
cyninges dagum Herodes, þā cōmon þā tungolwītegan fram ēastdǣle tō

Jerusalem,   and   said   Where   is   the   Jews'   king   who   born   is?
Hierusalem, 2 and cwǣdon, "Hwǣr ys sē Iūdēa Cyning þe ācenned ys?

Truly   we   saw   his   star   in   east-part,   and   we   came   us   to   him   to
Sōðlīce wē gesāwon hys steorran on ēastdǣle, and wē cōmon ūs him tō

humble.   When Herod that   heard,   then became he   disturbed   and   all
geēadmēdenne." 3 Đā Herodes þæt gehȳrde, ðā wearð hē gedrēfed and eal

Jerusalem-people with him.   And then   gathered   Herod   all   leaders   of the
Hierosolimwaru mid him. 4 And þā gegaderode Herodes ealle ealdras þǣra

priests and people's   scribes,   and   asked   where Christ   born would be (or was). Then
sācerda and folces writeras, and āxode hwǣr Crist ācenned wǣre.   5 Đā

said they to him, "In   Jewish   Bethlehem;   truly   thus   is   written   by   the
sǣdon hī him, "On Iūdēiscere Bethlem; witodlīce þus ys āwriten þurh þone

prophet: 'And you Bethlehem   Jews' land,   certainly   not are you least in Judah
wītegan: 6 'And þū Bethleem, Iūdēa land, witodlīce ne eart þū lǣst on Iūda

[25] The relation of British to American English is discussed by Baugh, pp. 406–465; Pyles, pp. 217–261.
[26] On the presentation of the texts, see below, p. 36.

leaders; from you forth shall go the general who will care for my people Israel.'"
ealdrum; of ðē forð gǣð sē heretoga sē þe recð mīn folc Israhel' ".

Herod then called in private-speech the astronomers, and asked them
7 Herodes þā clypode on sundersprǣce ðā tungolwītegan, and befrān hī

eagerly when the star to them appeared. And he sent them to Bethlehem,
georne hwænne sē steorra him ætēowde. 8 And hē āsende hī tō Bethlem,

and thus said:
and ðus cwæð:

"Go and ask eagerly about the child; and when you it find,
"Farað and āxiað geornlīce be þām cilde; and þonne gē hyt gemētað,

tell later to me, that I may come and to him pray." When they the order
cȳþað eft mē, þæt ic cume and mē tō him gebidde." 9 Ðā hī þæt gebod

heard, then went they and truly the star which they in east-part saw
gehȳrdon, þā fērdon hī; and sōþlīce sē steorra þe hī on ēastdǣle gesāwon

them before went, until it stood over where the child was. Truly when the
him beforan fērde, oð hē stōd ofer þǣr þæt cild wæs. 10 Sōþlīce þā ðā

astronomers the star saw, (they) rejoiced very great joy.
tungelwītegan þone steorran gesāwon, fægenodon swȳðe myclum gefēan.

And going into the house they found the child with Mary its
11 And gangende intō þām hūse hī gemētton þæt cild mid Marian hys

mother; and they prostrated them, and to him prayed; and they opened
mēder; and hī āðenedon hī, and hī tō him gebǣdon; and hi untȳndon

their goldhoards, and to him presents brought, that was gold and incense and myrrh.
hyra goldhordas, and him lāc brōhton, þæt wæs gold and rēcels and myrre.

And they received answer in dreams that they back to Herod not turn;
12 And hī āfēngon andsware on swefnum þæt hī eft tō Herode ne hwyrfdon;

but they on other way to their kingdom went. When they then went then appeared
ac hī on ōðerne weg on hyre rīce fērdon. 13 Þā hī þā fērdon, þā ætȳwde

God's angel to Joseph in dreams and thus said: "Arise and take the
Drihtnes engel Iosepe on swefnum, and þus cwæð: "Ārīs and nim þæt

child and its mother, and flee to Egyptians' land, and be there till that I you
cild and his mōdor, and flēoh on Egypta land, and bēo þǣr oð þæt ic ðē

tell; future is that Herod will seek the child to destroy." He arose
secge; tōweard ys þæt Herodes sēcð þæt cild tō forspillenne." 14 Hē ārās

then and took the child and its mother in night, and went to Egypt; and
þā and nam þæt cild and his mōdor on niht, and fērde on Egyptum; 15 and

was there till Herod's death: that should be fulfilled which concerning God
wæs þǣr oð Herodes forðsīð: þæt wǣre gefylled þæt ðe fram Drihtne

spoken   was   by   the   prophet: "From   Egypt   I   my   son   called."
gecweden wæs þurh ðone wītegan: "Of Egyptum ic mīnne sunu geclypode."

Wycliffite (Purvey)

1 Therfor whanne Jhesus was borun in Bethleem of Juda, in the daies of King Eroude, lo! astromyenes camen fro the eest to Jerusalem, 2 and seiden, Where is he, that is borun King of Jewis? For we han seyn his sterre in the eest, and we comen to worschipe him. 3 But King Eroude herde, and was trublid, and al Jerusalem with hym. 4 And he gaderide to gidre alle the prynces of prestis, and scribis of the puple, and enqueride of hem, where Crist shulde be borun. 5 And thei seiden to hym, In Bethleem of Juda; for so it is writun bi a profete. 6 And thou, Bethleem, the lond of Juda, art not the leest among the prynces of Juda; for of thee a duyk schal go out, that schal gouerne my puple of Israel. 7 Thanne Eroude clepide pryueli the astromyens, and lernyde bisili of hem the tyme of the sterre that apperide to hem. 8 And he sente hem in to Bethleem, and seide, Go ȝe, and axe ȝe bisili of the child, and whanne ȝee han foundon, telle ȝe it to me, that Y also come, and worschipe hym. 9 And whanne thei hadden herd the Kyng, thei wenten forth. And lo! the sterre, that thei siȝen in the eest, wente bifore hem, til it cam, and stood aboue, where the child was. 10 And thei siȝen the sterre, and ioyeden with a ful greet ioye. 11 And thei entriden in to the hous, and founden the child with Marie his modir; and thei felden doun, and worschipiden him. And whanne thei hadden openyd her tresouris, thei offryden to hym ȝiftis, gold, encense, and myrre. 12 And whanne thei hadden take an aunswere in sleep, that thei schulden not turne aȝen to Eroude, thei turneden aȝen bi anothir weie in to her cuntrey. 13 And whanne thei weren goon, lo! the aungel of the Lord apperide to Joseph in sleep, and seide, Rise vp, and take the child and his modir, and fle in to Egipt, and be thou there, til that I seie to thee; for it is to come, that Eroude seke the child, to destrie hym. 14 And Joseph roos, and took the child and his modir bi nyȝt, and wente in to Egipt, 15 and he was there to the deeth of Eroude; that it shulde be fulfillid, that was seid of the Lord bi the profete, seiynge, Fro Egipt Y haue clepid my sone.

King James

1 Now when Jesus was borne in Bethlehem of Judea, in the dayes of Herod the king, behold, there came Wise men from the East to Hierusalem,

2 Saying, Where is he that is borne King of the Jewes? for we haue seene his Starre in the East, and are come to worship him. 3 When Herod the king had heard these things, he was troubled, and all Hierusalem with him. 4 And when he had gathered all the chiefe Priests and Scribes of the people together, hee demanded of them where Christ should be borne. 5 And they said vnto him, In Bethlehem of Judea: For thus it is written by the Prophet; 6 And thou Bethlehem in the land of Juda, art not the least among the Princes of Juda: for out of thee shall come a Gouernour, that shall rule my people Israel. 7 Then Herod, when he had priuily called the Wise men, enquired of them diligently what time the Starre appeared: 8 And he sent them to Bethlehem, and said, Goe, and search diligently for the yong child, and when ye haue found him, bring me word againe, that I may come and worship him also. 9 When they had heard the King, they departed, and loe, the Starre which they saw in the East, went before them, till it came and stood ouer where the young childe was. 10 When they saw the Starre, they reioyced with exceeding great ioy. 11 And when they were come into the house, they saw the yong child with Mary his mother, and fell downe, and worshipped him: and when they had opened their treasures, they presented vnto him gifts, gold, and frankincense, and myrrhe. 12 And being warned of God in a dreame, that they should not returne to Herode, they departed into their owne countrey another way. 13 And when they were departed, behold, the Angel of the Lord appeareth to Joseph in a dreame, saying, Arise and take the young childe, and his mother, and flee into Egypt, and bee thou there vntill I bring thee word: for Herode will seeke the young childe, to destroy him. 14 When he arose, he tooke the yong childe and his mother by night, and departed into Egypt: 15 And was there vntill the death of Herode, that it might be fulfilled which was spoken of the Lord by the Prophet, saying, Out of Egypt haue I called my sonne.

New English Bible

1 Jesus was born at Bethlehem in Judaea during the reign of Herod. After his birth astrologers from the east arrived in Jerusalem, 2 asking, 'Where is the child who is born to be king of the Jews? We observed the rising of his star, and we have come to pay him homage.' 3 King Herod was greatly perturbed when he heard this; and so was the whole of Jerusalem. 4 He called a meeting of the chief priests and lawyers of the Jewish people, and put before them the question: 'Where is it that the Messiah is to be born?' 5 'At Bethlehem in Judaea', they replied; and they referred him to the prophecy which reads: 6 'Bethlehem in the land of Judah, you are far from least in the eyes of the rulers of Judah; for out of you shall come a leader to

be the shepherd of my people Israel.' 7 Herod next called the astrologers to meet him in private, and ascertained from them the time when the star had appeared. 8 He then sent them on to Bethlehem, and said, 'Go and make a careful inquiry for the child. When you have found him, report to me, so that I may go myself and pay him homage.' 9 They set out at the king's bidding; and the star which they had seen at its rising went ahead of them until it stopped above the place where the child lay. 10 At the sight of the star they were overjoyed. 11 Entering the house, they saw the child with Mary his mother, and bowed to the ground in homage to him; then they opened their treasures and offered him gifts: gold, frankincense, and myrrh. 12 And being warned in a dream not to go back to Herod, they returned home another way. 13 After they had gone, an angel of the Lord appeared to Joseph in a dream, and said to him, 'Rise up, take the child and his mother and escape with them to Egypt, and stay there until I tell you; for Herod is going to search for the child to do away with him.' 14 So Joseph rose from sleep, and taking mother and child by night he went away with them to Egypt, 15 and there he stayed till Herod's death. This was to fulfil what the Lord had declared through the prophet: 'I called my son out of Egypt.'

NOTES

2   NEB offers the alternative 'Where is the king of the Jews who has just been born?', which is the OE translation also.
6   For 'least in the eyes of' NEB also offers 'least among.'
7   Note that the ME (Purvey) translates this somewhat differently.
15 In the OE *fram* can mean either 'concerning' or 'by'; both the ME and the KJ have the former, but the NEB implies 'by,' having put the verb into the active instead of the passive.

SPECIMEN ANALYSIS

Before beginning an examination of any particular aspect of the language of parallel texts, the student should carefully read through the preliminary remarks above, and through the following analysis. The tabular layout is probably the most useful starting point, but it is naturally less practical in the case of word order or some features of syntax. Sometimes an extra column may be needed — for instance, in the section on vocabulary I have used an extra column for "related words surviving in MnE" by the side of the OE column. It would be impossible to find texts that illustrate every aspect of the development of the language; I have therefore added comments on other things to be looked for, even though these passages do not illustrate them.

ORTHOGRAPHY

a) *Letter forms.* Three OE letters and one ME letter do not survive into MnE: OE þ, equivalent to later *th:* 5 OE *þus*, King James *thus;* 15 OE *þæt*, ME *that.* This letter was often used in other ME texts, and is sometimes found in early printed books as *y*, e.g., *y*ᵉ for *the.*

OE ð (capital Đ), also equivalent to later *th:* 6 OE *forð*, 9 ME *forth.* OE scribes did not distinguish between ð and þ, e.g., 2 *sōðlīce*, 10 *sōþlīce.* OE æ (capital Æ) produces several results in later English. Short OE æ̆ usually produces MnE *a*, e.g., 1 OE *wæs*, ME *was*, 15 *þæt*, ME *that;* very rarely it results in *e:* 7 OE *hwænne*, ME *whanne*, NEB *when.* Long OE ǣ (assuming that it remained long in ME) could produce *e, ea, ee:* e.g., 1 *Hǣlend* [MnE *healer*], 6 OE *lǣst*, ME *leest*, KJ and NEB *least*, 2 OE *hwǣr*, ME *where.* The reasons for this variation are to be found in the Germanic source of the OE ǣ or in later ME developments; shortened OE ǣ sometimes produced MnE *a* as in *Stratford.* The letter is found in early ME texts such as XXVII and XXVIII.

ME ʒ was used in OE MSS for *g* in all positions, and has not been printed in this book. In ME its usage was more precise; it is used either for the MnE sound *y*, e.g., 8 ME *ʒe*, KJ *ye*, or for the sound [h] after a vowel, as in 14 OE *niht*, ME *nyʒt*, KJ *night.* In some ME texts it is used where MnE would have *z.*

b) *Sounds and spellings.* The following table compares a few of the spellings for the same word:

	OE	ME	KJ	NEB
1	cyning(es)	king	king	—
2	steorra(n)	sterre	Starre	star
	ēast	eest	East	east
4	(ge)gaderode	gaderide	gathered	—
6	—	puple	people	people
5	(ā)writen	writun	written	—
	—	profete	Prophet	—
8	cild(e)	child	child	child
8	—	worschipe	worship	—
11	hūs(e)	hous	house	house
	—	ʒiftis	gifts	gifts
12	andsware	aunswere	—	—
	weg	weie	way	way
14	mōdor	modir	mother	mother
15	sunu	sone	sonne	son
	mīn(ne)	my	my	my

Purely orthographic features demonstrated by this list include the use of *k* to show [k] before a front vowel; the use of *ch* for [tʃ] instead of OE *c;* the use of a double consonant to indicate a preceding short vowel (*written*); the MnE use of *ph* for *f* (*prophet*); ME *ou* for the sound represented in OE by *ū* (*hous*); ME use of *o* for *u* to avoid confusion in writing with letters like *n, m, u* (*v*) in *sone.* Both *u* and *eo* in *puple, people,* indicate a rounded sound (as in modern French *heure*) in early ME.

Some changes in spelling are the result of changes in pronunciation: they include MnE *ar* in *star; d/th* alternation in *gather, mother; ʒiftis* beside MnE *gifts;* ME *aunswere* for OE *andsware;* the changes in *weg-way.*

The conservatism of English spelling will be readily observed if the assumed sounds of the words are written beside the words.

| 2 | east [ɛːə] | eest [ɛː] | east [eːɪ] | east [iː] |
| 11 | hus(e) [uː] | hous [uː] | house [ʌu] | house [au] |

NOTE: The student should beware of attributing any phonetic significance to variation between *i* and *j* (or *I* and *J*), which often depends on scribal or printing convention; similarly *u* and *v* vary in the King James version not according to pronunciation, as in MnE, but according to position in the word, e.g., *priuily, vnto.* The use of capital letters is also a printer's convention in origin.

VOCABULARY

The table on pp. 22–24 is the basis for any consideration of the development of English vocabulary, for loan words, word replacement, semantics, and so on. Such a list should include words that are carried through from OE to MnE, as this is a feature of the language fully as important as the loss of words. It should exclude prepositions and conjunctions, which come into a different category; unless there is any special reason for their inclusion, proper names should be omitted. In the following, words are not repeated after their first occurrence if the sequence of replacements, etc., is the same in every instance. It is useful to have an extra column after the OE showing any modern form that is derived from, or closely related to, the OE word.

Some words have continued through all versions, e.g., *king, star, sent, child, house, way, arise, night, son,* and others have been available at all periods, such as *ask, see.* It is important to remember that Purvey (ME) did not know the OE version, that the King James version made some slight use of the ME, and that the translators of the New English Bible by contrast, knew the King James very well. When considering the changes made in the vocabulary, constant reference should be made to the OED to see whether a word was available at the time of the translation — "available" here means "available in the sense required and without any undesirable connotations" as well as simply "existing in the language at the time."

The following OE words are not used in the ME version: *Hǣlend, ācenned, tungolwītega, (ēast-)dǣl, ge-ēadmēdan, ge-drēfed, ealdras, sācerd, wītega, heretoga, sundersprǣc, befrīnan (befrān), ǣtēowan* (or *ǣtȳwan*), *cȳþan, fēran, fǣgenian, gefēa, āðenian, untȳnan, lāc, rēcels, āfōn (āfēngon), hwyrfan, rīce, Drihten, engel, forspillan, forðsīð, reccan, swȳðe, gangan.* Many of these words did not survive long after the Conquest; some of them (e.g., *gang*) lived on in dialects but were evidently not the most acceptable to the ME translator. The following were extant in ME (some still survive) but were not used by Purvey: *cweðan* of which the past singular *quoth, quod,* is used by Chaucer; *writeras; folc; āxian* (used by the ME at 8), *georne* (the adverb is used by Chaucer), *faran, ge-mētan* (MnE would probably say *meet with*), *sōþlīce, myclum, goldhordas, brōhton* (from *bringan*), *swefnum* (frequent in Chaucer). The OE *engel,* which would have given MnE **engle* or **ingle,* is from Greek *angelos* (ἄγγελοσ), the source of the later borrowing *a(u)ngel* from French. Note that OE *ge-fylled* has been reinforced by *ful-* to produce *fulfilled.*

The use to be made of the OED may be illustrated by *ken* verb,[2] OE *(ā)cennan,* 'give birth to,' which occurs sporadically through the ME period; its last certain occurrence is in the late fourteenth century West Midland poem *Richard the Redeless.* OED records it in the *Towneley Plays* (MS of the fifteenth century), but the example is not certain; it was evidently only dialectal at the time of the ME Bible. All later versions replace *ācenned* by a form of *born.* The OED article on *bear* verb (42–43 and *born*) shows that the sense of bearing children derives from that of a tree carrying (bearing) fruit. It is first recorded in this sense in late OE, after which it quickly superseded the literal *ācenned.*

A few words are found in the OE and ME versions but not later: 7, 15, *clypode, clepide,* which survives later as a poetic archaism *yclept* 'named'; 8 *āxiað, axe* (MnE *ask*); 12 *andsware, aunswere* (MnE *answer*) translate Vulgate *responso.* The Greek New Testament seems to have had a word meaning "warned."

The ME replacements can be divided into (i) native words, (ii) foreign importations:

(i) *borun* (see above); *say,* etc. (OE *cweðan* occurred only rarely in late ME, except in the form *quoth, quod*); *worschipe* (this verb replaces the two OE reflexive verbs *ge-ēadmēdan* 'make one's *mōd,* heart, *ēad,* humble' and *ge-biddan* (OE had a noun *wurðscipe* but the verb is not found till 1200); *prestis* (OE *prēost* is itself a loan word); *lernyde; go* (8); *bisili* (the early uses of this word all involve the notion of anxiety); *han foundon; telle* (OE *tellan* had the sense 'reckon'); *wenten* (OE *wendan* 'turn'); *ful* (ME *swithe* has the sense 'swiftly'); *greet; felden doun; openyd; ȝiftis; offryden; turne aȝen* (for both *hwyrfdon* and *fērdon*); *weren goon* (OE could not have used this form); *Lord; deeth; sleep.*

	OE	[MnE]	ME	KJ	NEB
1	Hǣlend	[healer]	Jhesus	Jesus	Jesus
	ācenned	[cp. kin]	borun	borne	born
	dagum^a	[day]^a	daies	dayes	reign
	cōmon tō	[came]	camen to	came to	arrived in
	tungolwitegan		astromyenes	Wise men	astrologers
	Ēastdǣle	[-deal]	eest	East	east
2	cwǣdon	[quoth, bequeath]	seiden	saying	asking
	cyning	[king]	King	King	king
	ge-sāwon^b	[saw]^b	han seyn	haue seene	observed
	steorran	[star]	sterre	Starre	star
3	ge-ēadmēdenne, refl. vb.		worschipe	worship	pay homage
	ge-hȳrde	[heard]	herde	had heard	heard
	ge-drēfed		trublid	troubled	perturbed
	eal		al	all	the whole of
4	ge-gaderode	[gathered]	gaderide	gathered	called a meeting of
	ealdras	[aldermen]	prynces	chiefe	chief
	sācerda^c	[cp. sacerdotal]^c	prestis	Priests	priests
	folces	[folk]	puple	people	people
	writeras	[writers]	scribis	Scribes	lawyers
	āxode	[asked]	enqueride	demanded	put the question
5	sǣdon^d	[said]^d	seiden	said	replied
	āwriten	[written]	writun	written	—
	witegan	[cp. wit]	profete	Prophet	(prophecy)
6	ealdrum	[aldermen]	prynces	Princes	rulers
	forð gǣð	[goes forth]	go out	come	come
	heretoga		duyk	Gouernour	leader
7	recð	[reck]	gouerne	rule	(be the shepherd of)
	clypode	[arch. yclept]	clepide	called	called
	on sundersprǣce	[cp. asunder]	pryueli	priuily	in private
	befrān		lernyde	enquired	ascertained
	georne	[cp. yearn]^e	bisili	diligently	—
8	æt-ēowde		apperide	appeared	appeared
	āsende	[sent]	sente	sent	sent
	cwæð	[quoth]	seide	said	said

	Old English		Middle English		Modern English
	faraδ	[fare]	go	goe	go
	āxiaδ be	[ask]	axe of	search for	make a careful inquiry for
	geornlice		bisili	diligently	
	cilde	[cp. yearn]	child	yong child	child
	ge-mētaδ	[child]	han foundon	haue found	have found
	cȳþaδ	[meet]	telle	bring word	report
	cume	[come]	come	come	go
9	gebidde, f refl.	[bid]	worschipe	worship	pay homage
	þæt gebod		(the kyng)	(the King)	the king's bidding
	ge-hȳrdon	[heard]g	hadden herd	had heard	—
	fērdon		wenten forth	departed	set out
	on ēastdæle	[-deal]	in the eest	in the East	at its rising
	fērde		wente	went	went
	stōd	[stood]	(cam and) stood	(came and) stood	stopped
	wæs	[was]	was	was	lay
10	ge-sāwon	[saw]	siȝen	saw	(at the sight of)
	fægenodon	[fain]	ioyeden	reioyced	were overjoyed
	swȳðe myclum	[much, mickle]	a ful greet	exceeding great	
	gefēan		ioye	ioy	
11	gangende	[gang]	entriden	were come into	entering
	hūse	[house]	hous	house	house
	ge-mētton	[met]	founden	saw	saw
	āðenedon, refl.		felden doun	fell downe	bowed to the ground
	ge-bǣdon, f refl.	[bid]	worschipiden	worshipped	(in homage)
	untȳndon		openyd	opened	opened
	goldhordas	[gold-hoards]	tresouris	treasures	treasures
	lāc		ȝiftis	gifts	gifts
	brōhton	[brought]	offryden	presented	offered
	gold	[gold]	gold	gold	gold
	rēcels	[cp. reek]	encense	frankincense	frankincense
	myrre	[myrrh]	myrre	myrrhe	myrrh
12	āfēngon		(hadden) take	being warned	being warned
	andsware	[answer]	aunswere		
	swefnum	[sweven]	sleep	dreame	dream
	eft hwyrfdon		turne aȝen	returne	go back
	weg	[way]	weie	way	way

OE	[MnE]	ME	KJ	NEB
rīce	[cp. bishopric]	cuntrey	countrey	home
fērdon		turneden aȝen	departed	returned
13 fērdon		weren goon	were departed	had gone
ætȳwde		apperide	appeareth	appeared
Drihtnes		Lord	Lord	Lord
engel	[cp. angel]	aungel	Angel	angel
ārīs	[arise]	rise vp	arise	rise up
nim	[cp. nimble, numb]	take	take	take
mōdor	[mother]	modir	mother	mother
flēoh	[flee]	fle	flee	escape
bēo	[be]	be	bee	stay
secge	[say]	seie	bring word	tell
tōweard ys	[toward]	it is to come	—	
sēcð	[seek]	seke	seeke	search for
forspillenne	[spill]	destrie	destroy	do away with
14 ārās	[arose]	roos	arose	rose (from sleep)
nam		took	tooke	taking
on niht	[night]	bi nyȝt	by night	by night
fērde		wente	departed	went away
15 wæs	[was]	was	was	stayed
forðsīð		deeth	death	death
ge-fylled	[filled]	fulfillid	fulfilled	(to) fulfill
ge-cweden	[cp. bequeath]	seid	spoken	(declared)
wītegan	[cp. wit]	profete	Prophet	prophet
sunu	[son]	sone	sonne	son
ge-clypode	[yclept]	clepid	called	called

a MnE *day* comes from OE singular forms with *dæg*(-); the OE plural *dag-* produced ME *dawe(s)*: compare *dawn* from OE *dagung*.

b MnE *saw* comes from the past singular *seah*.

c The OE word is from Latin, as is *sacerdotal*, but the latter is an independent borrowing made much later.

d MnE *said* comes from the earlier OE *sægd(on)*, of which *sǣd(on)* is a development; present *say* comes from forms with postvocalic *g*, such as present third person singular *segð*, past *sægde*.

e MnE *yearn* comes directly from OE verb *giernan*, non-West Saxon *gernan*.

f OE *biddan-bæd-bǣdon-beden*, class V, with weak present.

g MnE *hear(d)* comes from non-West Saxon *hēran* (West Saxon *hīeran, hȳran*).

(ii) *astromyenes, trublid, prynces, scribis, puple, enqueride, profete, duyk, gouerne, pryueli, apperide, ioyeden, ioye, entriden, tresouris, encense, cuntrey, destrie, aungel* (see above on OE *engel*); all of these words are from French except perhaps *scribis,* which could be directly from Latin *scriba.* ON *taka* has replaced both *āfēngon* (from *āfōn*) and *niman.*

The distinction between native and foreign is perhaps less worth making in 1611, but some words introduced during ME possibly took a long time to be accepted as native. The same division is followed:

(i) *wise men, come* (6, for *go out,* Vulgate *exiet*), *called, bring word, were come into, saw* (for *foundon*), *being warned, dreame, spoken.*

(ii) *chiefe, demanded, gouernour, rule, enquired, diligently, search, departed, reioyced, exceeding, presented, frankincense, returne* (in which the French prefix *re-* replaces English *aȝen* 'back'), *destroy* (a later French form for earlier *destrie*). The *g* in *gifts* (ME *ȝiftis*) is from ON. Most of these words were in the language at the time of the Purvey translation.

Perhaps the most interesting replacements are those of the New English Bible. None of the words in the King James passage have dropped from the language, but many of them, now having a more or less archaic ring, were therefore "unavailable" to the translators of the New English Bible, whose aim was to approximate to "the idiom of contemporary English." Many alterations have been made through the syntax. The New English Bible replacements can be seen readily from the table. Their origin and date should be checked with the OED, but in many cases the New English Bible has simply made use of an idiomatic phrase or word that has been in the language for a long time (e.g., *arrive, perturb, observe*), sometimes going back to the ME translation (e.g., 11 *offered*). The tendency to use phrases of verb + noun is notable: e.g., *called a meeting of* (for *gathered*), *put the question, make a careful enquiry for. Pay homage to* replaces *worship,* which, according to the OED, had lost its secular sense of 'honour' (–1579), 'salute' (–1737), 'honour with gifts' (–1482). Stylistic motives (linguistically as important as any other motive) account for 9 *lay,* 13, 14 *stayed* (KJ *be, was*) and for 5 *replied* (KJ *said*). Modern connotations have been avoided by the substitution of *rulers* for *princes,* and *leader* for *gouernour.*

With the New English Bible the modern student is at an advantage. The translation is so recent that all the alternative forms of expression are easily known. In linguistic terminology, the translation can be viewed *synchronically;* that is, the resources of the language can be assessed without any historical reference, and alternative translations can be weighed against each other. For instance, for 13 *rise up* the translator could have used *get up,* or *set off* for 9 *set out.* One's aim should be to approach this enviable vantage point as nearly as possible for all periods of the language.

MORPHOLOGY

This section is divided into: A. Inflexions, including endings of nouns and verbs, declension of pronouns, conjugations of strong verbs, etc., and B. Resolved forms. This division, while fairly practical, is unreal, in that B is in many ways just an aspect of A.

A. *Inflexions*

i) *Nouns.* These passages do not give many examples of the simplification of noun declension. By the time of the ME passage all the features are those of modern declension (e.g., 1 *dagum, daies, dayes*), and none of the examples illustrate the loss of distinct noun classes. Note that foreign words conform to the common pattern of plural in -(*e*)*s*.

ii) *Articles, demonstratives, adjectives.* Again, as it happens, these passages do not show any interesting developments. The declension of the definite article has of course disappeared in the ME (for the implications for grammatical gender, see pp. 29–30), and the gradual emergence of the indefinite article is not illustrated. The OE declension of adjectives has disappeared (e.g., 4 *ealle*, 12 *ōðerne*). Other passages in the book should be examined for the forms of MnE *this–these, that–those*, etc.

iii) *Pronouns.* In analyzing personal pronouns, remember that OE distinguished the accusative and dative of *hē* (*hine–him*), *hēo* (*hi–hire*), *hit* (*hit–him*), plural *hī* (*hī–him*); the problem may be further complicated by the use of prepositions taking (in OE) accusative or dative. In ME and later, English had only nominative, genitive and objective (direct object, indirect object, or after prepositions). Care should therefore be taken when comparing the use of pronouns in parallel passages. An additional complication may be the loss of grammatical gender in favor of natural gender (*steorra, cild*).

			OE		ME		KJ		NEB
15	1 sg. nom.		ic		Y		I		I
6	1 sg. poss.		mīn (neut.)		my		my		my
15	(adj.)		mīnne (masc.)						
6	2 sg. nom.		þū		thou		thou		you
6	2 sg. obj.	(of)	ðē	(of)	thee	(out of)	thee	(out of)	you
13	2 sg. dat.		ðē	(to)	thee		thee		you
3	3 sg. masc. nom.		hē	(4)	he		he		he
2	3 sg. masc. gen.		hys		his		his		his
3	3 sg. masc. obj.	(mid)	him	(with)	hym	(with)	him		—
2	1 pl. nom.		wē		we		we		we
8	2 pl. nom.		gē		ȝe		ye		you
5	3 pl. nom.		hī		thei		they		they
8	3 pl. acc.		hī		hem		them		them
7	3 pl. dat.		him	(to)	hem		—		—
9	3 pl. obj.	(before)	him		hem		them		them
11	3 pl. gen.		hyra		her		their		their
12	3 pl. gen.		hyre		her		their owne		—

This table shows that MnE replaces both the second person singular pronoun (in all cases) and the second person plural nominative by the originally accusative/objective second person plural form *you*. The gradual replacement of OE *h-* forms of the third person plural by ON *th-* forms is shown by ME and King James, where the former has *th-* in the nominative, but otherwise *h-*, whereas King James has *th-* forms throughout. On the declension of *hit* see below on grammatical gender. Although the genitive of *hit* does not occur in these passages, particular attention should be paid to it whenever it does: OE has *his*, and MnE *its*, but intermediate forms include *it* and the periphrastic *thereof* (see I, 15 *n.* and the references there). Note any occurrence of the possessive form such as *theirs*, *ours* and compare VIII, 3, where the ME has *herne* 'theirs.'

iv) *Verbs*. The possibility of resolved forms and the replacement of words makes this table somewhat shorter than it might be; a hypothetical table could be made to show what the MnE form of an OE verb would be if it had been used. In some longer passages it would perhaps also be advisable to classify the type of verb (e.g., strong, weak, irregular). Only recorded forms are included in this list.

		OE	ME	KJ	NEB
7	pt. 3 sg.	clypode	clepide	—	—
8	pt. 3 sg.	āsende	sente	sent	sent
9	pt. 3 sg.	stōd	stood	stood	—
14	pt. 3 sg.	ārās	roos	arose	rose
1	pt. 3 pl.	cōmon	camen	came	—
5	pt. 3 pl.	sǣdon	seiden	said	—
10	pt. 3 pl.	ge-sāwon	siȝen	saw	—
11	pt. 3 pl.	—	felden	fell	—
2	pt. 1 pl.	cōmon	comen	—	—
8	imper. pl.	āxiað	axe ȝe	—	—
13	subj. pr. 1 sg.	secge	seie	—	—
11	pr. pp.	gangende	(cp. 15 seiynge)	(2 saying)	(entering)
2	pt. pp.	—	seyn	seene	(9) seen
2	pt. pp.	—	borun	borne	born
5	pt. pp.	āwriten	writun	written	—
8	pt. pp.	—	foundon	found	found

The following points should be noted: unvoicing of *nd* > *nt* in *sent*, which serves as an indication of the past tense; the *a* in ME *camen* (beside *comen* 2), which may be from an unrecorded OE past singular **cam*, the expected past singular for a verb of Class IV; *siȝen* comes from OE (Anglian) *sēgon;* note the ME tendency to add the pronoun to the imperative; the absence of the *y*-prefix (OE *ge-*) in the ME.

Other texts yield information on the gradual loss of all endings in the present except *-s*, the loss of some strong verbs to the weak conjugations, and the analogical leveling of the singular and plural past of strong verbs under the same vowel. Note that all verbs of foreign origin conform to the weak pattern, except *take*, which retains its strong ON past *took*.

v) *Adverbs.* OE adverbs normally end in -*e*, but the later formation in -*ly* is already indicated by 8 *geornlīce* beside 7 *georne*. Other texts show the reformation of OE adverbs to this pattern. The use of MnE adverbial phrases (see also p. 31 on syntax) is seen in 7 *on sundersprǣce — pryueli — priuily — in private.*

B. *Resolved forms*

i) *Prepositional substitutes.* Such substitutions are so common that only a few examples are given.

	OE	ME	KJ	NEB
1	on Iūdēiscre Bethleem	in B. of Judea	in B. of J.	at B. in J.
1	þæs cyninges dagum	the daies of k.	the dayes of H.	the reign of H.
2	Iūdēa Cyning	king of Jewis	king of the J.	king of the J.
4	folces writeras	scribis of the p.	s. of the p.	lawyers of the . . . p.
5	sǣdon him	seiden to hym	said vnto him	—
9	him beforan	bifore hem	before them	ahead of them
10	gefēan	with . . . ioye	with . . . ioy	—
11	him . . . brōhton	offryden to hym	presented vnto	offered him
12	on ōðerne weg	bi anothir weie	another way	another way
13	Drihtnes engel	the a. of the Lord	the a. of the L.	an a. of the L.
13	Iosepe	to Joseph	to Joseph	to Joseph
13	ðē secge	seie to thee	bring thee word	tell you
15	Herodes forðsīð	the deeth of Eroude	the death of H.	Herod's death

Note that although MnE reverts to *Herod's death*, some constructions of this kind are not now acceptable, or at any rate less likely (e.g., *the people's lawyers*). In this context, note the appearance in later English of "group genitives" such as *the Wife of Bath's Tale*, where ME has *the Wife's Tale of Bath;* the resolved form would be *the Tale of the Wife of Bath.* A curious kind of resolved genitive found in ME and early MnE is the use of the pronoun: *the Wife of Bath her Tale;* this form was more common with *his*, perhaps because it sounded like the inflexion -*ys*, -*es*.

ii) *Resolved verbs.* The words in this list are taken out of context. There are syntactical reasons for the use of some of them. The list is divided into indicative, subjunctive, and passive.

	OE	ME	KJ	NEB
2	gesāwon	han seyn	haue seene	observed
	cōmon	comen	are come	have come
3	gehȳrde	herde	had heard	heard
6	gǣð	schal go	shall come	shall come
	recð	schal gouerne	shall rule	(to be . . .)
8	gemētað	han foundon	haue found	have found
9	gehȳrdon	hadden herd	had heard	—
	gesāwon	siȝen	saw	had seen
10	fægenodon	ioyeden	reioyced	were overjoyed
13	fērdon	weren goon	were departed	had gone
15	geclypode	haue clepid	haue called	called
4	ācenned wǣre	shulde be borun	should be borne	(is to be born)
8	cume . . . gebidde	come . . . worschipe	may come and worship	may go and pay homage
12	ne hwyrfdon	schulden not turne	should not returne	not to go back
15	wǣre gefylled	shulde be fulfillid	might be fulfilled	to fulfil
1	ācenned wæs	was borun	was borne	was born
5	ys āwriten	is writun	is written	—
15	gecweden wæs	was seid	was spoken	—
3	wearð gedrēfed	was trublid	was troubled	was perturbed

The origin of the perfect and pluperfect tenses should be checked; note also the MnE use of *have* with a verb of motion. OE lacks a distinctive future tense. The MnE tendency to use *to* + infinitive for purpose clauses has its origin in the OE *tō* + inflected infinitive (2 *ūs him tō geēadmēdenne*, 13 *tō forspillenne*). Late OE (as here) often forms the passive as in MnE, but at all periods an indefinite pronoun and active verb could be used (in OE *man*, in ME *me* or *men*, in MnE *one* in a more restricted way). Note the supplying of *it* as the subject of *is writun*. An important feature not seen in these passages is the use of the verb *do* as an auxiliary. In ME it is common and often pleonastic; in MnE it is usually reserved to negative sentences, questions, and emphatic uses.[27] The variation of tenses in adverbial clauses of time is a matter of syntax.

SYNTAX

Only a few significant topics are dealt with in this section.

i) *Grammatical gender.* In OE the grammatical gender of a noun may be seen by the gender of the definite article or the indefinite adjective, e.g., masculine *sē steorra*, *ōðerne weg*, neuter *þæt cild*. In ME only pronouns give any indication of the gender of a noun.

9	(star)	hē	it	it	it
8	(child)	hyt	(hym)	him	him

[27] See above, p. 9.

Natural gender gradually supersedes grammatical gender, but sometimes in ME we can see the retention of OE grammatical gender, or even of its replacement by French or Latin grammatical gender.[28] On the difficulty of using the genitive *his* as a sign of gender, see above on morphology, p. 27.

ii) *Relative pronouns*. Normally, pronouns that are the subject of the relative clause should be divided from those that are the direct or indirect object or are governed by prepositions.

(a)	2	þe	that	that	who
	6	sē þe	that	that	—
	15	þæt ðe	that	which	(object *what*)
(b)	9	þe	that	which	which
	9	ofer þǣr	aboue, where	ouer where	above the place where

The reason for the division is that MnE often omits the object relative pronoun. The New English Bible could have written 9 *the star they had seen;* in contrast, ME sometimes omits the subject pronoun.[29] The most important feature is the use in late ME and MnE of the originally interrogative pronouns (*who, which,* etc.) as relatives.

iii) *Parataxis versus Subordination*. The alternative methods of expression can be illustrated by 10. The Vulgate has *videntes autem stellam, gavisi sunt* 'seeing the star they rejoiced'; the OE and King James translate the present participle by a *when* clause: *þā . . . gesāwon, fægenodon; when they saw . . . , they reioyced.* The ME has parataxis: *and thei sizen the sterre and ioyeden;* the New English Bible has a form of subordination in the adverbial phrase *at the sight of.* At 4 and 7 KJ has a *when* clause where the others have parataxis. In making such comparisons, remember that the translators are to some extent limited by the syntax of their original. The OE correlative pair *þā . . . þā . . .* 'when . . . then . . .' is probably in origin paratactic (i.e., *then . . . then . . .*), but normally word order distinguishes the subordinate clause (see below). For the conjunctions used in subordinate clauses, see also below.

iv) *Conjunctions*. The conjunction *and* appears in all passages (see above on parataxis). *But* only becomes a conjunction introducing an independent clause in ME (3). It is immediately evident that the New English Bible has tried to cut down the number of *and's* and has avoided the use of *and* to introduce a new sentence. The OE *ac* 'but' (12) is seldom used after the early ME period.

---

[28] An example of such replacement is seen in *sēo sunne* (feminine) and *sē mōna* (masculine) 'moon,' which in ME become respectively masculine and feminine, partly because Latin *sol* 'sun' is masculine, but *luna* 'moon' is feminine, and perhaps also because of the mythological association of the sun with Phoebus Apollo and the moon with Diana (Cynthia). See XXVI, 13 *n.*

[29] See above, p. 9.

The following selective list is of conjunctions used to introduce subordinate clauses:

1 þā ... (þā ...)	whanne ... (lo ...)	when ... (behold ...)	—
9 Đā ... (þā ...)	whanne ...	when ...	—
13 þā ... (þā ...)	whanne ... (lo ...)	when ... (behold ...)	after ...
8 þonne ...	whanne ...	when ...	when ...
9 oð ...	til ...	till ...	until ...
13 oð þæt ...	til that ...	vntill ...	until ...
8 þæt ...	that ...	that ...	so that ...

The New English Bible frequently replaces a subordinate clause by an adverbial phrase, etc., e.g., 1 *After his birth*, 9 *at the king's bidding*.

Other passages may provide examples of adverbial clauses of concession (*although*, *even if*, etc.), comparison (*just as*, etc.), cause (*because*), result (*so that*), or condition. This last type produces a huge variety of ways of introducing the *if* clause (*and*, *if*, reversal of subject-verb, etc.).

v) *Prepositions*. Although almost all MnE prepositions are of native origin, many of them have changed meaning, as the following table illustrates.

1	on	in	in	at
	on	in	in	during
	fram	fro	from	from
	tō	to	to	(arrived) in
3	mid	with	with	—
5	þurh	bi	by	—
6	on	among	among	(in the eyes of)
	of	of	out of	out of
8	(āxiað) be	(axe) of	(search) for	(inquiry) for
9	him beforan	bifore hem	before them	ahead of them
	ofer	aboue	ouer	above
11	intō	in to	into	—
	mid	with	with	with
12	on ... weg	bi ... weie	another way	another way
	on ... rīce	in to	into	(home)
13	on swefnum	in	in	in
	on E. land	in to	into	to
14	on niht	bi ny3t	by night	by night
15	oð	to	vntill	till
	fram	of	of	(*by* implied)
	þurh	bi	by	through
	of	fro	out of	out of

The origin of *during* is the Latin present participle in phrases like *vita durante* 'while life lasts, during life'; ME *fro* is from ON. The OE *mid* survives in *midwife;* it is replaced by *with* which meant 'against' in OE. The OE word order *him beforan* illustrates the originally adverbial nature of English prepositions. In 15 NEB *through* means 'through the mouth of' whereas in the OE passage *þurh* = 'by.' The emergence of other prepositional uses (such as possessive *of*) can be seen in the section on resolved forms above. On the origin of *except*, see XXX, 11 *n.*

vi) *Tense.* The type of table necessary for an analysis of verbal tense is that used above for "resolved verbal forms." It indicates that OE had basically only two forms, the present (also used for the future) and the simple preterite. Later English developed auxiliaries that indicated completed action (*have* and *be* with the past participle), continuous action (*be* with present participle), and future tense (*shall, will, be going to,* etc.). There is some variation in the use of tenses within adverbial clauses of time: contrast 3 KJ *when . . . had heard* and NEB *when he heard.* At 8, OE has *þonne gē hyt gemētað* (with future reference); all other versions have the perfect: ME *whanne ȝee han foundon,* KJ *when ye haue found,* NEB *when you have found;* it would, however, be perfectly idiomatic English to say *when you find.*

vii) *Use of subjunctive.* The emergence of auxiliary "modal" verbs to form the subjunctive is shown in the section on resolved verbal forms above, where it is seen that the NEB has avoided the subjunctive three times by the use of the infinitive. All the possible occurrences of the subjunctive mood in OE and ME cannot be indicated here. Many such uses are dropped in MnE in favor of the indicative mood, and these changes should be noted carefully. The subjunctive is often found in indirect speech (statements, commands, questions, etc.). For this reason, in 4 there is no way of telling whether the OE means 'where Christ had been born' or 'where he was to be born.' In conditional clauses (*if, unless,* etc.), MnE uses the subjunctive only for unlikely or uncertain hypotheses, and uses the past subjunctive (virtually indistinguishable from the simple past: *if you went, you would find*), whereas ME, for instance, often uses the present subjunctive in the *if* clause of "probable" hypotheses. Also of importance are *whoever* clauses, introduced in OE by *swā hwā swā,* etc., which may have the subjunctive.

viii) *Introductory adverbs and conjunctions.* The use of these connectives is of course largely determined by the originals, but the OE translator seems to have felt himself free to interpose adverbs to convey the relevant tone; in the NEB almost all these connectives have been removed, a characteristic of *literary* English.

1	ergo	eornustlīce	therfor	now	—
	ecce	—	lo	behold	—
2	enim	sōðlīce	for	for	—
3	autem	—	but	—	—
5	enim	witodlīce	for	for	—
6	enim	—	for	for	for
10	autem	sōþlīce	—	—	—
13	enim	—	for	for	for

In 4 and 14 OE has added the adverb *þā* 'then,' which is not in the Latin, and at 14 NEB begins *So*, a common MnE connective. It is doubtful that *for* is often used as a connective in spoken MnE.

WORD ORDER

In these passages the word order of OE calls for most comment; in most ways the order of ME is hardly distinct from that of MnE. Because the OE passage is late Old English, it exhibits some variation and anticipates some later developments.

i) *Main clause.* It is almost standard OE practice for an adverb or adverbial clause to be followed by the order verb-subject: e.g., 9 *þā fērdon hī*, 13 *þā ætȳwde Drihtnes engel Iosepe*. In both these sentences, later versions have the order adverb-subject-verb. The OE order survives in 6: e.g., the New English Bible *for out of you shall come a leader*. It is also found after *there:* e.g., 1 King James *behold, there came Wise men from the East;* the emergence of the adverb *there* to introduce the order verb-subject is a ME development. The word order verb-subject is also normal in OE in questions, 2 *Hwǣr ys sē Iūdea Cyning?*, as in later English — MnE use of the auxiliary *do* obscures the order somewhat. OE also has this order after the negative, 6 *ne eart þū lǣst*, but not invariably.

ii) *Dependent clause.* OE tends to interpose other elements of the sentence between subject and verb in such clauses, and also after *and* and *ac:* e.g., 9 *Đā hī þæt gebod gehȳrdon*, 12 *ac hī on ōðerne weg on hyre rīce fērdon*. The modern order, however, is more usual after *and* and is also found in the relative clause in 6 *sē þe recð mīn folc.*

iii) *Pronoun placing.* In early OE it is common for direct and indirect object pronouns to be placed immediately before the verb in clauses with the order subject-verb. In this passage other considerations obscure this placing, such as the order subject . . . verb after *and* and in dependent clauses, e.g., 8 *þæt ic cume and mē tō him gebidde*. There are also several occurrences of the modern order subject-verb-object: 8 *And hē āsende hī tō Bethlem*, 11 *and hī āðenedon hī.*

iv) *Other features.* Some orders in OE are no less notable because they correspond to MnE practice: *sē Iūdea Cyning* 'the Jews' king,' *Drihtnes engel* 'God's angel.' Note the separation in *on þæs cyninges dagum Herodes*. This order is made possible by the genitive inflexion; on group genitives see Morphology, p. 28. The placing of *they replied* in the New English Bible should perhaps be regarded as a feature of modern literary writing. In OE there is a strong tendency for nonfinite parts of the verb (infinitive, participle) to be near the end of the clause. This order ceases to be normal in ME except in verse.

In other passages, note the position of the negative particle, adverbs, "prepositions" (which in OE often are at the end of the sentence, indicating their originally separate emphatic function), and "link words," such as *however*, which in MnE may be first, or may come after the first separable element of the sentence. American usage often places *however* near, or at, the end of the sentence.

MISCELLANEOUS

In the preceding sections I have tried to outline an economical division of attention to be paid to areas of linguistic interest in the analysis of parallel passages. The selection has to some extent been limited, however, by the specimens chosen. Other topics that will arise include: formation of negative sentences (e.g., repeated negatives in OE and ME), comparison (by inflexion or by use of comparative adverbs such as *more*), impersonal verbs, and problems of concord (as with multiple or divided subjects, or words denoting groups, such as *government*). A subject that has not been touched at all in this analysis is the influence of the prescriptive rules, referred to above,[30] on English syntax and grammar. No one should feel limited to this outline. Several passages will themselves suggest alternative methods of analysis, new divisions, and subdivisions. The only important rule is that the basis of analysis should be historical and comparative.

SOME AIDS TO READING OLD ENGLISH

Even without any previous knowledge of Old English, a modern reader can recognize MnE words in their OE dress, once he is aware of certain equivalences. As already noted, OE *þ* and *ð* correspond to MnE *th*, and OE *æ* to MnE *a* or *e*, so that OE *þæt, pæð* are clearly MnE *that, path*. A few other correspondences make the task of recognition easier: OE *ā* > MnE [o:], spelled *o, oa*, so that OE *stān* > MnE *stone*. OE *ǣ* often produces the MnE spelling *ea*, so *lǣdan* > MnE verb *lead*. OE *y* normally produces MnE *i*, so OE *hyll* > *hill*. OE *sc(e)* = MnE *sh*, so OE *sceadu* > MnE *shade*. OE *c* before *e* and *i* (and some other vowels) often produces MnE *ch*, so that OE *cild* = MnE *child*. Sometimes OE *g* before *e* and *i* produces MnE *y*, as in OE *gēar*, MnE *year*, or OE *giernan*, MnE *yearn*. OE *cg* corresponds to MnE *dg*, so OE *ecg* > MnE *edge*. The *h* disappears from the OE initial consonant groups *hl, hn, hr*, so that *hlēapan* > verb *leap, hnutu* > *nut, hræfn* > *raven*. The OE initial *hw* group, however, produces MnE *wh*, so that OE *hwā* > *who*. Between vowels OE *f* was voiced and pronounced as MnE *v*, so that *drīfan* > verb *drive*.

[30] Pp. 12-14.

ME, followed by MnE, often used the letter *o* for OE *u* simply to avoid spelling confusion in words that had several "minims" (*i, m, n, u, w*); thus it is often possible to recognize a MnE word by substituting *o* for *u*, so that OE *sunu, lufu* can be seen to correspond to MnE *son, love* (see p. 20).

Many words can be recognized more easily once they are stripped of their prefixes and suffixes. The perfective prefix *ge-* can always be ignored: OE *gedrifen* > *driven*. Many other prefixes, such as *ā-, be-* (not, of course, without meaning in OE) can be mentally removed in order to reveal a MnE word; thus, OE *ābītan* conceals MnE *bite*, or OE *bemurnan* without its prefix > MnE *mourn*.

It is important to recognize the OE inflexional suffixes: *-de, -ede, -ode* are past endings, so that *geopenode, gemacode = open(ed), make(d)* > *made.* The student will find his task much easier if he familiarizes himself at an early stage with the principal inflexional endings of nouns, adjectives, and verbs; he should also know the declension of the definite article and the personal pronouns, and the conjugation of the verb *bēon* 'be' as well as common auxiliary verbs such as *cann, mæg, sceal*, etc.[31] A glossary of some very common Old English words, which the student is advised to learn as soon as he begins to read the Old English texts, is included at the end of the book.

SELECTION AND PRESENTATION OF TEXTS

The aim of the *Reader* is to enable the student to study the general development of the language rather than any idiosyncrasies of style. Most of the texts have been selected with this in mind, in that they are not self-consciously literary. No doubt the translators of the Bible, Boethius, and Bede have always aimed at a style elegant enough to please educated readers; on the whole, however, they seem to have been content to present the meaning of their originals in lucid, idiomatic English, and not to have sought praise for their eloquence. Exceptions among I through XVII include the Old English verse rendering of *Psalm 102* (VI), the modern Fontana translations of the *Psalms*, the passage from Chaucer's *Troilus* (XIV), and the verse translations (particularly the Old English and Walton) of Boethius *Consolation* II, meter 5 (XV). Almost all the passages from the section of "free" writing (XXII through XXXIV) are samples of nonliterary English, in that their aim is expository rather than stylistic. Exceptions are the homiletic pieces (XXVI and XXVIII), the turgidly complicated prose of Pecock (XXXI), and perhaps the elegant preface of Caxton (XXXIV), although Caxton was capable of far more elevated prose and made frequent use of long Latinate ("inkhorn") words. The translations of Vergil's *Aeneid*

---

[31] See Baugh, pp. 64–71, Pyles, pp. 113–133.

(XVIII through XXI) have been included to give the student a chance of observing some of the changing fashions and styles in poetry from Gavin Douglas in the fifteenth century to C. Day Lewis in modern times.

The punctuation, capitalization, etc., of Old and Middle English has been made to conform to modern practice, to the extent of adding quotation marks even where they are not used by the most recent editors. The Old English abbreviation 7 has been expanded to *ond* in early West Saxon texts but *and* in later passages. In accordance with the practice of most modern editors I have printed the OE w-rune (*wynn*) as *w*, and the OE flat-topped ȝ as *g*. In all later passages (except those provided with modern punctuation by their modern editors), the original punctuation has been followed carefully. For example, the ampersand has been retained in the King James Bible.

In I through XII, the verse numbering of the King James has been followed, and the verse numbers inserted into the text of other translations which lack them (e.g., Tyndale and the New English Bible). In the prose passages of Boethius and Bede (XIII, XIV and XVI, XVII) I have numbered the sentences arbitrarily and inserted the numbers in the texts in parentheses, to facilitate comparison between versions. In all passages where the original is in verse (XV, and XVIII through XXI), the line numbering of the original is used for all the translations.

The texts have been prepared from modern editions, without reference to the original MSS or printed incunabula; the text of the King James Bible was made from the facsimile edition of 1911.

FOOTNOTE GLOSSARY

The glossary to I through XXI does not aim at completeness. It does not normally include words that are given in the word list at the end of this volume, or words that can easily be recognized by following the principles outlined above (pp. 34–35). It excludes the definite article, the demonstrative pronouns and adjectives, the personal pronouns, most conjunctions, etc. Its purpose is to guide the student through the Old English while he is comparing it with later versions; therefore, it is very selective. The meaning of most words can usually be discovered from the other passages. In the case of verbs whose forms change considerably throughout their paradigm, the infinitive is often given in parentheses. Sometimes closely related words in Modern English are given in brackets before the gloss. It is assumed that no one will attempt to study the passages in Part Two, for which no glossary is provided, until he is fairly competent in Old English.

PART
ONE

I - VI

੭੭੭੭੭੭੭੭੭੭੭੭੭੭੭੭੭੭੭੭੭੭੭੭੭੭੭੭੭

THE OLD TESTAMENT

The Old English passages from *Genesis* and *Numbers* are taken from the *Old English Heptateuch*, ed. S. J. Crawford, EETS o.s. 160 (1921). These portions of the translation were almost certainly written by the famous Ælfric, abbot of Eynsham, at the end of the tenth century. The Old English Psalms are from the early eleventh century Paris Psalter, in which the first fifty psalms are in prose [*West-Saxon Psalms*, ed. J. W. Bright and R. L. Ramsay (Boston: D. C. Heath and Company, 1907)]. The remainder, found in *The Paris Psalter and the Meters of Boethius*, (Anglo-Saxon Poetic Records, V. New York: Columbia University Press, 1932), are in verse. The second version of the two psalms is from the *English Psalter* by Richard Rolle (ca. 1340), ed. H. R. Bramley (Oxford: Clarendon Press, 1884).

The later Middle English translations are from the "Wycliffite" Bible, *The Holy Bible . . . made from the Latin Vulgate by John Wycliffe and his followers*, ed. J. Forshall and F. Madden, 4 vols. (Oxford: Oxford University Press, 1850). All the extracts here, and from the New Testament, are from the revised version of the late fourteenth century, usually ascribed to John Purvey, a strong supporter of Wycliffe. This later version is in the right-hand column in the Forshall and Madden edition.

Quotations from the King James *Authorized Version* are from the first edition of 1611, and so preserve the original orthography. They are taken from the facsimile edition, with Introduction by A. W. Pollard (Oxford: Oxford University Press, 1911).

The modern version of the extracts from *Genesis* and *Numbers* is from *The Bible: an American translation*, by J. M. Powis Smith and others (Chicago: University of Chicago Press, 1923). The two modern versions of the psalms are from *The Psalms: a new translation* (London: Fontana Books, 1963).

It is very important to note that the Old English versions, Rolle's *Psalter*, and the Wycliffite Bible are all based on the Latin Vulgate by Jerome (fourth century), whereas later translations were made directly from the Hebrew. The main differences are indicated in the Notes at the end of each section; the apparatus would have been overburdened if notice had been taken of all such variations — for instance, medieval MSS of the

Vulgate frequently differ, and tend to be contaminated by the Old Latin version (pre-Jerome) and by the Greek Septuagint. On the whole subject of biblical translations, see the collection of essays in *The Bible in its Ancient and English versions*, ed. H. W. Robinson (Oxford: Clarendon Press, 1940).

I

GENESIS 3: 1-19

୶୶୶୶୶୶୶୶୶୶୶୶୶୶

The Fall of Man

Vulgate

1 Sed et serpens erat callidior cunctis animantibus terrae quae fecerat Dominus Deus. Qui dixit ad mulierem: Cur praecepit vobis Deus ut non comederetis de omni ligno paradisi? 2 Cui respondit mulier: De fructu lignorum quae sunt in paradiso, vescimur; 3 De fructu vero ligni, quod est in medio paradisi, praecepit nobis Deus ne comederemus, et ne tangeremus illud, ne forte moriamur. 4 Dixit autem serpens ad mulierem: Nequaquam morte moriemini. 5 Scit enim Deus quod in quocumque die comederetis ex eo, aperientur oculi vestri; et eritis sicut dii, scientes bonum et malum. 6 Vidit igitur mulier quod bonum esset lignum ad vescendum, et pulchrum oculis, aspectuque delectabile; et tulit de fructu illius, et comedit, deditque viro suo, qui comedit. 7 Et aperti sunt oculi amborum; cumque cognovissent se esse nudos, consuerunt folia ficus, et fecerunt sibi perizomata. 8 Et cum audissent vocem Domini Dei deambulantis in paradiso ad auram post meridiem, abscondit se Adam et uxor eius a facie Domini Dei in medio ligni paradisi. 9 Vocavitque Dominus Deus Adam, et dixit ei: Ubi es? 10 Qui ait: Vocem tuam audivi in paradiso; et timui eo quod nudus essem, et abscondi me. 11 Cui dixit: Quis enim indicavit tibi quod nudus esses, nisi quod ex ligno de quo praeceperam tibi ne comederes, comedisti? 12 Dixitque Adam: Mulier, quam dedisti mihi sociam, dedit mihi de ligno, et comedi. 13 Et dixit Dominus Deus ad mulierem: Quare hoc fecisti? Quae respondit: Serpens decepit me, et comedi. 14 Et ait Dominus Deus ad serpentem: Quia fecisti hoc, maledictus es inter omnia animantia et bestias terrae; super pectus tuum gradieris, et terram comedes cunctis diebus vitae tuae. 15 Inimicitias ponam inter te et mulierem, et semen tuum et semen illius; ipsa conteret caput tuum, et tu insidiaberis calcaneo eius. 16 Mulieri quoque dixit: Multiplicabo aerumnas tuas, et conceptus tuos; in dolore paries filios, et sub viri potestate eris, et ipse dominabitur tui. 17 Adae vero dixit: Quia audisti vocem uxoris tuae, et comedisti de ligno, ex quo praeceperam tibi ne comederes,

maledicta terra in opere tuo; in laboribus comedes ex ea cunctis diebus vitae tuae. 18 Spinas et tribulos germinabit tibi, et comedes herbam terrae. 19 In sudore vultus tui vesceris pane, donec revertaris in terram de qua sumptus es; quia pulvis es, et in pulverem reverteris.

Old English Heptateuch

1 Ēac swylce sēo nǣddre wæs gēapre ðonne ealle ðā ōðre nȳtenu ðe God geworhte ofer eorðan. And sēo nǣddre cwæð tō ðām wīfe: "Hwī forbēad God ēow ðæt gē ne ǣton of ǣlcon trēowe binnan Paradīsum?" 2 Þæt wīf andwyrde: "Of ðǣra trēowa wæstme ðe synd on Paradīsum wē etað, 3 and of ðæs trēowes wæstme þe is on middan neorxnawange God bebēad ūs ðæt wē ne ǣton, ne wē ðæt trēow ne hrepedon ðī lǣs ðe wē swelton." 4 Ðā cwæð sēo nǣdre eft tō ðām wīfe: "Ne bēo gē nāteshwōn dēade, ðēah ðe gē of ðām trēowe eton. 5 Ac God wāt sōðlīce ðæt ēowre ēagan bēoð geopenode on swā hwylcum dæge swā gē etað of ðām trēowe, and gē bēoð ðonne englum gelīce, witende ǣgðer gē gōd gē yfel." 6 Ðā geseah ðæt wīf ðæt ðæt trēow wæs gōd tō etenne, be ðām ðe hyre ðūhte, and wlitig on ēagum and lustbǣre on gesyhðe, and genam ðā of ðæs trēowes wæstme and geæt and sealde hyre were; hē æt ðā. 7 And heora bēgra ēagan wurdon geopenode; hī oncnēowon ðā ðæt hī nacode wǣron, and sywodon him ficlēaf and worhton him wǣdbrēc. 8 Eft ðā ðā God cōm, and hī gehȳrdon his stemne ðǣr hē ēode on neorxnawange ofer midne dæg, ðā behȳdde Adam hine, and his wīf ēac swā dyde fram Godes gesihðe on middan ðām trēowe neorxnanwonges. 9 God clypode ðā Adam and cwæð: "Adam, hwǣr eart ðū?" 10 Hē cwæð: "Ðīne stemne ic gehīre, lēof, on neorxnawange, and ic ondrǣde mē, for ðām ðe ic eom nacod, and ic behȳde mē." 11 God cwæð: "Hwā sǣde ðē ðæt ðū nacod wǣre, gyf ðū ne ǣte of ðām trēowe ðe ic ðē bebēad ðæt-ðū ne ǣte?" 12 Adam cwæð: "Ðæt wīf ðe ðū mē forgēafe tō

---

1 gēap(re): *more astute;* nȳten(u): *animals;* eorð(an): *earth;* forbēad (forbēodan): *forbade;* ǣton (etan): *pt. pl. subj., eat;* binnan: *within*

2 andwyrde: *answered;* wæstm(e): *fruit*

3 neorxnawang(e): *paradise;* bebēad (bebēodan): *ordered;* hrepedon: *pt. pl. subj., touch;* ðī lǣs ðe: *lest;* swelton: *pt. pl. subj., die*

4 nāteshwōn: *by no means;* dēade: *dead;* ðēah ðe: *although*

5 ēagan: *eyes;* engl(um): *angels;* witende: *knowing*

6 be ðām ðe: *as;* ðūhte: *seemed;* wlitig: *beautiful;* lustbǣre: *pleasant;* gesyhð-(e): *sight;* genam: *took;* geæt: *ate;* sealde [sold]: *gave;* wer(e): *man*

7 bēgra: *gen., both;* oncnēowon: *knew;* ficlēaf: *figleaves;* wǣdbrēc [weeds, breeches]: *breeches*

8 gehȳrdon: *heard;* stemn(e): *voice;* ðǣr: *where;* behȳdde: *hid*

10 gehīre: *hear;* lēof: *dear (one);* ondrǣde mē: *am afraid*

12 forgēafe: *pt. 2 sg., gave;* gefēra(n): *companion*

gefēran, sealde mē of ðām trēowe and ic ætt." 13 God cwæð tō ðām wīfe: "Hwī dydestu ðæt?" Hēo cwæð: "Sēo nædre bepæhte mē and ic ætt." 14 God cwæð tō ðære næddran: "For ðan ðe ðū ðis dydest, ðū bist āwyrged betwēox eallum nȳtenum and wildēorum; ðū gǣst on ðīnum brēoste and etst ðā eorðan eallum dagum ðīnes līfes. 15 Ic sette fēondrǣdene betwux ðē and ðām wīfe and ðīnum ofspringe and hire ofspringe; hēo tobrȳtt ðīn hēafod and ðū syrwst ongēan hire hō." 16 Tō ðām wīfe cwæð God ēac swylce: "Ic gemænifylde ðīne yrmða and ðīne geēacnunga; on sārnysse ðū ācenst cild and ðū bist under weres anwealde and hē gewylt ðē." 17 Tō Adame hē cwæð: "For ðan ðe ðū gehȳrdes ðīnes wīfes stemne, and ðū æte of ðām trēowe ðe ic ðē bebēad ðæt ðū ne æte, is sēo eorðe āwyrged on ðīnum weorce: on geswyncum ðū etst of ðære eorðan eallum dagum ðīnes līfes. 18 Ðornas and bremelas hēo āsprȳt ðē and ðū ytst ðære eorðan wyrta. 19 On swāte ðīnes andwlitan ðū brȳcst ðīnes hlāfes, oð ðæt ðū gewende tō eorðan of ðære ðe ðū genumen wære, for ðan ðe ðū eart dust and tō duste gewyrst.

Wycliffite (Purvey)

1 But and the serpent was feller than alle lyuynge beestis of erthe, whiche the Lord God hadde maad. Which serpent seide to the womman, "Why comaundide God to ȝou, that ȝe schulden not ete of ech tre of paradis?" 2 To whom the womman answerde, "We eten of the fruyt of trees that ben in paradis; 3 sothely God comaundide to vs, that we schulden not ete of the fruyt of the tre, which is in the myddis of paradijs, and that we schulden not touche it, lest perauenture we dien." 4 Forsothe the serpent seide to the womman, "ȝe schulen not die bi deeth; 5 for whi God woot that in what euere dai ȝe schulen ete therof, ȝoure iȝen schulen be opened, and ȝe schulen be as Goddis, knowynge good and yuel." 6 Therfor the womman seiȝ that the tre was good, and swete to ete, and fair to the iȝen, and delitable

---

13 bepǣhte: *deceived*
14 āwyrged: *cursed;* wildēor(um): *wild animals;* gǣst (gān): *will go*
15 fēondrǣden(e): *enmity;* tōbrȳtt: *will break apart;* hēafod: *head;* syrwst (sierwan): *pr. 2 sg., will plot;* hō: *heel*
16 gemænifylde: *will multiply;* yrmð(a): *miseries;* geēacnung(a): *pregnancies;* sārnyss(e): *sorrow;* ācenst: *pr. 2 sg., will bear;* anweald(e): *power;* gewylt

(gewealdan): *pr. 3 sg., will rule over*
17 weorc(e): *labor;* geswync(um): *toils*
18 bremel(as): *brambles;* āsprȳt [sprout]: *will produce;* ytst = etst; wyrt(a) [worts]: *plants*
19 swāt(e): *sweat;* andwlita(n): *face;* brȳcst (brūcan): *pr. 2 sg., have the use of;* hlāf(es) [loaf]: *bread;* oð ðæt: *until;* gewende: *turn;* gewyrst (geweorðan): *pr. 2 sg., will become*

1 feller: *more clever*
3 sothely: *truly;* perauenture: *by chance*

5 woot: *knows*

in biholdyng; and sche took of the fruyt therof, and eet, and ȝaf to hir hosebonde, and he eet. 7 And the iȝen of bothe weren openid; and whanne thei knewen that thei weren nakid, thei sewiden the leeues of a fige tre, and maden brechis to hem silf. 8 And whanne thei herden the vois of the Lord God goynge in paradijs at the wynd after myddai, Adam and his wijf hidden hem fro the face of the Lord God in the middis of the tre of paradijs. 9 And the Lord God clepide Adam, and seide to hym, "Where art thou?" 10 And Adam seide, "Y herde thi vois in paradijs, and Y drede, for Y was nakid, and Y hidde me." 11 To whom the Lord seide, "Who forsothe schewide to thee that thou were nakid? — no but for thou hast ete of the tre of which Y comaundide to thee that thou schuldist not ete." 12 And Adam seide, "The womman which thou ȝauest felowe to me, ȝaf me of the tre, and Y eet." 13 And the Lord seide to the womman, "Whi didist thou this thing? Which answerde, "The serpent disseyued me, and Y eet." 14 And the Lord God seide to the serpent, "For thou didist this, thou schalt be cursid among alle lyuynge thingis and vnresonable beestis of erthe; thou schalt go on thi brest, and thou schalt ete erthe in alle daies of thi liif; 15 Y schal sette enemytees bitwixe thee and the womman, and bitwixe thi seed and hir seed; sche schal breke thin heed, and thou schalt sette aspies to hir heele." 16 Also God seide to the womman, "Y schal multiplie thi wretchidnessis and thi conseyuyngis; in sorewe thou schalt bere thi children; and thou schalt be vndur power of the hosebonde, and he schal be lord of thee." 17 Sothely God seyde to Adam, "For thou herdist the voys of thi wijf, and hast ete of the tree, of which Y comaundide to thee that thou schuldist not ete, the erthe schal be cursid in thi werk; in traueylis thou schalt ete therof in alle daies of thi lijf; 18 it schal brynge forth thornes and breris to thee, and thou schalt ete eerbis of the erthe; 19 in swoot of thi cheer thou schalt ete thi breed, til thou turne aȝen in to the erthe of which thou art takun; for thou art dust, and thou schalt turne aȝen in to dust."

King James

1 Now the serpent was more subtill then any beast of the field, which the Lord God had made, and he said vnto the woman, Yea, hath God said, Ye shall not eat of euery tree of the garden? 2 And the woman said vnto the serpent, Wee may eate of the fruite of the trees of the garden: 3 But

---

11   no but for: *not unless because*   18   breris: *briars;* eerbis: *herbs*
15   aspies: *spies*   19   swoot: *sweat;* cheer: *face*
17   traueylis: *toils*

of the fruit of the tree, which is in the midst of the garden, God hath said, Ye shal not eate of it, neither shall ye touch it, lest ye die. 4 And the Serpent said vnto the woman, Ye shall not surely die. 5 For God doeth know, that in the day ye eate thereof, then your eyes shalbee opened: and yee shall bee as Gods, knowing good and euill. 6 And when the woman saw, that the tree was good for food, and that it was pleasant to the eyes, and a tree to be desired to make one wise, she tooke of the fruit thereof, and did eate, and gaue also vnto her husband with her, and hee did eate. 7 And the eyes of them both were opened, & they knew that they were naked, and they sewed figge leaues together, and made themselues aprons. 8 And they heard the voyce of the Lord God, walking in the garden in the coole of the day: and Adam and his wife hid themselues from the presence of the Lord God, amongst the trees of the garden. 9 And the Lord God called vnto Adam, and said vnto him, Where art thou? 10 And he said, I heard thy voice in the garden: and I was afraid, because I was naked, and I hid myselfe. 11 And he said, Who told thee, that thou wast naked? Hast thou eaten of the tree, whereof I commanded thee, that thou shouldest not eate? 12 And the man said, The woman whom thou gauest to be with mee, shee gaue me of the tree, and I did eate. 13 And the Lord God said vnto the woman, What is this that thou hast done? And the woman said, The Serpent beguiled me, and I did eate. 14 And the Lord God said vnto the Serpent, Because thou hast done this, thou art cursed aboue all cattel, and aboue euery beast of the field: vpon thy belly shalt thou goe, and dust shalt thou eate, all the dayes of thy life. 15 And I will put enmitie betweene thee and the woman, and betweene thy seed and her seed: it shall bruise thy head, and thou shalt bruise his heele. 16 Vnto the woman he said, I will greatly multiply thy sorowe and thy conception. In sorow thou shalt bring forth children: and thy desire shall be to thy husband, and hee shall rule ouer thee. 17 And vnto Adam he said, Because thou hast hearkened vnto the voyce of thy wife, and hast eaten of the tree, of which I commaunded thee, saying, Thou shalt not eate of it: cursed is the ground for thy sake: in sorow shalt thou eate of it all the dayes of thy life. 18 Thornes also and thistles shall it bring forth to thee: and thou shalt eate the herbe of the field. 19 In the sweate of thy face shalt thou eate bread, till thou returne vnto the ground: for out of it wast thou taken, for dust thou art, and vnto dust shalt thou returne.

Modern American

1 Now the serpent was the most clever of all the wild beasts that the Lord God had made. "And so God has said that you are not to eat from any

tree of the garden?" he said to the woman. 2 "From the fruit of the trees of the garden we may eat," the woman said to the serpent; 3 "it is only concerning the fruit of the tree which is in the middle of the garden that God has said, 'You may not eat any of it, nor touch it, lest you die.' " 4 But the serpent said to the woman, "You would not die at all; 5 for God knows that the very day you eat of it, your eyes will be opened, and you will be like gods who know good from evil." 6 So when the woman realized that the tree was good for food and attractive to the eye, and further, that the tree was desirable for its gift of wisdom, she took some of its fruit, and ate it; she also gave some to her husband with her, and he ate. 7 Then the eyes of both of them were opened, and they realized that they were naked; so they sewed fig-leaves together, and made themselves girdles. 8 But when they heard the sound of the Lord God taking a walk in the garden for the breezes of the day, the man and his wife hid themselves from the Lord God among the trees of the garden. 9 The Lord God called to the man. "Where are you?" he said to him. 10 "I heard the sound of thee in the garden," he replied, "and I was afraid, because I was naked; so I hid myself." 11 "Who told you that you were naked?" he said. "Have you eaten from the tree from which I commanded you not to eat?" 12 The man said, "The woman whom thou didst set at my side, it was she who gave me fruit from the tree; so I ate it." 13 Then the Lord God said to the woman, "What ever have you done?" The woman said, "It was the serpent that misled me, and so I ate it." 14 So the Lord God said to the serpent,

> Because you have done this,
> The most cursed of all animals shall you be,
> And of all wild beasts.
> On your belly you shall crawl, and eat dust,
> As long as you live.
> 15   I will put enmity between you and the woman,
> And between your posterity and hers;
> They shall attack you in the head,
> And you shall attack them in the heel."

16 To the woman he said,

> "I will make your pain at child-birth very great;
> In pain shall you bear children;
> And yet you shall be devoted to your husband,
> While he shall rule over you."

17 And to the man he said, "Because you followed your wife's suggestions, and ate from the tree from which I commanded you not to eat,

Cursed shall be the ground through you,
In suffering shall you gain your living from it as
    long as you live;
18 Thorns and thistles shall it produce for you,
So that you will have to eat wild plants.
19 By the sweat of your brow shall you earn your
    living,
Until you return to the ground,
Since it was from it that you were taken;
For dust you are,
And to dust you must return."

NOTES

1 The literalness of Purvey is illustrated by *But and* for Vulgate
Sed et.

3 OE *neorxnawange* (but 1 *Paradisum*): this is a common OE gloss for
Paradise (which means 'enclosed garden'); *wang* 'plain'; first element
is uncertain.

6 Vulgate *aspectu delectabile* more or less repeats *pulchrum oculis;*
note that the Vulgate (and dependent versions) contain no reference
to wisdom. OE *be ðām ðe hyre ðūhte* emphasizes the illusory nature
of the tree.

7 The Geneva Bible (1560) was known as the "Breeches Bible" because of its use of the word "breeches" here; note that both the
OE (*-brǣc*) and Purvey also use the word, as did Coverdale (1535).

9ff. These verses illustrate the development of the second person
singular personal pronoun *thou.* The modern version is the only one
to make a distinction between addresses to God and to Adam. The
"plural of polite address" (*ye, you*) was hardly ever used in speaking
to God (perhaps an indication of the intimacy of prayers), and in
modern literary English *thou* has somehow acquired a flavor of
formality, unlike the general *you.*

10 Most MSS of the OE have the past tense here (as Vulgate, etc.). The
sense of *lēof* 'dear (one)' is probably no more than 'sir': in the plural
it is common at the beginning of sermons (compare 'dearly beloved
brethren').

11 The curious syntax of the OE and Purvey is explained by the Vulgate.

13 The desire to supply a direct object for *ate* has led the modern version
into an unfortunate ambiguity.

15 Vulgate *insidiaberis* 'plot against, lay traps for' is accurately rendered

by OE *syrwst*, but Purvey's *sette aspies* is poor. Note that in the Vulgate, the OE and Purvey, the heel is that of the woman, not of the seed (as in the later versions).

KJ *his heel:* MnE would use *its* but this form was not yet fully established at this date: compare Shakespeare, *King Lear* I, iv, 239 'it head, it young.' In late ME and early MnE if the use of *his* appeared to imply natural gender, *thereof* was often used: compare 6 above, and XXXI, 7-8.

16 Vulgate *sub viri potestate* does not imply 'desire' as KJ and the modern text.

II

GENESIS 8: 6-18

ᏇᏇᏇᏇᏇᏇᏇᏇᏇᏇᏇᏇ

The Exit from the Ark

Vulgate

6 Cumque transissent quadraginta dies, aperiens Noe fenestram arcae, quam fecerat, dimisit corvum; 7 Qui egrediebatur, et non revertebatur, donec siccarentur aquae super terram. 8 Emisit quoque columbam post eum, ut videret si iam cessassent aquae super faciem terrae. 9 Quae cum non invenisset ubi requiesceret pes eius, reversa est ad eum in arcam; aquae enim erant super universam terram; extenditque manum, et apprehensam intulit in arcam. 10 Expectatis autem ultra septem diebus aliis, rursum dimisit columbam ex arca. 11 At illa venit ad eum ad vesperam, portans ramum olivae virentibus foliis in ore suo. Intellexit ergo Noe quod cessassent aquae super terram. 12 Expectavitque nihilominus septem alios dies; et emisit columbam, quae non est reversa ultra ad eum. 13 Igitur sexcentesimo primo anno, primo mense, prima die mensis, imminutae sunt aquae super terram; et aperiens Noe tectum arcae, aspexit, viditque quod exsiccata esset superficies terrae. 14 Mense secundo, septimo et vigesimo die mensis, arefacta est terra. 15 Locutus est autem Deus ad Noe, dicens: 16 Egredere de arca, tu et uxor tua, filii tui et uxores filiorum tuorum tecum. 17 Cuncta animantia quae sunt apud te, ex omni carne, tam in volatilibus quam in bestiis et universis reptilibus quae reptant super terram, educ tecum, et ingredimini super terram: crescite et multiplicamini super eam. 18 Egressus est ergo Noe, et filii eius, uxor illius, et uxores filiorum eius, cum eo.

Old English Heptateuch

6 Ðā æfter fēowertigum dagum undyde Noe his ēahðyrl, ðe hē on ðām arce gemacode. 7 and āsende ūt ǣnne hremn: sē hrem flēah ðā ūt, and

---

6   undyde [undid]: *unfastened;* ēahðyrl: *window;* gemacode: *made*

7   hremn: *raven;* flēah: *flew;* nolde: *would not;* cyrran: *turn;* ǣr ðan ðe: *before;* ādrūwodon: *dried up*

49

nolde eft ongēan cyrran, ǣr ðan ðe ðā wæteru ādrūwodon ofer eorðan. 8 Hē āsende ðā eft ūt āne culfran, ðæt hēo scēawode gyf ðā wætera ðāgȳt geswicon ofer ðǣre eorðan brādnysse. 9 Hēo ðā flēah ūt and ne mihte findan hwǣr hēo hire fōt āsette, for ðan ðe ðā wætera wǣron ofer ealle eorðan; and hēo gecyrde ongēan tō Noe, and hē genam hī in tō ðām arce. 10 Hē ābād ðā gȳt ōðre seofan dagas and āsende ūt eft culfran. 11 Hēo cōm ðā on æfnunge eft tō Noe and brōhte ān twig of ānum elebēame mid grēnum lēafum on hyre mūðe. Ðā undergeat Noe ðæt ðā wætera wǣron ādrūwode ofer eorðan. 12 and ābād swā ðēah seofan dagas and āsende ūt culfran; swā hēo ne gecyrde ongēan tō him. 13 Ðā geopenode Noe ðæs arces hrōf, and behēold ūt and geseah ðæt ðǣre eorðan brādnis wæs ādrūwod. 15 God ðā spræc tō Noe, ðus cweðende: 16 "Gang ūt of ðām arce, ðū and þīn wīf and ðīne suna and heora wīf; 17 and eal ðæt ðǣr inne is mid ðē, lǣd ūt mid ðē ofer eorðan, and weaxe gē and bēoð gemǣnifylde ofer eorðan." 18 Noe ðā ūt ēode of ðām arce, and hī ealle ofer eorðan.

Wycliffite (Purvey)

6 And whanne fourti daies weren passid, Noe openyde the wyndow of the schip which he hadde maad, 7 and sente out a crowe, which ȝede out, and turnede not aȝen til the watris weren dried on erthe. 8 Also Noe sente out a culuer aftir hym, to se if the watris hadden ceessid thanne on the face of erthe; 9 and whanne the culuer foond not where hir foot schulde reste, sche turnede aȝen to hym in to the schip, for the watris weren on al erthe; and Noe helde forth his hoond, and brouȝte the culuer takun in to the schip. 10 Sotheli whanne othere seuene daies weren abedun aftirward, eft he leet out a culuer fro the schip; 11 and sche cam to hym at euentid, and bare in hir mouth a braunche of olyue tre with greene leeuys. Therfor Noe vndirstood that the watris hadden ceessid on erthe; 12 and neuerthelesse he abood seuene othere daies, and sente out a culuer, which turnede no more aȝen to hym. 13 Therfor in the sixe hundrid and o ȝeer of the lijf of Noe, in the firste monethe, in the firste day of the monethe,

---

8 culfr(an): *dove;* scēawode: *pt. 3 sg. subj., might see;* ðāgȳt: *yet;* geswicon: *ceased*
9 āsette: *pt. 3 sg. subj., set;* genam (geniman): *took*
10 ābād (ābīdan) [abode]: *waited*
11 æfnung(e): *evening;* brōhte (bringan):

7 ȝede: *went*
8 culuer: *dove*

brought; elebēam(e): *olive tree;* undergeat: *understood*
12 swā ðēah: *nevertheless*
13 hrōf: *roof;* behēold [beheld]: *looked*
16 Gang: *imper., go*
17 weaxe: *subj. = imper., increase;* gemǣnifylde [manifold]: *multiplied*

10 weren abedun: *lit., had been waited*
13 o: *one*

watris weren decreessid on erthe; and Noe openede the roof of the schip, and bihelde and sei3 that the face of the erthe was dried. 14 In the secunde monethe, in the seuene and twentithe dai of the monethe, the erthe was maad drie. 15 Sotheli the Lord spak to Noe; and seide, "Go out of the schip, thou, and thi wijf, thi sones, and the wyues of thi sones with thee; 17 and lede out with thee alle lyuynge beestis that ben at thee of ech fleisch, as wel in volatilis as in vnresonable beestis, and alle reptils that crepen on erthe; and entre 3e on the erthe, encreesse 3e, and be 3e multiplied on erthe." 18 Therfor Noe 3ede out, and hise sones, and his wijf, and the wyues of hise sones with hym.

King James

6 And it came to passe at the end of forty dayes, that Noah opened the window of the Arke which he had made. 7 And he sent forth a Rauen, which went foorth to and fro, vntill the waters were dried vp from off the earth. 8 Also hee sent foorth a doue from him, to see if the waters were abated from off the face of the ground. 9 But the doue found no rest for the sole of her foote, and she returned vnto him into the Arke: for the waters were on the face of the whole earth. Then he put foorth his hand, and tooke her, and pulled her in vnto him, into the Arke. 10 And hee stayed yet other seuen dayes; and againe hee sent foorth the doue out of the Arke. 11 And the doue came in to him in the euening, and loe, in her mouth was an Oliue leafe pluckt off: So Noah knew that the waters were abated from off the earth. 12 And hee stayed yet other seuen dayes, and sent forth the doue, which returned not againe vnto him any more. 13 And it came to passe in the sixe hundredth and one yeere, in the first moneth, the first day of the moneth, the waters were dryed vp from off the earth: and Noah remooued the couering of the Arke, and looked, and behold, the face of the ground was drie. 14 And in the second moneth, on the seuen and twentieth day of the moneth, was the earth dried. 15 And God spake vnto Noah, saying, 16 Goe foorth of the Arke, thou, and thy wife, and thy sonnes, and thy sonnes wiues with thee: 17 Bring foorth with thee euery liuing thing that is with thee, of all flesh, both of fowle, and of cattell, and of euery creeping thing that creepeth vpon the earth, that they may breed abundantly in the earth, and be fruitfull, and multiply vpon the earth. 18 And Noah went foorth, and his sonnes, and his wife, and his sonnes wiues with him.

---

17   volatilis: *birds*

Modern American

6 At the end of forty days Noah opened the window that he had made in
the ark, 7 and released a raven, which went flying back and forth until the
waters had dried off the earth. 8 Then he released a dove, to see whether
the waters had subsided from the surface of the land; 9 but the dove could
find no resting-place for the sole of her foot, so she came back to him into
the ark; for there was water all over the earth. He put out his hand, and
catching her, drew her into the ark with him. 10 After waiting another
seven days, he again released the dove from the ark; 11 in the evening the
dove came back to him, and there, in her beak, was a freshly picked olive
leaf! So Noah knew that the waters had subsided off the earth. 12 After
waiting another seven days, he released the dove, but she never came back
to him. 13 By the first day of the first month of the six hundred and first
year of Noah's life the waters had dried off the earth. So Noah removed
the covering of the ark and found that the surface of the ground was quite
dry. 14 By the twenty-seventh day of the second month the earth was dry.

15 Then God said to Noah, 16 "Come out of the ark, your wife, your
sons, and your sons' wives accompanying you; 17 bring out with you every
animal of every sort that is with you, birds, quadrupeds, and all land
reptiles, that they may breed freely on the earth, and be fruitful and
multiply on the earth." 18 So Noah came out, his sons, his wife, and his
sons' wives accompanying him.

NOTES

In this, and the next two extracts, the OE version abbreviates the Vulgate
considerably, but usually with no loss of sense. Verse 14 is omitted entirely.

 6   Note the different assumptions about the antecedent of the relative
     pronoun: the Vulgate allows either, as both 'window' and 'ark' are
     feminine in Latin.
15   Purvey *sotheli* glosses *autem*, a connecting word: compare I, 3, 4, etc.
17   As in I, 14, Purvey glosses *bestiae* by *vnresonable beestis*.

III

GENESIS 22: 1-18

෨෨෨෨෨෨෨෨෨෨෨෨෨෨෨

Abraham and Isaac

Vulgate

1 Quae postquam gesta sunt, tentavit Deus Abraham, et dixit ad eum: Abraham! Abraham! At ille respondit: Adsum. 2 Ait illi: Tolle filium tuum unigenitum, quem diligis, Isaac, et vade in terram visionis, atque ibi offeres eum holocaustum super unum montium quem monstravero tibi. 3 Igitur Abraham de nocte consurgens, stravit asinum suum, ducens secum duos iuvenes, et Isaac filium suum; cumque concidisset ligna in holocaustum, abiit ad locum quem praeceperat ei Deus. 4 Die autem tertio, elevatis oculis, vidit locum procul. 5 Dixitque ad pueros suos: Expectate hic cum asino; ego et puer illuc usque properantes, postquam adoraverimus, revertemur ad vos. 6 Tulit quoque ligna holocausti, et imposuit super Isaac filium suum; ipse vero portabat in manibus ignem et gladium. Cumque duo pergerent simul, 7 Dixit Isaac patri suo: Pater mi. At ille respondit: Quid vis, fili? Ecce, inquit, ignis et ligna; ubi est victima holocausti? 8 Dixit autem Abraham: Deus providebit sibi victimam holocausti, fili mi. Pergebant ergo pariter. 9 Et venerunt ad locum quem ostenderat ei Deus, in quo aedificavit altare, et desuper ligna composuit; cumque alligasset Isaac filium suum, posuit eum in altare super struem lignorum. 10 Extenditque manum, et arripuit gladium, ut immolaret filium suum. 11 Et ecce angelus Domini de caelo clamavit, dicens: Abraham! Abraham! Qui respondit: Adsum. 12 Dixitque ei: Non extendas manum tuam super puerum, neque facias illi quidquam; nunc cognovi quod times Deum, et non pepercisti unigenito filio tuo propter me. 13 Levavit Abraham oculos suos, viditque post tergum arietem inter vepres haerentem cornibus, quem assumens obtulit holocaustum pro filio. 14 Appelavitque nomen loci illius, Dominus videt. Unde usque hodie dicitur: In monte Dominus videbit. 15 Vocavit autem angelus Domini Abraham secundo de caelo, dicens: 16 Per memet ipsum juravi, dicit Dominus: quia fecisti hanc rem, et non pepercisti filio tuo unigenito propter me, 17 Benedicam tibi, et multiplicabo semen tuum sicut stellas caeli, et velut arenam quae est in littore maris;

possidebit semen tuum portas inimicorum suorum. 18 Et benedicentur
in semine tuo omnes gentes terrae, quia obedisti voci meae.

Old English Heptateuch

1 God wolde þā fandian Abrahames gehȳrsumnysse, and clypode hys
naman, 2 and cwæð him ðus tō: "Nym ðīnne āncennedan sunu Isaac, þe
ðū lufast, and far tō þām lande Visionis hraðe, and geofra hyne þǣr uppan
ānre dūne." 3 Abraham ðā ārās on þǣre ylcan nihte and fērde mid twām
cnapum tō þām fyrlenum lande, and Isaac samod, on assum rīdende.
4 Þā on ðone ðriddan dæg, þā hī ðā dūne gesāwon, ðǣr ðǣr hī tō sceoldon
tō ofslēane Isaac, 5 ðā cwæð Abraham tō þām cnapum ðus: "Anbīdiað
ēow hēr mid þām assum sume hwīle: ic and þæt cild gāð unc tō gebiddenne,
and wē syððan cumað sōna eft tō ēow." 6 Abraham þā hēt Isaac beran
þone wudu tō þǣre stōwe, and hē sylf bær hys swurd and fȳr. 7 Isaac ðā
āxode Abraham hys fæder: "Fæder mīn, ic āxige hwǣr sēo offrung sȳ?
hēr ys wuda and fȳr." 8 Him andwyrde sē fæder: "God foresceāwað, mīn
sunu, him sylf ðā offrunge." 9 Hī cōmon þā tō ðǣre stōwe þe him
geswutelode God, and hē ðǣr wēofod ārǣrde on ðā ealdan wīsan, and þone
wudu gelōgode, swā swā hē hyt wolde habban tō hys suna bærnette syððan
hē ofslagen wurde. Hē geband þā hys sunu, 10 and hys swurd ātēah þæt
hē hyne geoffrode on þā ealdan wīsan. 11 Mid ðām ðe hē wolde þæt weorc
begynnan, ðā clypode Godes engel ardlīce of heofonum, "Abraham!"
Hē andwyrde sōna. 12 Sē engel him cwæð tō: "Nē ācwel ðū þæt cild, nē þīne
hand ne āstrece ofer hys swuran: nū ic oncnēow sōðlīce, þæt ðū swȳðe
ondrǣtst God, nū þū þīnne āncennedan sunu ofslēan woldest for him." 13 Ðā
beseah Abraham sōna underbæc, and geseah ðǣr ǣnne ram betwux þām

---

1 fandian: *test;* gehȳrsumnyss(e): *obedience*

2 Nym: *imper., take;* āncenned(an): *only-begotten;* far [fare]: *imper., go;* hraðe: *quickly;* dūn(e) [down]: *hill*

3 fērde: *went;* cnap(um): *boys;* fyrlen-(um): *distant;* samod: *together*

4 tō sceoldon: *had to (go) to;* ofslēan(ne): *kill*

5 Anbīdiað: *imper., wait;* gāð: *pr. 1 pl., will go;* unc tō gebiddenne: *to pray;* sōna [soon]: *immediately*

6 hēt (hātan): *pt. 3 sg., ordered;* beran: *bear;* stōw(e): *place;* bær (beran): *pt. 3 sg., bore*

8 andwyrde: *answered;* foresceāwað: *lit., see before, provide*

9 geswutelode: *showed;* wēofod: *altar;* ārǣrde [rear]: *raised up;* wīs(an): *fashion;* gelōgode [lodge]: *arranged;* suna: *gen., son's;* bærnett(e): *burning;* ofslagen wurde [slain]: *pt. pp. + pt. 3 sg. subj.* (weorðan), *had been killed;* geband (gebindan): *tied*

10 ātēah (ātēon): *pt. 3 sg., drew*

11 Mid ðām ðe: *while;* ardlīce: *quickly*

12 ācwel: *imper., kill;* āstrece: *imper., stretch;* swur(an): *neck;* oncnēow: *know*

13 beseah (besēon): *looked;* underbæc: *behind;* bremel(um): *brambles;* gehæft: *fastened;* āhefde: *lifted up;* ofsnāð (of-snīðan): *pt. 3 sg., cut up;* God(e) tō lāc(e): *as a sacrifice to God*

bremelum be ðām hornum gehæft, and hē āhefde ðone ram tō ðǣre offrunge and hyne þǣr ofsnāð Gode tō lāce for hys sunu Isaac. 14 Hē hēt þā þā stōwe *Dominus vidit*, þæt ys "God gesȳhð", and gȳt ys gesǣd swā: *In monte Dominus vidit*, þæt ys "God gesȳhð on dūne". 15 Eft clypode sē engel Abraham, and cwæð: 16 "Ic swerige ðurh mē sylfne, sǣde sē Ælmihtiga, nū ðū noldest ārian þīnum āncennedan suna, ac ðē wæs mīn ege māre þonne hys līf: 17 ic ðē nū blētsige and ðīnne ofspringe gemenigfylde swā swā steorran on heofonum and swā swā sandceosel on sǣ; þīn ofsprincg sceal āgan heora fēonda gatu, 18 and on þīnum sǣde bēoð ealle ðēoda geblētsode, for þan ðe þū gehȳrsumodest mīnre hǣse ðus."

Wycliffite (Purvey)

1 And aftir that these thingis weren don, God assaiede Abraham, and seide to hym, "Abraham! Abraham!" He answerde, "Y am present." 2 God seide to him, "Take thi sone oon gendrid, whom thou louest, Ysaac; and go into the lond of visioun, and offre thou hym there in to brent sacrifice, on oon of the hillis whiche Y schal schewe to thee." 3 Therefor Abraham roos bi niȝt, and sadlide his asse, and ledde with hym twey ȝonge men, and Ysaac his sone; and whanne he hadde hewe trees in to brent sacrifice, he ȝede to the place which God hadde comaundid to him. 4 Forsothe in the thridde dai he reiside hise iȝen, and seiȝ a place afer; 5 and he seide to hise children, "Abide ȝe here with the asse; Y and the child schulen go thidur; and aftir that we han worschipid, we schulen turne aȝen to ȝou." 6 And he took the trees of brent sacrifice, and puttide on Ysaac his sone; forsothe he bar fier, and a swerd in hise hondis. And whanne thei tweyne ȝeden togidere, 7 Isaac seide to his fadir, "My fadir!" And he answerde, "What wolt thou, sone?" He seide, "Lo! fier and trees, where is the beeste of brent sacrifice?" 8 Abraham seide, "My sone, God schal puruey to hym the beeste of brent sacrifice." Therfor thei ȝeden to gidere, 9 and camen to the place whiche God hadde schewid to hym, in which place Abraham bildide an auter, and dresside trees aboue; and whanne he hadde bounde togidere Ysaac, his sone, he puttide Ysaac in the auter,

---

14 hēt: *called;* gesȳhð: *sees;* gesǣd: *pt. pp., called*
16 swerige: *swear;* noldest: *did not desire;* ārian: *spare;* ege: *fear*
17 blētsige: *bless;* gemenigfylde: *pr. 1 sg., will increase;* sandceosel: *gravel;* āgan [owe, own]: *possess;* fēonda: *gen., enemies*
18 ðēoda: *peoples;* gehȳrsumodest: *obeyed;* hǣs(e): *command*

1 assaiede: *tested*
2 oon gendrid: *only-begotten*
3 hewe: *pt. pp., cut down;* ȝede: *went*
4 iȝen: *eyes;* seiȝ: *saw;* afer: *far off*
8 puruey: *provide*
9 dresside: *arranged*

on the heep of trees. 10 And he helde forth his hond, and took the swerd
to sacrifice his sone. 11 And lo! an aungel of the Lord criede fro heuene, and
seide, "Abraham! Abraham!" Which answerde, "I am present." 12 And
the aungel seide to hym, "Holde thou not forth thin honde on the child,
nether do thou ony thing to him; now Y haue knowe that thou dredist
God, and sparidist not thin oon gendrid sone for me." 13 Abraham reiside
hise iȝen, and he seiȝ bihynde his bak a ram cleuynge bi hornes among
breris, which he took, and offride brent sacrifice for the sone. 14 And he
clepide the name of that place, "The Lord seeth"; wherfore it is seyd, til
to dai, "The Lord schal see in the hil." 15 Forsothe the aungel of the Lord
clepide Abraham the secounde tyme fro heuene, and seide, 16 "The Lord
seith, Y haue swore bi my silf, for thou hast do this thing, and hast not
sparid thin oon gendrid for me, 17 Y schal blesse thee, and Y schal multiplie
thi seed as the sterris of heuene, and as grauel which is in the brynk of the
see; thi seed schal gete the ȝatis of hise enemyes; 18 and alle the folkis of
erthe schulen be blessid in thi seed, for thou obeiedist to my vois."

King James

1 And it came to passe after these things, that God did tempt Abraham,
and said vnto him, Abraham. And hee said, Beholde, heere I am. 2 And
he said, Take now thy sonne, thine onely sonne Isaac, whom thou louest,
and get thee into the land of Moriah: and offer him there for a burnt offering
vpon one of the Mountaines which I will tell thee of. 3 And Abraham rose
vp earely in the morning, and sadled his asse, and tooke two of his yong
men with him, and Isaac his sonne, and claue the wood for the burnt offering, and rose vp, and went vnto the place of which God had told him. 4 Then
on the third day Abraham lift vp his eyes, and saw the place afarre off.
5 And Abraham said vnto his yong men, Abide you here with the asse,
and I and the lad will goe yonder and worship, and come againe to you.
6 And Abraham tooke the wood of the burnt offering, and layd it vpon
Isaac his sonne: and he tooke the fire in his hand, and a knife: and they
went both of them together. 7 And Isaac spake vnto Abraham his father,
and said, My father: and he said, Here am I, my sonne. And hee said,
Behold the fire and wood: but where is the lambe for a burnt offring? 8 And
Abraham said, My sonne, God will prouide himselfe a lambe for a burnt
offering: so they went both of them together. 9 And they came to the place
which God had tolde him of, and Abraham built an Altar there, and layd
the wood in order, and bound Isaac his sonne, and layde him on the Altar

---

13   cleuynge: *sticking*   14   clepide: *called*

vpon the wood. 10 And Abraham stretched foorth his hand, and tooke the knife to slay his sonne. 11 And the Angel of the Lord called vnto him out of heauen, and said, Abraham, Abraham. And he said, Here am I. 12 And he said, Lay not thine hand vpon the lad, neither do thou any thing vnto him: for now I know that thou fearest God, seeing thou hast not withhelde thy sonne, thine onely sonne from mee. 13 And Abraham lifted vp his eyes, and looked, and beholde, behinde him a Ramme caught in a thicket by his hornes: And Abraham went and tooke the Ramme, and offered him up for a burnt offering, in the stead of his sonne. 14 And Abraham called the name of that place Jehouah-ijreh, as it is said to this day, In the Mount of the Lord it shalbe seene. 15 And the Angel of the Lord called vnto Abraham out of heauen the second time, 16 And said, By my selfe haue I sworne, saith the Lord, for because thou hast done this thing, and hast not withheld thy sonne, thine onely sonne, 17 That in blessing I will blesse thee, and in multiplying, I will multiply thy seed, as the starres of the heauen, and as the sand which is vpon the sea shore, and thy seed shall possesse the gate of his enemies. 18 And in thy seed shall all the nations of the earth be blessed, because thou hast obeyed my voice.

Modern American

1 Some time after this God put Abraham to the test. "Abraham!" he said to him. "Here am I," he said. 2 "Take your son," he said, "your only son, whom you love, Isaac, and go to the land of Moriah, and there offer him as a burnt-offering on one of the hills which I shall designate to you." 3 So next morning Abraham rose early, and harnessing his ass, he took two of his servants with him and his son Isaac, and having cut wood for the burnt-offering, he started off for the sanctuary which God had designated to him. 4 On the third day, when Abraham raised his eyes, he saw the sanctuary in the distance. 5 So Abraham said to his servants, "Stay here with the ass, while I and the boy go yonder to perform our devotions, after which we shall return to you." 6 So Abraham took the wood for the burnt-offering and put it on the back of his son Isaac, while he carried in his own hand the fire and the knife. So the two of them went off together.

7 "Father!" said Isaac to his father Abraham. "Yes, my son," he responded. "Here are the fire and the wood," he said, "but where is the sheep for a burnt-offering?" 8 "God will provide himself with the sheep for a burnt-offering, my son," said Abraham. Thereupon the two of them proceeded on their way together. 9 When they arrived at the sanctuary which God had designated to him, Abraham built the altar there, arranged the wood, and binding his son Isaac, laid him on the altar on top of the wood.

10 But as Abraham put out his hand to grasp the knife to slay his son,
11 the angel of the Lord called to him from the heavens, "Abraham,
Abraham!" "Here am I," he replied. 12 "Do not lay hands on the boy,"
he said, "do nothing of the sort to him; for I know now that you revere
God, in that you have not withheld your son, your only son, from me."

13 When Abraham raised his eyes, he saw behind him a ram caught in
the brushwood by its horns! 14 So Abraham went and took the ram, and
offered it up as a burnt-offering in place of his son. Then Abraham called
the name of that sanctuary Yahweh-jireh, which is today interpreted as "At
the hill of the Lord provision is made." 15 A second time the angel of the
Lord called to Abraham from the heavens, 16 "I swear by myself" — it is
the oracle of the Lord — "that since you have done this, and have not
withheld your son, your only son, 17 I will indeed bless you, and will surely
make your descendants as numerous as the stars of the sky, or the sands
that are on the seashore, so that your descendants shall take possession of
the cities of their enemies, 18 and through your descendants all the nations
of the earth shall invoke blessings on one another — just because you
heeded my injunction."

NOTES

2   The Vulgate has interpreted the Hebrew place-name by *Visio(nis)*
     'vision, sight,' but the OE and Purvey have left the Latin form: con-
     trast 14 and IV, 3.

3   The OE has omitted the reference to loading the ass, but assumed that
     they were riding on asses: it uses a plural again in 5. Note Purvey *trees*
     for *ligna* 'timber' here and in 6, 9, etc.

8   OE *hym sylf* need not be an example of the use in combination ('God
     himself'): *sylf* agrees with the subject, but *hym* may be the indirect
     object: 'God himself will provide for himself.'

9   The OE has altered this verse considerably: the addition *on ðā ealdan
     wīse* 'in the old fashion' may be intended to indicate that human
     sacrifice was only a very primitive practice.

12   OE 'over his neck' appears to be for dramatic effect. Vulgate *propter
     me* shows that the angel is speaking God's words; the OE, however,
     separates God and the angel as is shown by *him*.

13   Purvey obscures the fact that *holocaustum* is predicative, 'as a sacri-
     fice.'

14   OE past *vidit* is clearly an error: two MSS read *videt*. Note the different
     interpretations of the place-name: the sense 'provision' is the most
     likely.

16 Vulgate *per* probably indicates the object by which the oath is sworn; this is not made clear in all versions. OE *nū* is causal/temporal, 'now (that).' Note the objective genitive *mīn ege* 'fear of me.'

18 The American version is interpreting rather than translating.

IV

NUMBERS 11: 1-15

᪸᪸᪸᪸᪸᪸᪸᪸᪸᪸᪸᪸᪸᪸᪸᪸᪸᪸

The Israelites in the Desert

Vulgate

1 Interea ortum est murmur populi, quasi dolentium pro labore, contra Dominum. Quod cum audisset Dominus, iratus est; et accensus in eos ignis Domini devoravit extremam castrorum partem. 2 Cumque clamasset populus ad Moysen, oravit Moyses ad Dominum, et absorptus est ignis; 3 Vocavitque nomen loci illius *Incensio*, eo quod incensus fuisset contra eos ignis Domini. 4 Vulgus quippe promiscuum, quod ascenderat cum eis, flagravit desiderio, sedens et flens, junctis sibi pariter filiis Israel, et ait: Quis dabit nobis ad vescendum carnes? 5 Recordamur piscium quos comede-bamus in Aegypto gratis; in mentem nobis veniunt cucumeres, et pepones, porrique et caepe, et allia. 6 Anima nostra arida est, nihil aliud respiciunt oculi nostri nisi man. 7 Erat autem man quasi semen coriandri, coloris bdellii. 8 Circuibatque populus, et colligens illud, frangebat mola; sive terebat in mortario, coquens in olla, et faciens ex eo tortulas saporis quasi panis oleati. 9 Cumque descenderet nocte super castra ros, descendebat pariter et man. 10 Audivit ergo Moyses flentem populum per familias, singulos per ostia tentorii sui. Iratusque est furor Domini valde; sed et Moysi intoleranda res visa est, 11 Et ait ad Dominum: Cur afflixisti servum tuum? quare non invenio gratiam coram te? et cur imposuisti pondus universi populi huius super me? 12 Numquid ego concepi omnem hanc multitudinem, vel genui eam, ut dicas mihi: Porta eos in sinu tuo, sicut portare solet nutrix infantulum, et defer in terram pro qua jurasti patribus eorum? 13 Unde mihi carnes ut dem tantae multitudini? Flent contra me, dicentes: Da nobis carnes ut comedamus. 14 Non possum solus sustinere omnem hunc populum, quia gravis est mihi. 15 Sin aliter tibi videtur, obsecro ut interficias me, et inveniam gratiam in oculis tuis, ne tantis afficiar malis.

Old English Heptateuch

1 Gemang ðām ārās micel murcnung on ðām folce ongēan Drihten, and hī wǣron sārie for heora geswince. Þā hē þæt gehȳrde, ðā wearð hē yrre, and Drihtnes fȳr wearð onǣled and forbærnde þone ȳtemestan dæl þæs folces. 2 Þā clypode þæt folc tō Moyse, and Moyses gebæd tō Drihtne, and þæt fȳr geswāc, 3 and hē nemde þǣre stōwe naman "Onāl" for þan þe Drihtnes fȳr wæs ðǣr onǣled ongēan þæt folc. 4 Ðæt gemengede folc wearð gefylled mid gȳfernysse, and sǣton and wēopon mid Israhela folce, and cwǣdon: "Hwā sylð ūs flǣsc tō etanne? 5 Wē gemunon hū fela fixa wē hæfdon tō gyfe on Egypta lande, and wē hæfdon cucumeres, þæt sind eorðæpla, and pepones and porlēac and ennelēac and manega ōþre þinge. 6 Nū wē synd hlǣne; nabbe wē nān þincg tō etene būtan man." 7 Swā hī hēton þone heofonlīcan mete þe hī God mid fēdde; þæt wæs swilce coriandran sǣd, hwītes blēos swā cristalla. 8 Þæt hī gaderodon and grundon on cwyrne oððe brȳtton and sudon on croccan and worhton hlāfas ðǣrof: þā wǣron swylce hī wǣron elebacene. 9 Þonne ðæt dēaw cōm on niht, ðonne cōm ðǣrmid sē heofonlīca mete þe hī "man" hēton. 10 Moyses gehȳrde ðæt ðæt folc wēop, ælc æt his geteldes dura, and Godes yrre āstāh swȳðe, and hit ðūhte Moyse swȳðe hefitȳme. 11 And hē cwæð tō Drihtne: "Hwī geswenctest ðū þīnne ðēow? Hwī nabbe ic nāne gyfe beforan ðē, and hwī settest ðū þises folces swārnysse uppan mē? 12 Cwyst ðū, geēacnode ic hī ealle oþþe ācende ic hī, þæt ðū mē bude þæt ic hī bǣre on mīnum bōsme, swā fōstormōdor dēð cild, and þæt ic bǣre on þæt land, þe ðū hyra fæderum foreswōre? 13 Hwanan sceolde mē cuman flǣsc, ðæt ic sylle ðison folce? Hī wēpað ongēan mē, and cweðað: 'Syle ūs flǣsc tō etanne.' 14 Ne mæg ic āna ācuman eall þis folc; hit is mē swȳðe hefig. 15 Būtan ðū elles wylle, ic

---

1 Gemang ðām [among]: *in the mean-time;* ārās (ārīsan): *arose;* Drihten: *God;* sārie: *sorry;* geswinc(e): *toil;* gehȳrde: *heard;* yrre: *angry;* onǣled: *kindled;* forbærnde: *burnt up;* ytemest-(an): *outermost;* dæl [deal]: *part*

2 gebæd (gebiddan): *prayed;* geswāc (geswīcan): *ceased*

3 stōw(e): *gen., place;* Onāl: *burning*

4 gemengede: *mixed;* gȳfernyss(e): *greed;* sǣton (sittan): *pt. 3 pl., sat;* wēopon (wēpan): *wept;* sylð (sellan): *will give*

5 gemunon: *remember;* fela: *many;* tō gyfe: *as a gift, free;* cucumeres: *cucumbers;* eorðæpl(a): *earth apples;* pepones: *melons;* porlēac: *leeks;* ennelēac: *onions*

6 hlǣn(e): *lean;* nabbe: *do not have*

7 hēton (hātan): *pt. 3 pl., called;* mete [meat]: *food;* blēos: *gen., color*

8 gaderodon: *gathered;* grundon (grindan): *pt. 3 pl., ground;* cwyrn(e) [quern]: *handmill;* brȳtton: *broke;* sudon (sēoðan) [seethe, sodden] *boiled;* elebacene: *baked in oil*

9 dēaw: *dew;* ðǣrmid: *therewith*

10 geteldes: *gen., tent's;* yrre: *anger;* āstāh (āstīgan): *arose;* ðūhte: *seemed;* hefitȳme: *grievous*

11 geswenctest: *pt. 2 sg., troubled;* ðēow: *servant;* gyf(e): *grace;* swārnyss(e): *oppression*

12 geēacnode: *conceived;* ācende: *gave birth to;* bude (bēodan): *pt. 2 sg., ordered;* bǣre: *pt. 1 sg. subj., bear;* foreswōre [swore]: *pt. 2 sg., promised*

13 Hwanan: *whence;* sylle [sell]: *pr. 1 sg. subj., give*

14 āna: *alone;* ācuman: *support*

15 elles: *otherwise;* wylle: *pr. 2 sg. subj., wish;* ofslēa: *pr. 2 sg. subj., kill*

bidde ðē ðæt ðū mē ofslēa and ic hæbbe gyfe beforan ðē, þæt ic ne sȳ mid swā miclum yfele geswenct."

Wycliffite (Purvey)

1 Yn the meene tyme the grutchyng of the puple, as of men sorewynge for trauel, roos aȝens the Lord. And whanne Moises hadde herd this thing, he was wrooth; and the fier of the Lord was kyndelid on hem, and deuouride the laste part of the tentis. 2 And whanne the puple hadde cried to Moises, Moises preiede the Lord, and the fier was quenchid. 3 And he clepid the name of that place *Brennyng*, for the fier of the Lord was kyndlid aȝens hem. 4 And the comyn puple of malis and femalis, that hadde stied with hem, brent with desire of fleischis, and sat, and wepte with the sones of Israel ioyned togidere to hem, and seide, "Who schal ȝyue to vs fleischis to ete? 5 We thenken on the fischis whiche we eten in Egipt freli; gourdis, and melouns, and lekis, and oyniouns, and garlekis comen in to mynde to vs; 6 oure soule is drie; oure iȝen byholden noon other thing no but manna." 7 Forsothe manna was as the seed of coriaundre, of the colour of bdellyum, which is whijt and briȝt as cristal. 8 And the puple ȝede aboute, and gaderide it, and brak with a queerne stoon, ether pownede in a morter, and sethide in a pot; and made therof litle cakis of the sauour, as of breed maad with oile. 9 And whanne dew cam doun in the niȝt on the tentis, also manna cam doun togidere. 10 Therfor Moises herde the puple wepynge bi meynees, and alle bi hem silf bi the doris of her tentis; and the woodnesse of the Lord was wrooth greetli, but also the thing was seyn vnsuffrable to Moises. 11 And he seide to the Lord, "Whi hast thou turmentid thi seruaunt? whi fynde Y not grace bifor thee? and whi hast thou put on me the burthun of al this puple? 12 whethir Y conseyuede al this multitude, ethir gendride it, that thou seie to me, Bere thou hem in thi bosum as a nurise is wont to bere a litil ȝong child, and bere thou in to the lond for which thou hast swore to the fadris of hem. 13 Wherof ben fleischis to me, that Y ȝyue to so greet multitude? Thei wepen bifore me, and seyn, 'ȝyue thou fleischis to vs that we ete'; 14 I mai not aloone suffre al this puple, for it is greuouse to me. 15 If in other maner it semeth to thee, Y biseche that thou sle me, and that Y fynde grace in thin iȝen, that Y be not punyschid bi so grete yuelis."

---

1 trauel: *sorrow*	8 ȝede: *went;* queerne [quern]: *mill;*
3 clepid: *called*	ether: *or*
4 stied: *gone up*	10 bi meynees: *in companies;* woodnesse:
6 iȝen: *eyes*	*madness;* was seyn: *was seen, seemed*

King James

1 And when the people complained, it displeased the Lord: and the Lord heard it: and his anger was kindled, and the fire of the Lord burnt among them, and consumed them that were in the vttermost parts of the campe. 2 And the people cried vnto Moses, and when Moses prayed vnto the Lord, the fire was quenched. 3 And hee called the name of the place Taberah: because the fire of the Lord burnt among them. 4 And the mixt multitude that was among them, fell a lusting, and the children of Israel also wept againe, and said, Who shal giue vs flesh to eate? 5 We remember the fish which wee did eate in Egypt freely: the cucumbers, and the melons, and the leekes, and the onions, and the garlicke. 6 But now our soule is dried away, there is nothing at all, besides this Manna, before our eyes. 7 And the Manna was as Coriander seed, and the colour thereof as the colour of Bdelium: 8 And the people went about, and gathered it, and ground it in milles, or beat it in a morter, and baked it in pans, and made cakes of it: and the taste of it was as the taste of fresh oyle. 9 And when the dew fell vpon the campe in the night, the Manna fell vpon it. 10 Then Moses heard the people weepe throughout their families, euery man in the doore of his tent, and the anger of the Lord was kindled greatly, Moses also was displeased. 11 And Moses said vnto the Lord, Wherefore hast thou afflicted thy seruant? and wherefore haue I not found fauour in thy sight, that thou layest the burden of all this people vpon me? 12 Haue I conceiued all this people? haue I begotten them, that thou shouldest say vnto me, Cary them in thy bosome (as a nursing father beareth the sucking child) vnto the land which thou swarest vnto their fathers? 13 Whence should I haue flesh to giue vnto all this people? for they weep vnto me, saying, Giue vs flesh, that we may eate. 14 I am not able to beare all this people alone, because it is too heauie for mee. 15 And if thou deale thus with mee, kill me, I pray thee out of hand, if I haue found fauour in thy sight, and let me not see my wretchednesse.

Modern American

1 Now the people were complaining of misfortune in the hearing of the Lord; and when the Lord heard it, his anger blazed, so that the fire of the Lord burned among them, and consumed some of the best parts of the camp. 2 Then the people cried to Moses; so Moses prayed to the Lord, and the fire abated. 3 Hence the name of that place came to be called Taberah (burning), because the fire of the Lord had burned among them.

4 Now the rabble among them had a craving for flesh, and the Israelites

also wept, and said, "O that we had flesh to eat! 5 We remember the fish that we used to eat for nothing in Egypt, the cucumbers, the melons, the leeks, the onions, and the garlic; 6 but now we are hungry, and there is not a thing, except that we have the manna to look at." 7 Now the manna was like coriander seed, and its color was like that of resinous gum. 8 The people used to go about and gather it, then grind it between millstones or pound it in a mortar, boil it in a pot, and make cakes of it; its taste was like that of a cake baked with oil. 9 Whenever the dew fell on the camp at night, the manna used to fall with it.

10 Moses heard the people weeping, family by family, each at the doorway of his tent; the anger of the Lord blazed exceedingly, and Moses was displeased. 11 "Why hast thou been so hard on thy servant?" said Moses to the Lord. "Why have I not found favor with thee, that thou shouldst put the burden of all this people on me? 12 Was it I who conceived all this people? Or was it I who gave them birth, that thou shouldst say to me, 'Carry them in your bosom, as a nurse would carry a sucking child, to the land which thou didst promise on oath to their fathers'? 13 Where can I get flesh to give to all this people? For they weep on my shoulder, saying, 'Give us flesh to eat.' 14 I am not able to carry all this people by myself, because they are too heavy for me. 15 If this is the way thou art going to deal with me, pray kill me at once, if I find any favor with thee, and let me see no more of my trouble."

NOTES

1   Purvey *Moises* is against Vulgate *Dominus*; both OE and Purvey may have had a text of the Vulgate in which the subject of *audisset* was omitted, making it unclear who the subject should be.

3   The Hebrew place-name is translated by the Vulgate, by the OE (*on-āl* is the noun from which the verb *on-ǣlan* 'burn' was formed) and by Purvey, but not by KJ and the American version. This contrast between medieval and modern translation practice is also seen in the treatment of technical terms such as Hebrew religious offices.

4   The Vulgate and the original Hebrew clearly differ. Purvey *stied* (OE *stīgan*) is a literal translation of *ascenderat* 'went up.' Vulgate *promiscuum* probably means 'racially mixed,' not of both sexes (as Purvey).

5   Note that the OE (or its text of the Vulgate) has committed a howler by taking *allia* 'garlic' as though it were *alia* 'other things.'

7   Probably the OE and Purvey had a text of the Vulgate which commented on the color of *bdellium* (the vine-palm, noted for its gum, or the gum itself) as being like crystal; the OE has substituted a more familiar plant.

8 OE *elebacene* '(loaves) baked in oil,' not to be associated with *bacon*.

10 Note the literalness of Purvey *was seyn* for *videbatur* 'seemed.' Vulgate *sui tentorii* could mean 'each man's tent' (as Purvey), but Moses' tent is more likely.

12 OE *Cwyst* often introduces a question implying disbelief, as Latin *Num(quid)*: compare XII, 17 and *n.*; loosely it means 'do you say?'; Purvey *Whethir* is a common introduction to a direct question in ME. All versions except the OE treat the phrase 'which you promised to their ancestors' as part of God's hypothetical speech, in which case *you* = Moses; the OE, by putting the words into indirect speech, has made God the subject of *foreswōre* 'promised.'

14 Purvey misses the image of carrying implied by *sustinere* and *gravis*.

15 Texts derived from the Vulgate differ from later ones here.

V

PSALM 8

෯෯෯෯෯෯෯෯෯

Lord our Lord, how Excellent Is Thy Name

Vulgate

1 Domine, Dominus noster, quam admirabile est nomen tuum in universa terra! Quoniam elevata est magnificentia tua super caelos. 2 Ex ore infantium et lactentium perfecisti laudem propter inimicos tuos, ut destruas inimicum et ultorem. 3 Quoniam videbo caelos tuos, opera digitorum tuorum, lunam et stellas quae tu fundasti, 4 Quid est homo, quod memor es eius? aut filius hominis, quoniam visitas eum? 5 Minuisti eum paulo minus ab angelis; gloria et honore coronasti eum; 6 Et constituisti eum super opera manuum tuarum. Omnia subiecisti sub pedibus eius, 7 oves et boves universas, insuper et pecora campi, 8 volucres caeli, et pisces maris qui perambulant semitas maris. 9 Domine, Dominus noster, quam admirabile est nomen tuum in universa terra!

Old English

1 Ēalā Drihten, ūre God, hū wundorlīc þīn nama ys geond ealle eorðan! For þām āhefen ys þīn myclung ofer heofonas; 2 gē furðum, of ðæra cilda mūðe þe meolc sūcað þū byst hered. 3 Þæt hī dōð tō bysmore þīnum fēondum; for ðām þū tōwyrpest þīne fȳnd, and ealle þā þe unrihtwīsnesse lādiað and scyldað. 3 Ic ongite nū þæt weorc þīnra fingra, þæt synd heofonas and mōna and steorran, þā þū āstealdest. 4 Drihten, hwæt is sē mann þe þū swā myclum āmanst? oþþe hwæt is sē mannes sunu þe þū oft rǣdlīce

---

1 wundorlīc: *wonderful;* āhefen (āhebban): *pt. pp., lifted up;* myclung:
   greatness
2 gē furðum: *yea moreover;* þe meolc
   sūcað: *that suck milk;* hered: *pt. pp.,
   praised;* tō bysmore: *as an insult;*

tōwyrpest (tōweorpan): *overthrow;* un-
rihtwīsness(e): *unrighteousness;* lādiað:
excuse; scyldað: *sin*
3 ongite: *perceive;* āstealdest: *founded*
4 āmanst (onmunan): *pr. 2 sg., remember;*
nēosast: *visit*

nēosast? 5 Þū hine gedēst lȳtle lǣssan þonne englas; þū hine gewuldrast
and geweorðast, and him sylst hēafodgold tō mǣrðe; 6 and þū hine gesetest
ofer þīn handgeweorc. Ealle gesceafta þū legst under his fēt, and under his
anwald; 7 scēap and hrȳðera and ealle eorðan nȳtenu; 8 flēogende fuglas
and sǣfiscas, þā farað geond þā sǣwegas. 9 Drihten, Drihten, ūre God,
hū wuldorlīc þīn nama ys geond ealle eorðan!

Richard Rolle

1 Lord, oure lord, what thi name is wondirful in all the erth. For liftid is
thi worship abouen heuens. 2 Of the mouth of noght spekand and sowkand
thou has made louynge for thi enmys, that thou distroy the enmy and the
vengere. 3 For I sall see thi heuens, werkis of thi fyngirs, the mone and the
sternes the whilk thou grundid. 4 What is man that thou ert mynand of
him? or son of man for thou visites him? 5 Thou lessid hym a litel fra
aungels; with ioy and honour thou coround him, 6 and thou sett him abouen
the werkis of thi hend. All thyngis thou vndirkast vndir his fete, 7 shepe
and oxin all, ouer that and the bestis of the feld. 8 Foghlis of heuen and
fischis of the see, that gas the wayes of the se. 9 Lord, oure lord, what thi
name is wondirful in all the erth.

Wycliffite (Purvey)

1 Lord, thou art oure Lord; thi name is ful wonderful in al erthe. For thi
greet doyng is reisid, aboue heuenes. 2 Of the mouth of ȝonge children,
not spekynge and soukynge mylk, thou madist perfitli heriyng, for thin
enemyes; that thou destrie the enemy and avengere. 3 For Y schal se thin
heuenes, the werkis of thi fyngris; the moone and sterris, whiche thou hast

---

5 gedēst (gedōn): *make;* gewuldrast,
  geweorðast: *honor;* sylst (sellan): *give;*
  hēafodgold [head-gold]: *crown;* tō
  mǣrðe: *for (his) honor*
6 gesceafta: *creation(s);* legst (lecgan):

  pr. 2 sg., place; anwald: *power*
7 nȳten(u): *animals*
8 flēogende: *flying;* fuglas [fowls]: *birds;*
  farað [fare]: *go*
9 wuldorlīc: *glorious*

1 what: *lo!*
2 sowkand: *sucking;* louynge: *praise*
3 sall: *shall;* sternes: *stars;* the whilk:
  which

4 mynand: *remembering*
6 hend: *hands*
8 Foghlis: *birds;* gas: *go*

2 perfitli heriyng: *perfect praise*

foundid. 4 What is a man, that thou art myndeful of hym; eithir the sone of a virgyn, for thou visitist hym? 5 Thou hast maad hym a litil lesse than aungels; thou hast corouned hym with glorie and onour, 6 and hast ordeyned hym aboue the werkis of thin hondis. Thou hast maad suget alle thingis vndur hise feet; 7 alle scheep and oxis, ferthermore and the beestis of the feeld; 8 the briddis of the eir, and the fischis of the see; that passen bi the pathis of the see. 9 Lord, thou art oure Lord; thi name is wondurful in al erthe.

King James

1 O Lord our Lord, how excellent is thy name in all the earth! who hast set thy glory aboue the heauens. 2 Out of the mouth of babes and sucklings hast thou ordained strength, because of thine enemies, that thou mightest still the enemie and the auenger. 3 When I consider thy heauens, the worke of thy fingers, the moone and the starres which thou hast ordained; 4 What is man, that thou art mindfull of him? and the sonne of man, that thou visitest him? 5 For thou hast made him a little lower then the Angels; and hast crowned him with glory and honour. 6 Thou madest him to haue dominion ouer the workes of thy hands; thou hast put all things vnder his feete. 7 All sheepe and oxen, yea and the beasts of the field. 8 The foule of the aire, and the fish of the sea, and whatsoeuer passeth through the paths of the seas. 9 O Lord our Lord, how excellent is thy name in all the earth!

Fontana

1   How great is your name, O Lord our God,
     through all the earth!
     Your majesty is praised above the heavens;
2   on the lips of children and of babes
     you have found praise to foil your enemy,
     to silence the foe and the rebel.
3   When I see the heavens, the work of your hands,
     the moon and the stars which you arranged,
4   what is man that you should keep him in mind,
     mortal man that you care for him?

---

6   suget: *subject*

5 Yet you have made him little less than a god;
   with glory and honour you crowned him,
6 gave him power over the works of your hand,
   put all things under his feet.
7 All of them, sheep and cattle,
   yes, even the savage beasts,
8 birds of the air, and fish
   that make their way through the waters.
9 How great is your name, O Lord our God,
   through all the earth!

NOTES

1 Rolle *what* is an exclamation. Note Rolle's literal interpretation of *magnificentia* as *greet doyng*, typical of all his translation (compare 2, 5, 7).

2 OE interprets and elucidates *propter inimicos:* 'they do this as an insult to your enemies.' Note that Rolle *louynge* is not 'loving' (OE verb *lufian*) but 'praising' (OE *lōfung*). The ME use of *o* for *u*, to avoid confusion in writing with letters such as *u, n, m*, resulted in much confusion between the words for 'love' and 'praise.' Note the Northern present participle in *-and*. Both Rolle and Purvey translate *in-fantium* literally, as 'not speaking.'

4 Purvey *sone of a virgyn* improbably interprets the common biblical phrase "son of man" (i.e., mortal man) as referring to Christ.

5 OE *sylst hēafodgold* 'give a crown (head-gold)' renders *coronasti* closely.

9 OE here uses *wuldorlīc* 'glorious' rather than *wundorlīc* 'wonderful' (1) to translate *admirabile*.

VI

PSALM 102: 1-12

༺෴෴෴෴෴෴෴෴෴෴෴༻

Hear my Prayer, O Lord

Vulgate

1 Domine, exaudi orationem meam, et clamor meus ad te veniat. 2 Non avertas faciem tuam a me; in quacumque die tribulor, inclina ad me aurem tuam. In quacumque die invocavero te, velociter exaudi me. 3 Quia defecerunt sicut fumus dies mei, et ossa mea sicut cremium aruerunt. 4 Percussus sum ut foenum, et aruit cor meum, quia oblitus sum comedere panem meum. 5 A voce gemitus mei adhaesit os meum carni meae. 6 Similis factus sum pellicano solitudinis; factus sum sicut nycticorax in domicilio. 7 Vigilavi, et factus sum sicut passer solitarius in tecto. 8 Tota die exprobrabant mihi inimici mei, et qui laudabant me adversum me jurabant. 9 Quia cinerem tanquam panem manducabam, et potum meum cum fletu miscebam; 10 A facie irae et indignationis tuae, quia elevans allisisti me. 11 Dies mei sicut umbra declinaverunt, et ego sicut foenum arui. 12 Tu autem, Domine, in aeternum permanes, et memoriale tuum in generationem et generationem.

Old English (verse)

1 Ðū mīn gebed,   mǣre drihten,
   gehȳr, heofenes weard,   and gehlȳde mīn
   tō ðē becume,   þēoda reccend.
2 Nā þū andwlitan   ǣfre þīnne
   āwend fram mē,   wuldres ealdor;
   gif ic geswenced sȳ,   þū swǣs tō mē

---

1 gebed: *prayer;* mǣre: *glorious;* gehȳr: *hear;* weard: *guardian;* gehlȳde: *voice;* þēoda: *gen., peoples;* reccend: *ruler*
2 andwlita(n): *face;* āwend: *turn;* wul- dres: *gen., glory;* ealdor: *prince;* geswenced: *tormented;* swǣs: *benevolent;* onhyld: *incline;* ofestlīce: *swiftly;* bēna(n): *pleader*

70

þīn ēare onhyld and mē ofestlīce
gehȳr, heofenes weard, helpys bēnan.

3 Forðon dagas mīne gedroren syndan
smēce gelīce, and forspyrcende synd
mīne mearhcofan, þæs þe mē þinceð,
swylce hī on cōcerpannan cōcas gehyrstan.

4 Ic eom hege gelīc, þām þe hraðe weornað,
ðonne hit byð āmāwyn mannes folmum;
is mīn heorte ēac hearde geswenced,
forðon ic ǣr forgeat, þæt ic etan sceolde

5 mīnne swētne hlāf; forðon mē is swǣre stefn
hefig gnorniende heortan getenge,
ætfēolen ēac mīn bān flǣsce mīnum.

6 Ic geworden eom pellicane gelīc,
sē on wēstene wunað; wāt ic ēac swīðe geare,
þæt ic genemned eam nihthrefne gelīc,

7 þe on scræfe eardað, and ic spearuwan swā some
gelīce gewearð, ānlīcum fugele.

8 Hwæt, mē ealne dæg edwitsprǣce on
mīne fēondas fæste brōhtan,
and ðā mē heredan, hī mē hraþe æfter
full swȳþe eft swerigean ongunnon.

9 Forðon ic ānlīc ætt æscean hlāfe,
and ic mīnne drinc mengde wið tēarum,

10 for andwlitan yrres þīnes;
fēor þū mē āhōfc and gehnǣctest eft.

11 Dagas mīne gedruran swā sē deorca scūa,
and ic hege gelīc, swā hit hraðe weornað.

12 Þū on ēcnysse wunast āwā, drihten;
wunað þīn gemynd, þenden woruld standeð.

---

3 gedroren (drēosan): *pt. pp., perished;*
smēc(e): *smoke;* forspyrcende: *drying
up;* mearhcofa(n) [marrow]: *bones;*
þæs þe mē þinceð: *as it seems to me;*
cōcerpann(an): *frying pans;* cōcas:
cooks; gehyrstan: *fried*

4 hraðe: *quickly;* weornað: *withers;*
āmāwyn: *mown;* folm(um): *hands;*
forgeat: *forgot;* etan: *eat;* swētne:
sweet

5 forðon: *therefore;* swǣre: *sad;* stefn:
voice; gnorniende: *sorrowing;* getenge:
burdensome to; ætfēolen: *pt. pp., stuck
to*

6 wēsten(e): *desert;* wunað: *dwells;*
geare: *readily;* genemned: *named;*

nihthrefn(e): *night raven;* scræf(e):
hole; eardað: *dwells*

7 spearuwan: *sparrow;* ānlīc(um) [only]:
solitary

8 edwitsprǣce on: *in insult;* fēondas:
enemies; brōhtan: *pt. 3 pl., brought;*
heredan: *pt. 3 pl., praised;* swerigean:
swear; ongunnon (onginnan): *began*

9 ætt: *ate;* æsc(ean): *ash;* mengde: *mixed*

10 yrres: *gen., anger;* feor: *far;* āhōfe
(āhebban): *pt. 2 sg., raised up;*
gehnǣctest: *brought down*

11 gedruran: *pt. 3 pl., passed away;* scūa:
shadow

12 ēcnyss(e): *eternity;* āwā: *forever;*
gemynd: *memory;* þenden: *while*

Richard Rolle

1 Lord here my prayere, and my cry cum til the. 2 Turne noght away thi face fra me: in what day that I am in anguys held til me thin ere. In what day that I hafe inkald the, swiftly thou here me. 3 For my dayes failyd as reke, and my banys as kraghan dryid. 4 Smytyn I am as hay and my hert dryed, for I forgat to ete my brede. 5 Fro the voice of my sorowynge: my bane droghe till my fleyss. 6 Like I am made til the pellicane of anly stede: I am made as nyght rauen in the house euysynge. 7 I woke, and I am made as sparow solitary in the hous. 8 All day vpbraydid til me my fas: and tha that louyd me agayns me thai sware. 9 For aske I ete as brede; and my drynke I mengid with gretynge. 10 Fra the face of the wreth of thi dedeyn: for vpliftand thou downsmate me. 11 My dayes as shadow heldid: and I dryed as hay. 12 Bot thou, lord, dwellis withouten end: and thi menynge in generacioun and generacioun.

Wycliffite (Purvey)

1 Lord, here thou my preier; and my crie come to thee. 2 Turne not awei thi face fro me; in what euere dai Y am troblid, bowe doun thin eere to me. In what euere day Y schal inwardli clepe thee, here thou me swiftli. 3 For my daies han failid as smoke; and my boonus han dried vp as critouns. 4 I am smytun as hei, and myn herte dried vp; for Y haue forȝete to eete my breed. 5 Of the vois of my weilyng my boon cleuede to my fleische. 6 I am maad lijk a pellican of wildirnesse; Y am maad as a niȝt crowe in an hous. 7 I wakide; and Y am maad as a solitarie sparowe in the roof. 8 Al dai myn enemyes dispisiden me; and thei that preisiden me sworen aȝens me. 9 For Y eet aschis as breed; and Y meddlide my drinke with weping. 10 Fro the face of the ire of thin indignacioun; for thou reisinge me hast hurtlid me doun. 11 Mi daies boweden awei as a schadewe; and Y wexede drie as hei. 12 But, Lord, thou dwellist with outen ende; and thi memorial in generacioun and in to generacioun.

---

1 til: *to*
2 held: *incline;* inkald: *called on*
3 reke [reek]: *smoke;* kraghan: *scraps*
5 droghe: *drew*
6 anly [only]: *lonely;* stede: *place;* euysynge: *eaves*

8 louyd: *praised*
9 aske: *ashes;* mengid: *mingled;* gretynge: *weeping*
10 dedeyn: *disdain;* downsmate: *struck down*
12 menynge: *memory*

2 clepe: *call*
3 critouns: *scraps, cracklings*

5 cleuede: *stuck*
11 wexede: *became*

King James

1 Heare my prayer, O Lord: and let my crie come vnto thee. 2 Hide not thy face from me in the day when I am in trouble, incline thine eare vnto me: in the day when I call, answere mee speedily. 3 For my dayes are consumed like smoke: and my bones are burnt as an hearth. 4 My heart is smitten, and withered like grasse: so that I forget to eate my bread. 5 By reason of the voice of my groning, my bones cleaue to my skinne. 6 I am like a Pelican of the wildernes: I am like an owle of the desert. 7 I watch, and am as a sparowe alone vpon the house top. 8 Mine enemies reproch me all the day: and they that are mad against me, are sworne against me. 9 For I haue eaten ashes like bread: and mingled my drinke with weeping. 10 Because of thine indignation and thy wrath: for thou hast lifted me vp, and cast me downe. 11 My dayes are like a shadow, that declineth: & I am withered like grasse. 12 But thou, O Lord, shalt endure for euer: and thy remembrance vnto all generations.

Fontana

1 O Lord, listen to my prayer
    and let my cry for help reach you.

2 Do not hide your face from me
    in the day of my distress.
    Turn your ear towards me
    and answer me quickly when I call.

3 For my days are vanishing like smoke,
    my bones burn away like a fire.

4 My heart is withered like the grass.
    I forget to eat my bread.

5 I cry with all my strength
    and my skin clings to my bones.

6 I have become like a pelican in the wilderness,
    like an owl in desolate places.

7 I lie awake and I moan
    like some lonely bird on a roof.

8 All day long my foes revile me;
    those who hate me use my name as a curse.

9 The bread I eat is ashes;
    my drink is mingled with tears.

10 In your anger, Lord, and your fury
    you have lifted me up and thrown me down.

11   My days are like a passing shadow
      and I wither away like the grass.
12   But you, O Lord, will endure for ever
      and your name from age to age.

NOTES

The OE version provides an example of OE versification technique; images
that can readily be expressed in traditional poetic vocabulary are fully
expanded.

2   The OE noun *bēna* 'petitioner (for something)' is best rendered by a
    present participle, 'hear me, asking for help.' It expresses very con-
    cisely the Vulgate *in quacumque die invocavero te* 'on whatever day I
    call on you.'

3   Vulgate *cremium* 'firewood' is rendered by Rolle and Purvey with
    words of roughly the same meaning ('dried out scraps'); clearly the
    Hebrew had a different word. The OE has expanded the domestic
    image considerably.

6   Vulgate *domicilio:* Purvey was content to translate 'house,' but Rolle
    gives 'in the eaves of the house' and OE *scræf* usually means something
    scraped out (compare *eorðscræf* 'cave').

7   Note that Vulgate *vigilavi*, Purvey *wakide*, Rolle *woke*, KJ *watched*,
    all refer to the continuous state of being awake, not the action of
    awakening.

8   Note the differences between Vulgate- and Hebrew-derived versions.
    Rolle *louyd* 'praised': compare V, 2 *n*. above.

9   Rolle *gretynge:* the verb *greet* 'lament' is still used in Northern dialects.

VII · XII

⧾⧾⧾⧾⧾⧾⧾⧾⧾⧾⧾⧾⧾⧾⧾⧾⧾⧾⧾⧾⧾⧾⧾⧾⧾⧾⧾

THE NEW TESTAMENT

For general remarks on English biblical translations, see the preface to the Old Testament selections, p. 39–40. The Old English passages are taken from the eleventh century late *West-Saxon Gospels*, ed. J. W. Bright (Boston: Belles Lettres Series, *St. John* and *St. Matthew*, 1904, *St. Luke*, 1906). For a full reference to the Wycliffite (Purvey) translation into Middle English, and to the King James *Authorized Version* of 1611, see p. 39 above. Passages are given from the 1534 revised version of Tyndale's *New Testament*, ed. N. H. Wallis (Cambridge: Cambridge University Press, 1938). The modern translation is from the *New English Bible: New Testament* (London: Oxford University Press and Cambridge University Press, 1961).

The Old English (West-Saxon) Gospels and the Wycliffite Bible are based on the Latin Vulgate by Jerome; later versions (including Tyndale) are translated directly from the original Greek. In some minor cases the *New English Bible* differs from the King James and Tyndale, because of modern textual revisions.

VII

MATTHEW 5: 1-10

❧❧❧❧❧❧❧❧❧❧❧❧❧❧❧

Blessed Are the Poor in Spirit

Vulgate

1 Videns autem Jesus turbas, ascendit in montem, et cum sedisset, accesserunt ad eum discipuli eius. 2 Et aperiens os suum docebat eos, dicens: 3 Beati pauperes spiritu quoniam ipsorum est regnum caelorum. 5 Beati mites, quoniam ipsi possidebunt terram. 4 Beati qui lugent, quoniam ipsi consolabuntur. 6 Beati qui esuriunt et sitiunt justitiam, quoniam ipsi saturabuntur. 7 Beati misericordes, quoniam ipsi misericordiam consequentur. 8 Beati mundo corde, quoniam ipsi Deum videbunt. 9 Beati pacifici, quoniam filii Dei vocabuntur. 10 Beati qui persecutionem patiuntur propter justitiam, quoniam ipsorum est regnum caelorum.

Old English

1 Sōðlīce þā sē Hǣlend geseh þā menigu, hē āstāh on þone munt; and þā hē sæt, þā genēalǣhton his leorningcnihtas tō him. 2 And hē ontȳnde his mūð and lǣrde hī, and cwæð, 3 "Ēadige synt þā gāstlīcan þearfan, for þām hyra ys heofena rice. 5 Ēadige synt þā līðan, for þām þe hī eorðan āgun. 4 Ēadige synt þā ðe nū wēpað, for þām þe hī bēoð gefrēfrede. 6 Ēadige synt þā ðe rihtwīsnesse hingriað and þyrstað, for þām þe hī bēoð gefyllede. 7 Ēadige synt þā mildheortan, for þām þe hī mildheortnysse begytað. 8 Ēadige synt þā clǣnheortan, for þām þe hī God gesēoð. 9 Ēadige synt þā gesybsuman, for þām ðe hī bēoð Godes bearn genemnede. 10 Ēadige synt þā þe ēhtnysse þoliað for rihtwīsnysse, for þām þe hyra ys heofonan rīce."

---

1 Hǣlend [healer]: *Savior;* menigu: *multitude;* āstāh (āstīgan): *went up;* genēalǣhton: *approached;* leorning-cnihtas [learning-knights]: *disciples*
2 ontȳnde: *opened;* lǣrde: *taught*
3 gāstlīc(an) [ghostly]: *spiritual(ly);* þearf(an): *needy;* heofena: *gen. pl., heavens*

5 līðan: *gentle;* āgun [own, owe]: *pr. 3 pl., possess*
4 gefrēfrede: *pt. pp., comforted*
6 rihtwīsnes(e): *righteousness*
7 begytað: *pr. 3 pl., obtain*
9 gesybsum(an): *peaceful;* genemnede: *pt. pp., named*
10 ēhtnyss(e): *persecution;* þoliað: *endure*

76

Wycliffite (Purvey)

1 And Jhesus, seynge the puple, wente vp in to an hil; and whanne he was set, hise disciplis camen to hym. 2 And he openyde his mouth, and tauȝte hem, and seide, 3 "Blessed ben pore men in spirit, for the kyngdom of heuenes is herne. 5 Blessid ben mylde men, for thei schulen welde the erthe. 4 Blessid ben thei that mornen, for thei schulen be coumfortid. 6 Blessid ben thei that hungren and thristen riȝtwisnesse, for thei schulen be ful-fillid. 7 Blessid ben merciful men, for thei schulen gete merci. 8 Blessid ben thei that ben of clene herte, for thei schulen se God. 9 Blessid ben pesible men, for thei schulen be clepid Goddis children. 10 Blessid ben thei that suffren persecusioun for riȝtfulnesse, for the kingdam of heuenes is herne."

Tyndale

1 When he sawe the people, he went vp into a mountayne, and when he was set, his disciples came to hym, 2 and he opened hys mouthe, and taught them sayinge: 3 Blessed are the povre in sprete: for theirs is the kyngdome of heven. 4 Blessed are they that morne: for they shalbe con-forted. 5 Blessed are the meke: for they shall inheret the erth. 6 Blessed are they which honger and thurst for rightewesnes: for they shalbe filled. 7 Blessed are the mercifull: for they shall obteyne mercy. 8 Blessed are the pure in herte: for they shall se God. 9 Blessed are the peacemakers: for they shalbe called the chyldren of God. 10 Blessed are they which suffre persecucion for rightwesnes sake: for theirs ys the kyngdome of heuen.

King James

1 And seeing the multitudes, he went vp into a mountaine: and when he was set, his disciples came vnto him. 2 And he opened his mouth, and taught them, saying, 3 Blessed are the poore in spirit: for theirs is the king-dome of heauen. 4 Blessed are they that mourne: for they shall be com-forted. 5 Blessed are the meeke: for they shall inherit the earth. 6 Blessed are they which doe hunger and thirst after righteousnesse: for they shall be filled. 7 Blessed are the mercifull: for they shall obtaine mercie. 8 Blessed

---

3   herne: *theirs*   5   welde [wield]: *rule*

are the pure in heart: for they shall see God. 9 Blessed are the peacemakers: for they shall bee called the children of God. 10 Blessed are they which are persecuted for righteousnesse sake: for theirs is the kingdome of heauen.

New English Bible

1 When he saw the crowds he went up the hill. There he took his seat, and when his disciples had gathered round him (2) he began to address them. And this is the teaching he gave:
3 How blest are those who know that they are poor;
          the kingdom of Heaven is theirs.
4 How blest are the sorrowful;
          they shall find consolation.
5 How blest are those of a gentle spirit;
          they shall have the earth for their possession.
6 How blest are those who hunger and thirst to see right prevail;
          they shall be satisfied.
7 How blest are those who show mercy;
          mercy shall be shown to them.
8 How blest are those whose hearts are pure;
          they shall see God.
9 How blest are the peacemakers;
          God shall call them his sons.
10 How blest are those who have suffered persecution for the cause of right;
          the kingdom of Heaven is theirs.

NOTES

2 Purvey *heuenes* (also in 10) is a literal translation of the plural *caelorum*.
3 The version of NEB may derive from a different original, unless it is simply a piece of interpretation by the translators.
    Purvey *herne* (also in 10): this form of the independent possessive pronoun (= MnE *theirs*) may have been formed by analogy with the *-n* of *min, thin,* or it may illustrate the extent to which the *-en(e)* ending, originally the OE genitive plural of weak nouns and of the definite declension of adjectives (*-ena*), had come to be used as an adjectival and possessive suffix. See Mustanoja, p. 164.
4–5 The Vulgate and dependent translations reverse these verses.

VIII

MATTHEW 6: 19-34

ᜒᜒᜒᜒᜒᜒᜒᜒᜒᜒᜒᜒᜒᜒᜒᜒᜒᜒᜒᜒᜒ

Lay not up for Yourselves Treasures upon Earth

Vulgate

19 Nolite thesaurizare vobis thesauros in terra, ubi aerugo et tinea de-molitur, et ubi fures effodiunt, et furantur. 20 Thesaurizate autem vobis thesauros in caelo, ubi neque aerugo neque tinea demolitur, et ubi fures non effodiunt, nec furantur. 21 Ubi enim est thesaurus tuus, ibi est et cor tuum. 22 Lucerna corporis tui est oculus tuus. Si oculus tuus fuerit simplex, totum corpus tuum lucidum erit. 23 Si autem oculus tuus fuerit nequam, totum corpus tuum tenebrosum erit. Si ergo lumen quod in te est, tenebrae sunt, ipsae tenebrae quantae erunt! 24 Nemo potest duobus dominis servire: aut enim unum odio habebit, et alterum diliget; aut unum sustinebit, et alterum contemnet. Non potestis Deo servire et mammonae. 25 Ideo dico vobis, ne solliciti sitis animae vestrae quid manducetis, neque corpori vestro quid induamini. Nonne anima plus est quam esca, et corpus plus quam vestimentum? 26 Respicite volatilia caeli, quoniam non serunt, neque metunt, neque congregant in horrea; et Pater vester caelestis pascit illa. Nonne vos magis pluris estis illis? 27 Quis autem vestrum cogitans potest adjicere ad staturam suam cubitum unum? 28 Et de vestimento quid solliciti estis? Considerate lilia agri quomodo crescunt: non laborant, neque nent. 29 Dico autem vobis, quoniam nec Salomon in omni gloria sua coopertus est sicut unum ex istis. 30 Si autem foenum agri quod hodie est, et cras in clibanum mittitur, Deus sic vestit: quanto magis vos modicae fidei! 31 Nolite ergo solliciti esse, dicentes: Quid manducabimus, aut quid bibemus, aut quo operiemur? 32 Haec enim omnia gentes inquirunt. Scit enim Pater vester, quia his omnibus indigetis. 33 Quaerite ergo primum regnum Dei, et justitiam eius, et haec omnia adjicientur vobis. 34 Nolite ergo solliciti esse in crastinum. Crastinus enim dies sollicitus erit sibi ipsi: sufficit diei malitia sua.

Old English

19 Nellen gē goldhordian ēow goldhordas on eorþan, þǣr ōm and moððe hit fornimð, and þǣr ðēofas hit delfað and forstelaþ. 20 Goldhordiað ēow sōþlīce goldhordas on heofenan, þǣr nāðor ōm nē moþðe hit ne fornimð, and ðār þēofas hit ne delfað nē ne forstelaþ; 21 witodlīce þǣr ðīn goldhord is, þǣr is ðīn heorte. 22 Ðīnes līchaman lēohtfæt is þīn ēage; gyf þīn ēage bið ānfeald, eall þīn līchama bið beorht. 23 Gif þīn ēage sōþlīce bið mānfull, eall þīn līchama byþ ðȳsterfull. Eornustlīce gyf þæt lēoht þe on ðē is synt þȳstru, hū mycle bēoþ ðā þȳstru! 24 Ne mæg nān man twām hlāfordum þēowian; oððe hē sōðlīce ǣnne hatað and ōðerne lufað, oððe hē bið ānum gehȳrsum and ōðrum ungehȳrsum. Ne magon gē Gode þēowian and woruldwelan. 25 For þām ic secge ēow þæt gē ne sīn ymbhȳdige ēowre sāwle hwæt gē eton, ne ēowrum līchaman mid hwām gē sȳn ymbscrȳdde. Hū nys sēo sāwl sēlre þonne mete, and ēower līchama betera þonne þæt rēaf? 26 Behealdað heofonan fuglas, for þām þe hig ne sāwað, nē hig ne rīpað, nē hig ne gadriað on berne; and ēower heofonlīca Fæder hig fēt. Hū ne synt gē sēlran þonne hig? 27 Hwylc ēower mæg sōþlīce geþencan þæt hē geēacnige āne elne tō hys anlīcnesse? 28 And tō hwī synt gē ymbhȳdige be rēafe? Bescēawiað æcyres lilian, hū hig weaxað; ne swincað hig, nē hig ne spinnað. 29 Ic secge ēow sōðlīce þæt furðon Salomon on eallum hys wuldre næs oferwrigen swā swā ān of ðyson. 30 Sōþlīce gyf æcyres wēod, þæt ðe tō dæg is and bið tō morgen on ofen āsend, God swā scȳrt, Ēala gē gehwædes gelēafan! þām mycle mā he scrȳt ēow. 31 Nellen gē eornustlīce bēon ymbhȳdige, þus cweþende, "Hwæt ete wē?" oððe, "Hwæt drince wē?" oþþe, "Mid hwām bēo wē oferwrogene?" 32 Sōþlīce ealle þās þing þēoda sēceað; witodlīce ēower Fæder wāt þæt gē eallra þyssa þinga beþurfon. 33 Eornustlīce sēceað ǣrest Godes rīce and hys

---

19 Nellen: *pr. 2 pl. subj.* = *imper. do not wish;* goldhordian [goldhoard]: *store up treasure;* ōm: *rust;* fornimð: *destroy;* forstelaþ: *steal*
20 nāðor . . . nē: *neither . . . nor*
22 līchama(n): *gen., body's;* lēohtfæt [light-vat]: *lamp;* ānfeald [one-fold]: *single*
23 mānfull: *sinful;* ðȳsterfull: *full of darkness*
24 þēowian: *serve;* oððe . . . oððe: *either . . . or;* hatað: *hates;* gehȳrsum: *obedient;* woruldwela(n): *worldly wealth*
25 sīn: *pr. 2 pl. subj.,* be; ymbhȳdig(e): *thoughtful;* sāwl(e): *dat., soul;* eton: *pr. 2 pl. subj.,* eat; ymbscrȳdde

[shroud]: *clothed;* sēlre: *better;* rēaf: *garment*
26 fuglas [fowls]: *birds;* rīpað: *reap;* gadriað: *gather;* fēt (fēdan): *pr. 3 sg., feeds*
27 geþencan: *think;* geēacnige: *pr. 3 sg. subj., add;* el(ne): *cubit*
28 æcyres [acre]: *gen., field;* weaxað: *grow*
29 furðon: *even;* wuldre: *glory;* oferwrigen (oferwrēon): *pt. pp., covered*
30 wēod: *weed;* tō dæg: *today;* tō morgen: *tomorrow;* scȳrt = scrȳt: *pr. 3 sg., clothes;* gelēafan: *gen., belief;* þām mycle mā: *by that much more*
32 þēoda: *peoples;* beþurfon: *need;* sēceað: *seek*

rihtwīsnesse, and ealle þās þing ēow bēoþ þǣr tō geēacnode. 34 Ne bēo gē nā hogiende ymb þā morgenlīcan nēode; sōðlīce sē morgenlīca dæg carað ymb hyne sylfne. Æghwylc dæg hæfð genōh on hys āgenum ymbhogan.

Wycliffite (Purvey)

19 Nile ʒe tresoure to ʒou tresouris in erthe, where ruste and mouʒte destrieth, and where theues deluen out and stelen; 20 but gadere to ʒou tresouris in heuene, where nether ruste ne mouʒte distrieth, and where theues deluen not out, ne stelen. 21 For where thi tresoure is, there also thin herte is. 22 The lanterne of thi bodi is thin iʒe; if thin iʒe be symple, al thi bodi shal be liʒtful; 23 but if thin iʒe be weiward, al thi bodi shal be derk. If thanne the liʒt that is in thee be derknessis, how grete schulen thilk derknessis be? 24 No man may serue tweyn lordis, for ethir he schal hate the toon, and loue the tother; ethir he shal susteyne the toon, and dispise the tothir. ʒe moun not serue God and richessis. 25 Therfor I seie to ʒou, that ʒe be not bisi to ʒoure lijf, what ʒe schulen ete; nether to ʒoure bodi, with what ʒe schulen be clothid. Whether lijf is not more than meete, and the bodie more than cloth? 26 Biholde ʒe the foulis of the eire, for thei sowen not, nethir repen, nethir gaderen in to bernes; and ʒoure fadir of heuene fedith hem. Whether ʒe ben not more worthi than thei? 27 But who of ʒou thenkynge mai putte to his stature o cubit? 28 And of clothing what ben ʒe bisye? Biholde ʒe the lilies of the feeld, how thei wexen. Thei trauelen not, nether spynnen; 29 and Y seie to ʒou, Salomon in al his glorie was not keuered as oon of these. 30 And if God clothith thus the hei of the feeld, that to day is, and to morewe is cast in to an ouen, hou myche more ʒou of litel feith? 31 Therfor nyle ʒe be bisi, seiynge, "What schulen we ete?" or, "What schulen we drinke?" or, "With what thing schulen we be keuered?" 32 For hethene men seken alle these thingis; and ʒoure fadir woot, that ʒe han nede to alle these thingis. 33 Therfor seke ʒe first the kyngdom of God, and his riʒtfulnesse, and alle these thingis shulen be cast to ʒou. 34 Therfor nyle ʒe be bisy in to the morew, for the morew shal be bisi to hym silf; for it suffisith to the dai his owen malice.

---

34 hogiende: *thinking;* morgenlīc(an): *adj., morning, tomorrow;* carað: *cares;*

genōh: *enough;* āgen(um): *own;* ymbhoga(n): *thought*

19 Nile: *do not wish;* mouʒte: *moth*
22 iʒe: *eye*
24 moun: *may*

29 keuered: *covered*
32 woot: *knows*

Tyndale

19 Se that ye gaddre you not treasure vpon the erth, where rust and mothes corrupte, and where theves breake through and steale. 20 But gaddre ye treasure togeder in heven, where nether rust nor mothes corrupte, and where theves nether breake vp nor yet steale. 21 For where soever youre treasure ys, there will youre hertes be also. 22 The light of the body is thyne eye. Wherfore yf thyne eye be syngle, all thy body shalbe full of light. 23 But and if thyne eye be wycked then all thy body shalbe full of derckenes. Wherefore yf the light that is in the, be darckenes: how greate is that darckenes. 24 No man can serve two masters. For ether he shall hate the one and love the other: or els he shall lene to the one and despise the other: ye can not serve God and mammon. 25 Therfore I saye vnto you, be not carefull for your lyfe, what ye shall eate, or what ye shall drincke, nor yet for youre body, what ye shall put on. ys not the lyfe more worth then meate, and the body more of value then rayment? 26 Beholde the foules of the ayer: for they sowe not, nether reepe, nor yet cary in to the barnes: and yet youre hevenly father fedeth them. Are ye not moche better then they? 27 Which of you (though he toke thought therfore) coulde put one cubit vnto his stature? 28 And why care ye then for rayment? Considre the lylies of the felde, how they growe. They labour not nether spynne. 29 And yet for all that I saye vnto you, that euen Salomon in all his royalte was not arayed lyke vnto one of these. 30 Wherfore yf God so clothe the grasse, which ys to daye in the felde, and to morowe shalbe caste into the fournace: shall he not moche more do the same vnto you, o ye of lytle fayth? 31 Therfore take no thought sayinge: what shall we eate, or what shall we drincke, or wherwith shall we be clothed? 32 After all these thynges seke the gentyls. For youre hevenly father knoweth that ye have neade of all these thynges. 33 But rather seke ye fyrst the kyngdome of heuen and the rightwisnes therof, and all these thynges shalbe ministred vnto you. 34 Care not then for the morow, but let the morow care for it selfe: for the daye present hath ever ynough of his awne trouble.

King James

19 Lay not vp for your selues treasures vpon earth, where moth and rust doth corrupt, and where theeues breake thorow, and steale. 20 But lay vp for your selues treasures in heauen, where neither moth nor rust doth corrupt, & where theeues doe not breake thorow, nor steale. 21 For where your treasure is, there will your heart be also. 22 The light of the body is the eye: If therefore thine eye be single, thy whole body shalbe full of light. 23

But if thine eye be euill, thy whole body shall be full of darknesse. If therfore the light that is in thee be darkenesse, how great is that darkenesse? 24 No man can serue two masters: for either he will hate the one and loue the other, or else hee will holde to the one, and despise the other. Ye cannot serue God and Mammon. 25 Therfore I say vnto you, Take no thought for your life, what yee shall eate, or what ye shall drinke, nor yet for your body, what yee shall put on: Is not the life more then meate? and the body then raiment? 26 Behold the foules of the aire: for they sow not, neither do they reape, nor gather into barnes, yet your heauenly father feedeth them. Are yee not much better then they? 27 Which of you by taking thought, can adde one cubite vnto his stature? 28 And why take ye thought for raiment? Consider the lillies of the field, how they grow: they toile not, neither doe they spinne. 29 And yet I say vnto you, that euen Solomon in all his glory, was not arayed like one of these. 30 Wherefore, if God so clothe the grasse of the field, which to day is, and to morrow is cast into the ouen: shall he not much more clothe you, O yee of little faith? 31 Therefore take no thought, saying, What shall we eate? or What shall we drinke? or Where-withall shall wee be clothed? 32 (For after all these things doe the Gentiles seeke:) for your heauenly father knoweth that ye haue neede of all these things. 33 But seeke ye first the kingdome of God, and his righteousnesse, and all these things shalbe added vnto you. 34 Take therefore no thought for the morrow: for the morrow shall take thought for the things of it selfe: sufficient vnto the day is the euill thereof.

New English Bible

19 Do not store up for yourselves treasure on earth, where it grows rusty and moth-eaten, and thieves break in to steal it. 20 Store up treasure in heaven, where there is no moth and no rust to spoil it, no thieves to break in and steal. 21 For where your wealth is, there will your heart be also. 22 The lamp of the body is the eye. If your eyes are sound, you will have light for your whole body; 23 if the eyes are bad, your whole body will be in darkness. If then the only light you have is darkness, the darkness is doubly dark. 24 No servant can be slave to two masters; for either he will hate the first and love the second, or he will be devoted to the first and think nothing of the second. You cannot serve God and Money. 25 Therefore I bid you put away anxious thoughts about food and drink to keep you alive, and clothes to cover your body. Surely life is more than food, the body more than clothes. 26 Look at the birds of the air; they do not sow and reap and store in barns, yet your heavenly Father feeds them. You are worth more than the birds! 27 Is there a man of you who by anxious thought can add a foot

to his height? 28 And why be anxious about clothes? Consider how the lilies grow in the fields; they do not work, they do not spin; 29 and yet, I tell you, even Solomon in all his splendour was not attired like one of these. 30 But if that is how God clothes the grass in the fields, which is there today, and tomorrow is thrown on the stove, will he not all the more clothe you? How little faith you have! 31 No, do not ask anxiously, "What are we to eat? What are we to drink? What shall we wear?" 32 All these are things for the heathen to run after, not for you, because your heavenly Father knows that you need them all. 33 Set your mind on God's kingdom and his justice before everything else, and all the rest will come to you as well. 34 So do not be anxious about tomorrow; tomorrow will look after itself. Each day has troubles enough of its own.

NOTES

19   The Vulgate singular *demolitur* 'destroys' after the "divided" subject *aerugo et tinea* 'rust and moth' has been followed by the OE and Purvey. Tyndale has a plural verb, but King James a singular *doth;* the NEB has rephrased the line. Prescriptive grammarians have often been concerned about the "correct" form of the verb after a "divided" subject.

20   OE *sōþlīce* (Vulgate *autem* 'however'): see II, 15 *n.* and Introduction, pp. 32–33.

22f.   The metaphor and the syllogism are only fully comprehensible in the NEB.

23   The awkward syntax of OE . . . *þe on ðē is synt* . . . and Purvey . . . *that is in thee be derknessis* is no less clumsy in the Vulgate. It is explained by the fact that the Latin for 'darkness' is plural *tenebrae.*

25   OE *sāwl* 'soul' for Vulgate *anima* is poor — 'life' is the correct rendering. Purvey *whether*: see IV, 12 *n.*
      The reference to drink is not in the Vulgate or versions dependent on it.

32   Vulgate *gentes* (compare King James *Gentiles*) implies separate, non-Jewish, people in most biblical contexts; this is not made clear by the OE *þēoda* 'people.'

33   In the Vulgate *justitiam eius*, the justice may be that of God or of the kingdom; this is also true of the OE, in which *rīce* 'kingdom' is neuter, (*his* = 'his' or 'its': see I, 15 *n.*) and of Purvey. Tyndale clearly implies 'the justice of the kingdom' by *therof*, but both KJ and NEB mean 'God's justice.'

34   The OE does not represent the full sense of the Vulgate in the last
      clause, omitting the reference to 'evil.'
      Note the formal subject *it* in Purvey — in comparable contexts MnE
      would use *there:* see Mustanoja, p. 132.
      Purvey *his* 'its': see 33 *n*.

IX

MATTHEW 14: 15-33

᭞᭞᭞᭞᭞᭞᭞᭞᭞᭞᭞᭞᭞᭞᭞᭞᭞᭞᭞᭞᭞

The Loaves and Fishes

Vulgate

15 Vespere autem facto, accesserunt ad eum discipuli eius, dicentes: Desertus est locus, et hora iam praeteriit; dimitte turbas, ut euntes in castella emant sibi escas. 16 Jesus autem dixit eis: Non habent necesse ire; date illis vos manducare. 17 Responderunt ei: Non habemus hic nisi quinque panes, et duos pisces. 18 Qui ait eis: Afferte mihi illos huc. 19 Et cum iussisset turbam discumbere super foenum, acceptis quinque panibus, et duobus piscibus, aspiciens in caelum benedixit et fregit, et dedit discipulis panes, discipuli autem turbis. 20 Et manducaverunt omnes, et saturati sunt. Et tulerunt reliquias, duodecim cophinos fragmentorum plenos. 21 Manducantium autem fuit numerus quinque millia virorum, exceptis mulieribus et parvulis. 22 Et statim compulit Jesus discipulos ascendere in naviculam, et praecedere eum trans fretum, donec dimitteret turbas. 23 Et dimissa turba, ascendit in montem solus orare. Vespere autem facto, solus erat ibi. 24 Navicula autem in medio mari iactabatur fluctibus; erat enim contrarius ventus. 25 Quarta autem vigilia noctis, venit ad eos ambulans super mare. 26 Et videntes eum super mare ambulantem, turbati sunt, dicentes: Quia phantasma est. Et prae timore clamaverunt. 27 Statimque Jesus locutus est eis, dicens: Habete fiduciam; ego sum, nolite timere. 28 Respondens autem Petrus dixit: Domine, si tu es, iube me ad te venire super aquas. 29 At ipse ait: Veni. Et descendens Petrus de navicula, ambulabat super aquam ut veniret ad Jesum. 30 Videns vero ventum validum, timuit, et cum coepisset mergi, clamavit, dicens: Domine, salvum me fac. 31 Et continuo Jesus, extendens manum, apprehendit eum; et ait illi: Modicae fidei, quare dubitasti? 32 Et cum ascendissent in naviculam, cessavit ventus. 33 Qui autem in navicula erant, venerunt et adoraverunt eum, dicentes: Vere Filius Dei es.

Old English

15 Sōðlīce þā hyt wæs æfen geworden, him tō genēalǣhton hys leorningcnihtas, and him tō cwǣdon, "Ðēos stōw ys wēste, and tīma is forð āgān; forlǣt þās mænegeo þæt hī faron intō þās burga and him mete bicgean." 16 Þā cwæð sē Hǣlend tō him, "Nabbað hī nēode tō farenne; sylle gē him etan." 17 Þā andswarodun hig, "Wē nabbað hēr būtun fīf hlāfas and twēgen fixas." 18 Þā cwæð sē Hǣlend, "Bringaþ mē hider þā." 19 And þā hē hēt þā menegu ofer þæt gærs hī sittan; and hē nam þā fīf hlāfas and twēgen fixas, and beseah on þone heofon, and blētsiende bræc þā hlāfas, and sealde his leorningcnihtum, and hī þām folce. 20 And hī ǣton ealle, and wǣron gefyllede; and hī nāmon þā lāfa, twelf wylian fulle þǣra gebrytsena. 21 Sōþlīce þǣra etendra getæl wæs fīf þūsenda wera, būtan wīfum and cildum. 22 And þā sōna hēt sē Hǣlend his leorningcnihtas on scyp āstīgan, and tōforan him faran ofer þone mūþan, oð þæt hē þā menegu forlēte. 23 And þā hē hig forlǣten hæfde, hē ēode on þone munt, and hyne þǣr āna gebæd; sōþlīce þā hyt æfen wæs, hē wæs āna þǣr. 24 Witodlīce wæs þæt scyp of þam ȳþum tōtorfod, for þām þe hyt wæs strang wind. 25 Þā cōm sē Hǣlend embe þone fēorþan hancrēd tō him, ofer þā sǣ gangende. 26 Ðā hī gesāwon þæt, hī wurdon þā gedrēfede, and for þām ege clypodon and cwǣdon þus, "Sōþlīce hyt ys scīnlāc." 27 Ðā sprǣc sē Hǣlend and cwæþ, "Habbaþ gelēafan; ic hyt eom; nellen gē ēow ondrǣdan." 28 Ðā andswarode him Petrus, and cwæð, "Drihten, gyf þū hyt eart, hāt mē cuman tō þē ofer þās wæteru." 29 Ðā cwæð hē, "Cum tō mē." Ðā ēode Petrus of þām scype ofer þæt wæter þæt hē tō þām Hǣlende cōme. 30 Þā hē geseh þone strangan wind, hē him ondrēd; ðā hē wearð gedofen, hē cwæð, "Drihten, gedō mē hālne." 31 And þā hrædlīce hē gefēng hyne, and

---

15 æfen: *evening;* geworden (weorðan): *pt. pp., become;* genēalǣhton: *approached;* stōw: *place;* āgān [ago]: *gone;* forlǣt: *release;* mænegeo: *company;* faron [fare]: *pr. 3 pl. subj., go;* bicgean: *buy*

16 Hǣlend [healer]: *Savior;* sylle [sell]: *pr. 2 pl. subj. = imper., give*

17 būtun: *except;* fixas: *fishes*

18 hider : *hither*

19 hēt (hātan): *ordered;* gærs: *grass;* nam (niman): *took;* beseah (besēon): *looked;* blētsiende: *blessing;* sealde [sold]: *gave*

20 ǣton (etan): *pt. 3 pl., ate;* lāf(a): *remainder;* wylia(n): *baskets;* gebrytsen(a): *fragments*

21 etendra: *gen. pl., eating;* getæl: *number;* wer(a): *men*

22 sōna: *immediately;* āstīgan: *go up;*

tōforan: *before;* mūþa(n) [mouth]: *estuary;* oð þæt: *until*

23 hyne ... gebæd: *prayed;* āna: *alone*

24 ȳþ(um): *waves;* tōtorfod: *thrown about*

25 embe: *about;* hancrēd: *cockcrow;* gangende: *walking*

26 ege: *fear;* scīnlāc: *specter*

27 gelēafan [belief]: *faith;* nellen: *pr. 1 pl. subj. = imper., do not (be willing);* ēow ondrǣdan: *be afraid*

28 hāt: *order*

29 cōme (cuman): *pt. 3 sg. subj., came*

30 geseh (gesēon): *pt. 3 sg., saw;* him ondrēd: *was afraid;* gedofen (dūfan) [dive]: *ducked;* gedō: *imper., make;* hāl(ne) [whole]: *safe*

31 hrædlīce: *quickly;* gefēng (gefōn): *seized;* twȳnedest: *doubted*

þus cwæð, "Lā lȳtles gelēafan, hwī twȳnedest þū?" 32 And þā hī wǣron on
þām scype, geswāc sē wind. 33 Sōþlīce þā þe on þām scype wǣron cōmon,
and tō him gebǣdon, and þus cwǣdon, "Sōþlīce þū eart Godes sunu."

Wycliffite (Purvey)

15 But whanne the euentid was com, hise disciplis camen to him, and seiden,
"The place is desert, and the tyme is now passid; lat the puple go in to
townes, to bye hem mete." 16 Jhesus seide to hem, "Thei han not nede to
go; ȝyue ȝe hem sumwhat to ete." 17 Thei answeriden, "We han not heere
but fyue looues and twei fischis." 18 And he seide to hem, "Brynge ȝe hem
hidur to me." 19 And whanne he hadde comaundid the puple to sitte to
meete on the heye, he took fyue looues and twei fischis, and he bihelde in to
heuene, and blesside, and brak, and ȝaf to hise disciplis; and the disciplis
ȝauen to the puple. 20 And alle eten, and weren fulfillid. And thei tooken
the relifs of brokun gobetis, twelue cofynes ful. 21 And the noumbre of
men that eten was fyue thousynde of men, outakun wymmen and lytle
children. 22 And anoon Jhesus compellide the disciplis to go vp in to a boot,
and go bifor hym ouer the see, while he lefte the puple. 23 And whanne the
puple was left, he stiede aloone in to an hil for to preie. But whanne the
euenyng was come, he was there aloone. 24 And the boot in the myddel of
the see was schoggid with wawis, for the wynd was contrarie to hem. 25
But in the fourthe wakyng of the niȝt, he cam to hem walkynge aboue
the see. 26 And thei, seynge hym walking on the see, weren disturblid, and
seiden, That "it is a fantum"; and for drede thei crieden. 27 And anoon
Jhesus spac to hem, and seide, "Haue ȝe trust, Y am; nyle ȝe drede." 28
And Petre answeride, and seide, "Lord, if thou art, comaunde me to come
to thee on the watris." 29 And he seide, "Come thou." And Petre ȝede
doun fro the boot, and walkide on the watris to come to Jhesu. 30 But he
siȝ the wynd strong, and was aferde; and whanne he bigan to drenche, he
criede, and seide, "Lord, make me saaf." 31 And anoon Jhesus helde forth
his hoond, and took Petre, and seide to hym, "Thou of litil feith, whi hast
thou doutid?" 32 And whanne he hadde stied in to the boot, the wynd
ceessid. 33 And thei, that weren in the boot, camen and worschipiden hym,
and seiden, "Verili, thou art Goddis sone."

---

32 geswāc (geswīcan): *ceased*	33 gebǣdon (gebiddan): *pt. 3 pl., prayed*
17 han: *have*	23 stiede: *went up*
20 eten: *ate;* relifs: *remainder;* cofynes: *baskets*	24 schoggid: *shaken;* wawis: *waves*
21 outakun: *except*	27 nyle: *do not (be willing)*
22 anoon: *immediately*	29 ȝede: *went*
	30 siȝ: *saw;* drenche: *drown*

Tyndale

15 When even was come, his disciples came to him sayinge. This is a deserte place, and the daye is spent: let the people departe, that they maye go in to the tounes, and bye them vytayllis. 16 But Iesus sayde vnto them. They have no neade to go awaye. Geve ye them to eate. 17 Then sayde they vnto him: we have here but v loves and two fysshes. 18 And he sayde: bringe them hyther to me. 19 And he commaunded the people to syt downe on the grasse: and toke the v loves, and the ii fysshes and loked vp to heven and blessed, and brake and gave the loves to his disciples, and the disciples gave them to the people. 20 And they dyd all eate, and were suffised. And they gadered vp of the gobbetes that remayned xii basketes full. 21 And they that ate, were in nombre about v M men, besyde wemen and chyldren. 22 And strayght waye Iesus made his disciples enter into a shippe, and to goo over before him, whill he sent the people awaye. 23 And assone as he had sent the people awaye, he went vp into a mountayne alone to praye. And when nyght was come, he was there him silf alone. 24 And the shippe was now in the middes of the see, and was toost with waves, for it was a contrary wynde. 25 In the fourthe watche of the night Iesus came vnto them walkynge on the see. 26 And when his disciples sawe him walkynge on the see, they were troubled, sayinge: it is some spirite, and cryed out for feare. 27 And streyghte waye Iesus spake vnto them sayinge: be of god cheare, it is I, be not a frayed. 28 Peter answered him, and sayde: master, if thou be he, bid me come vnto the on the water. 29 And he sayde, come. And when Peter was come doune out of the shippe, he walked on the water, to go to Iesus. 30 But when he sawe a myghty wynde, he was afrayed. And as he beganne to synke, he cryed sayinge: master save me. 31 And immediatly Iesus stretched forth his honde, and caught him, and sayde to him: O thou of lytell faith, wherfore diddest thou dout? 32 And assone as they were come in to the shippe, the wynde ceased. 33 Then they that were in the shippe, came and worshipped him, sayinge: of a truth thou arte the sonne of God.

King James

15 And when it was euening, his Disciples came to him, saying, This is a desert place, and the time is now past; send the multitude away, that they may goe into the villages, and buy themselues victuals. 16 But Jesus said vnto them, They neede not depart; giue yee them to eate. 17 And they say vnto him, We haue heere but fiue loaues, and two fishes. 18 He said, Bring them hither to me. 19 And hee commanded the multitude to sit downe on

the grasse, & tooke the fiue loaues, and the two fishes, and looking vp to
heauen, hee blessed, and brake, and gaue the loaues to his Disciples, and
the Disciples to the multitude. 20 And they did all eat, & were filled: and
they tooke vp of the fragments that remained twelue baskets full. 21 And
they that had eaten, were about fiue thousand men, beside women and
children. 22 And straightway Iesus constrained his Disciples to get into a
ship, and to goe before him vnto the other side, while he sent the multitudes
away. 23 And when he had sent the multitudes away, he went vp into a
mountaine apart to pray: and when the euening was come, he was there
alone: 24 But the ship was now in the midst of the Sea, tossed with waues:
for the wind was contrary. 25 And in the fourth watch of the night, Jesus
went vnto them, walking on the Sea. 26 And when the Disciples saw him
walking on the Sea, they were troubled, saying, It is a spirit: and they cried
out for feare. 27 But straightway Jesus spake vnto them, saying, Be of good
cheere: it is I, be not afraid. 28 And Peter answered him, and said, Lord, if it
be thou, bid me come vnto thee on the water. 29 And he said, Come. And
when Peter was come downe out of the ship, he walked on the water, to go
to Jesus. 30 But when he saw the wind boysterous, he was afraid: and
beginning to sinke, he cried, saying, Lord saue me. 31 And immediately
Jesus stretched foorth his hand, and caught him, and said vnto him, O thou
of little faith, wherefore didst thou doubt? 32 And when they were come into
the ship, the wind ceased. 33 Then they that were in the ship, came and
worshipped him, saying, Of a trueth thou art the sonne of God.

New English Bible

15 When it grew late the disciples came up to him and said, "This is a lonely
place, and the day has gone; send the people off to the villages to buy
themselves food." 16 He answered, "There is no need for them to go; give
them something to eat yourselves." 17 "All we have here," they said, "is
five loaves and two fishes." 18 "Let me have them," he replied. 19 So he
told the people to sit down on the grass; then, taking the five loaves and the
two fishes, he looked up to heaven, said the blessing, broke the loaves, and
gave them to the disciples; and the disciples gave them to the people. 20
They all ate to their hearts' content; and the scraps left over, which they
picked up, were enough to fill twelve great baskets. 21 Some five thousand
men shared in this meal, to say nothing of women and children. 22 Then he
made the disciples embark and go on ahead to the other side while he sent
the people away; 23 after doing that, he went up the hill-side to pray alone.
It grew late, and he was there by himself. 24 The boat was already well out
on the water, battling with a head-wind and a rough sea. 25 Between three

and six in the morning he came to them, walking over the lake. 26 When the disciples saw him walking on the lake they were so shaken that they cried out in terror: "It is a ghost!" 27 But at once he spoke to them: "Take heart! It is I; do not be afraid." 28 Peter called to him: "Lord, if it is you, tell me to come to you over the water." 29 "Come," said Jesus. Peter stepped down from the boat, and walked over the water towards Jesus. 30 But when he saw the strength of the gale he was seized with fear; and beginning to sink, he cried, "Save me, Lord." 31 Jesus at once reached out and caught hold of him, and said, "Why did you hesitate? How little faith you have!" 32 They then climbed into the boat; and the wind dropped. 33 And the men in the boat fell at his feet, exclaiming, "Truly you are the Son of God."

NOTES

15   Note the use of OE *hyt* as a 'formal subject,' which anticipates the later development in MnE 'it is raining' etc.

OE *bicgean* is either infinitive, loosely attached to the sentence to indicate purpose ('let them go . . . that they may go into the villages, and to buy . . .'), in which case one might have expected *tō* + inflected infinitive, *tō bicgeanne*, or it shows a reduced form of the third person plural subjunctive. *Faron . . . and . . . bicgean* would thus in early OE have appeared as *faren . . . bicgen*.

KJ *victuals* is a learned spelling based on Latin *victus*, but the MnE pronunciation is still *vittles*, deriving from the ME form.

17   This verse succinctly illustrates the development of the word *but* from OE *be-ūtan* 'outside of, except' (in this sense, therefore, permissible only after a negative) to early MnE 'only,' as in Tyndale and KJ. Its development as a conjunction is more or less parallel.

22   OE *mūþan* 'mouth' implies that the *fretum* is an estuary.

22–23   OE glosses Latin *dimittere* 'let go' by *forlætan* (as also in 15), which could also mean 'leave.' It is hard to see how Purvey came to use the verb *leave* as a translation of *dimittere*, unless *leave* had at some time been influenced by the senses of *forlætan*.

24   OE *strang* is hardly adequate for *contrarius*.

32   Purvey (*whanne he hadde stied*) may have had a Vulgate text with *ascendisset* singular instead of *ascendissent* plural.

X

LUKE 10: 25-37

᭷᭷᭷᭷᭷᭷᭷᭷᭷᭷᭷᭷᭷᭷᭷

The Good Samaritan

Vulgate

25 Et ecce quidam legisperitus surrexit tentans illum, et dicens: Magister,
quid faciendo vitam aeternam possidebo? 26 At ille dixit ad eum: In lege
quid scriptum est? quomodo legis? 27 Ille respondens dixit: Diliges Dominum
Deum tuum ex toto corde tuo, et ex tota anima tua, et ex omnibus viribus
tuis, et ex omni mente tua; et proximum tuum sicut teipsum. 28 Dixitque
illi: Recte respondisti: hoc fac, et vives. 29 Ille autem volens justificare
seipsum, dixit ad Jesum: Et quis est meus proximus? 30 Suscipiens autem
Jesus, dixit: Homo quidam descendebat ab Jerusalem in Jericho, et incidit
in latrones, qui etïam despoliaverunt eum, et plagis impositis, abierunt
semivivo relicto. 31 Accidit autem ut sacerdos quidam descenderet eadem
via; et viso illo, praeterivit. 32 Similiter et levita, cum esset secus locum, et
videret eum, pertransiit. 33 Samaritanus autem quidam iter faciens, venit
secus eum; et videns eum, misericordia motus est. 34 Et appropians
alligavit vulnera eius, infundens oleum et vinum, et imponens illum in
jumentum suum, duxit in stabulum, et curam eius egit. 35 Et altera die
protulit duos denarios, et dedit stabulario, et ait: Curam illius habe; et
quodcumque supererogaveris, ego cum rediero, reddam tibi. 36 Quis horum
trium videtur tibi proximus fuisse illi, qui incidit in latrones? 37 At ille
dixit: Qui fecit misericordiam in illum. Et ait illi Jesus: Vade, et tu fac
similiter.

Old English

25 Ðā ārās sum ǣglēaw man and fandode his, and cwæð, "Lārēow, hwæt
dō ic þæt ic ēce līf hæbbe?" 26 Ðā cwæþ hē tō him, "Hwæt is gewriten on

---

25 ārās (ārīsan): *arose;* ǣglēaw: *law-wise;*   *eternal;* hæbbe: *pr. 1 sg. subj., have*
      fandode: *tested;* Lārēow: *teacher;* ēce: 26   ǣ: *law;* rǣtst (rǣdan): *read*

þǣre ǣ? hū rǣtst þū?" 27 Ða andswarude hē, "Lufa Drihten þīnne God of
ealre þīnre heortan, and of ealre þīnre sāwle, and of eallum þīnum mih-
tum, and of eallum þīnum mǣgene; and þīnne nēhstan swā ðē sylfne." 28 Þā
cwæð hē, "Rihte þū andswarodest; dō þæt, þonne leofast þū." 29 Ða cwæþ
hē tō þām Hǣlende, and wolde hine sylfne gerihtwīsian, "And hwylc is mīn
nēhsta?" 30 Ða cwæþ sē Hǣlend, hine ūp besēonde, "Sum man fērde fram
Hierusalem tō Hiericho, and becōm on þā sceaðan, þā hine berēafodon, and
tintregodon hine, and forlēton hine sāmcucene. 31 Þā gebyrode hit þæt sum
sācerd fērde on þām ylcan wege; and þā hē þæt geseah, hē hine forbēh.
32 And eall swā sē dīacon, þā hē wæs wið þā stōwe and þæt geseah, hē hyne
ēac forbēah. 33 Ða fērde sum Samaritanisc man wið hine; þā hē hine geseah,
þā wearð hē mid mildheortnesse ofer hine āstyred. 34 Þā genēalǣhte hē,
and wrāð his wunda, and on āget ele and wīn, and hine on hys nȳten sette,
and gelǣdde on his lǣcehūs, and hine lācnude; 35 and brōhte ōðrum dæge
twēgen penegas, and sealde þām lǣce, and þus cwæð, 'Begȳm hys; and swā
hwæt swā þū māre tō gedēst, þonne ic cume, ic hit forgylde þē.' 36 Hwylc
þāra þrēora þyncð þē þæt sȳ þæs mǣg þe on ðā sceaðan befēoll?" 37 Ða
cwæð hē, "Sē ðe him mildheortnesse on dyde." Ða cwæþ sē Hǣlend, "Gā,
and dō eall swā."

Wycliffite (Purvey)

25 And lo! a wise man of the lawe ros vp, temptynge hym, and seiynge,
"Maister, what thing schal Y do to haue euerlastynge lijf?" 26 And he seide
to hym, "What is writun in the lawe? hou redist thou?" 27 He answeride,
and seide, "Thou schalt loue thi Lord God of al thin herte, and of al thi
soule, and of alle thi strengthis, and of al thi mynde; and thi neiȝbore as thi
silf." 28 And Jhesus seide to hym, "Thou hast answerid riȝtli; do this thing,
and thou schalt lyue." 29 But he willynge to iustifie hym silf, seide to

---

27 sāwl(e): *soul;* miht(um): *powers;*
    mǣgen(e) [main]: *strength;* nēhst(an)
    [next]: *neighbor;* sylf(ne): *self*
28 leofast (libban): *pr. 2 sg., live*
29 Hǣlend(e) [healer]: *Savior;* geriht-
    wīsian [righteous]: *justify*
30 hine ūp besēonde: *looking up;* fērde:
    went; becōm: *came;* sceaða(n): *robbers;*
    berēafodon [bereave]: *stripped;* tin-
    tregodon: *tortured;* forlēton: *aban-
    doned;* samcucen(e) [quick]: *half-alive*
31 gebyrode: *happened;* forbēh (for-
    būgan) [bow]: *turned from*
32 eall swā: *likewise;* wið: *opposite;* stōw-

(e): *place*
33 āstyred [stir]: *aroused*
34 genēalǣhte [near]: *approached;* wrāð
    (wrīðan): *pt. 3 sg., wrapped;* on āget
    (āgēotan): *poured on;* ele: *oil;* nȳten:
    animal; lǣcehūs [leech-house]: *hospital*
    (see Notes); lācnude: *healed*
35 brōhte: *brought;* twēgen: *two;* sealde
    [sold]: *gave;* Begȳm: *take care of;* swā
    hwæt swā: *whatever;* forgylde [yield]:
    repay; þrēo(ra): *gen., three;* þyncð:
    seems; mǣg: *kinsman;* befēoll (be-
    feallan): *pt. 3 sg., fell*

Jhesu, "And who is my neiȝbore?" 30 And Jhesu biheld, and seide, "A man cam doun fro Jerusalem in to Jerico, and fel among theues, and thei robbiden hym, and woundiden hym, and wente awei, and leften the man half alyue. 31 And it bifel, that a prest cam doun the same weie, and passide forth, whanne he hadde seyn hym. 32 Also a dekene, whanne he was bisidis the place, and saiȝ him, passide forth. 33 But a Samaritan, goynge the weie, cam bisidis hym; and he siȝ hym, and hadde reuthe on hym; 34 and cam to hym, and boond togidir hise woundis, and helde in oyle and wynne; and leide hym on his beest, and ledde in to an ostrie, and dide the cure of hym. 35 And another dai he brouȝte forth twey pans, and ȝaf to the ostiler, and seide, Haue the cure of hym; and what euer thou schalt ȝyue ouer, Y schal ȝelde to thee, whanne Y come aȝen. 36 Who of these thre, semeth to thee, was neiȝbore to hym, that fel among theues?" 37 And he seide, "He that dide merci in to hym." And Jhesus seide to hym, "Go thou, and do thou on lijk maner."

Tyndale

25 And beholde, a certayne Lawere stode vp, and tempted him sayinge: Master what shall I do, to inheret eternall life? 26 He sayd vnto him: What is written in the lawe? how redest thou? 27 And he answered and sayde: Loue thy Lorde God, with all thy hert, and with all thy soule, and with all thy strengthe, and with all thy mynde: and thy neghbour as thy sylfe. 28 And he sayde vnto him: Thou hast answered right. This do and thou shalt live. 29 He willinge to iustifie him silfe, sayde vnto Iesus: Who is then my neghbour? 30 Iesus answered and sayde: A certayne man descended from Hierusalem in to Hierico, and fell in to the hondes of theves, which robbed him of his rayment and wounded him, and departed levynge him halfe deed. 31 And by chaunce ther came a certayne preste that same waye, and when he sawe him, he passed by. 32 And lykewyse a Levite, when he was come nye to the place, went and loked on him, and passed by. 33 Then a certayne Samaritane, as he iornyed, came nye vnto him, and when he sawe him, had compassion on him, 34 and went to and bounde vp his woundes, and poured in oyle and wyne, and put him on his awne beaste, and brought him to a commen ynne, and made provision for him. 35 And on the morowe when he departed, he toke out two pence and gave them to the host, and sayde vnto him. Take cure of him, and whatsoever thou spendest moare,

---

32 saiȝ: *saw*
33 siȝ: *saw;* routhe: *pity*
34 helde: *poured;* ostrie: *inn;* cure: *care*

35 pans: *pennies;* ostiler: *innkeeper;* ȝelde: *pay*

when I come agayne, I will recompence the. 36 Which now of these thre, thynkest thou, was neighbour vnto him that fell into the theves hondes? 37 And he sayde: he that shewed mercy on him. Then sayde Iesus vnto him. Goo and do thou lyke wyse.

King James

25 And behold, a certaine Lawyer stood vp, and tempted him, saying, Master, what shall I doe to inherite eternall life? 26 He said vnto him, What is written in the law? how readest thou? 27 And he answering, said, Thou shalt loue the Lord thy God with all thy heart, and with all thy soule, and with all thy strength, and with all thy minde, and thy neighbour as thy selfe. 28 And he said vnto him, Thou hast answered right: this do, and thou shalt liue. 29 But he willing to iustifie himselfe, said vnto Jesus, And who is my neighbour? 30 And Jesus answering, said, A certaine man went downe from Hierusalem to Jericho, and fel among theeues, which stripped him of his raiment, and wounded him, and departed, leauing him halfe dead. 31 And by chaunce there came downe a certaine Priest that way, and when he saw him, he passed by on the other side. 32 And likewise a Leuite, when hee was at the place, came and looked on him, and passed by on the other side. 33 But a certaine Samaritane as he iourneyed, came where he was; and when hee saw him, hee had compassion on him, 34 And went to him, and bound vp his wounds, powring in oile and wine, and set him on his owne beast, and brought him to an Inne, and tooke care of him. 35 And on the morrow when he departed, hee tooke out two pence, and gaue them to the hoste, and saide vnto him, Take care of him, and whatsoeuer thou spendest more, when I come againe I will repay thee. 36 Which now of these three, thinkest thou, was neighbour vnto him that fell among the theeues? 37 And he said, He that shewed mercie on him. Then said Jesus vnto him, Goe, and doe thou likewise.

New English Bible

25 On one occasion a lawyer came forward to put this test question to him: "Master, what must I do to inherit eternal life?" 26 Jesus said, "What is written in the Law? What is your reading of it?" 27 He replied, "Love the Lord your God with all your heart, with all your soul, with all your strength, and with all your mind; and your neighbour as yourself." 28 "That is the

right answer," said Jesus; "do that and you will live." 29 But he wanted to
vindicate himself, so he said to Jesus, "And who is my neighbour?" 30
Jesus replied, "A man was on his way from Jerusalem down to Jericho when
he fell in with robbers, who stripped him, beat him, and went off leaving
him half dead. 31 It so happened that a priest was going down by the same
road; but when he saw him, he went past on the other side. 32 So too a
Levite came to the place, and when he saw him went past on the other side.
33 But a Samaritan who was making the journey came upon him, and when
he saw him was moved to pity. 34 He went up and bandaged his wounds,
bathing them with oil and wine. Then he lifted him on to his own beast,
brought him to an inn, and looked after him there. 35 Next day he produced
two silver pieces and gave them to the innkeeper, and said, "Look after
him; and if you spend any more, I will repay you on my way back." 36
Which of these three do you think was neighbour to the man who fell into
the hands of the robbers?" 37 He answered, "The one who showed him
kindness." Jesus said, "Go and do as he did."

NOTES

25   Note that OE *fandian* 'test' takes the genitive; compare XI, 23.

27   OE *mægene* 'strength' for Vulgate *mente* 'mind' is probably the result
of textual corruption.

30   Vulgate *suscipiens* 'taking up (his remark)' is more or less the sense
of all versions except the OE and Purvey, which may have had a
Vulgate text with *suspiciens* 'looking at.'

31   Compare the various translations of the Jewish religious orders.

34   Only the OE interprets *stabulum* ('inn') as a hospital (*læcehūs* < *læce*
'doctor' + *hūs* 'house'), and its keeper as a *læce*; this has led to the
interpretation *læcnude* 'healed' for 'took care of.'

35   Purvey *another dai* is an error. Normal ME for 'the next day' would be
the (or *that*) *other dai*.

36   Note the use of the subjunctive *sȳ* in the OE, arising from the supposed
uncertainty implied by 'seems to you.'
OE *mǣg* 'kinsman' narrows the concept of 'neighbor' a little; in 27
and 29 *nēhsta* 'nearest' renders *proximus* exactly.

XI

LUKE 20: 19-26

ৡ৾ঌৡ৾ঌৡ৾ঌৡ৾ঌৡ৾ঌৡ৾ঌৡ৾ঌ

Render unto Caesar

Vulgate

19 Et quaerebant principes sacerdotum, et scribae, mittere in illum manus illa hora; et timuerunt populum; cognoverunt enim quod ad ipsos dixerit similitudinem hanc. 20 Et observantes miserunt insidiatores, qui se iustos simularent, ut caperent eum in sermone, ut traderent illum principatui et potestati praesidis. 21 Et interrogaverunt eum, dicentes: Magister, scimus quia recte dicis et doces; et non accipis personam, sed viam Dei in veritate doces: 22 Licet nobis tributum dare Caesari, an non? 23 Considerans autem dolum illorum, dixit ad eos: Quid me tentatis? 24 Ostendite mihi denarium. Cuius habet imaginem et inscriptionem? Respondentes dixerunt ei: Caesaris. 25 Et ait illis: Reddite ergo quae sunt Caesaris, Caesari, et quae sunt Dei, Deo. 26 Et non potuerunt verbum eius reprehendere coram plebe; et mirati in responso eius, tacuerunt.

Old English

19 Ðā sōhton þāra sācerda ealdras and þā bōceras hyra handa on þǣre tīde on hine wurpun; and hig ādrēdon him þæt folc; sōðlīce hī ongēton þæt hē þis bigspell tō him cwæð. 20 Ðā sendun hig mid searwum þā ðe hig rihtwīse lēton, þæt hig hine gescyldgudun, and þæt hig hine gesealdon þām ealdron

---

19 sōhton (sēcan): *sought;* sācerd(a): *gen., priests;* ealdras: *leaders;* bōceras: *scribes;* tīd(e) [tide]: *time;* wurpun (inf. = weorpan): *throw;* ādrēdon: *feared;* ongēton (ongietan): *pt. 3 pl., understood;* bigspell: *parable*

20 sendun: *pt. 3 pl., sent;* mid searwum:

craftily; hig rihtwīse lēton: *made themselves out to be righteous;* gescyldgudun: *pt. 3 pl. subj., find guilty;* gesealdon [sold]: *pt. 3 pl. subj., give;* dōm(e): *judgment;* dēma(n): *judge;* anwald(e): *power*

tō dōme, and tō þæs dēman anwalde tō fordēmanne. 21 Ðā āhsodon hig
hine and cwǣdon, "Lāreow, wē witun þæt þū rihte sprycst and lǣrest, and
for nānon men ne wandast, ac Godes weg on sōðfæstnesse lǣrst; 22 ys hit
riht þæt man þām Cāsere gafol sylle, þe nā?" 23 Ðā cwæð hē tō him, þā hē
hyra fācen onget, "Hwī fandī gē mīn? 24 Ȳwað mē ānne pening. Hwæs
anlīcnesse hæfþ hē and ofergewrit?" Ðā cwǣdon hig, "Þæs Cāseres."
25 Ðā cwæð hē tō him, "Āgyfað þām Cāsere þā ðing þe ðæs Cāseres synt,
and Gode þā ðing þe Godes synt." 26 Ðā ne mihton hig his word befōn
beforan þām folce; þā suwudon hig, wundrigende be his andsware.

Wycliffite (Purvey)

19 And the princis of prestis, and scribis, souȝten to leye on hym hoondis
in that our, and thei dredden the puple; for thei knewen that to hem he
seide this liknesse. 20 And thei aspieden, and senten aspieris, that feyneden
hem iust, that thei schulden take hym in word, and bitaak hym to the
power of the prince, and to the power of the iustice. 21 And thei axiden
hym, and seiden, "Maister, we witen, that riȝtli thou seist and techist; and
thou takist not the persoone of man, but thou techist in treuthe the weie of
God. 22 Is it leueful to vs to ȝyue tribute to the emperoure, or nay? 23 And
he biheld the disseit of hem, and seide to hem, "What tempten ȝe me?
24 Shewe ȝe to me a peny; whos ymage and superscripcioun hath it? Thei
answerden, and seiden to hym, "The emperouris." 25 And he seide to hem,
"Ȝelde ȝe therfor to the emperoure tho thingis that ben the emperours, and
tho thingis that ben of God, to God." 26 And thei myȝten not repreue his
word bifor the puple; and thei wondriden in his answere, and heelden pees.

Tyndale

19 And the hye Prestes and the Scribes the same howre went about to laye
hondes on him, but they feared the people. For they perceaved that he had

---

21 āhsodon: *asked;* Lāreow: *teacher;*
    witun: *know;* sprycst (sprecan): *speak;*
    lǣrest: *teach;* nānon men: *dat., no man;*
    wandast: *stand in fear;* sōðfæstness(e):
    truth

22 gafol: *tribute;* sylle [sell]: *pr. 3 sg. subj.,
    give;* þe nā: *or not*

23 fācen: *trick;* fandī: *test*

24 Ȳwað: *imper., show;* anlīcness(e):
    likeness; ofergewrit [overwriting]: *su-
    perscription*

25 Āgyfað: *imper., give*

26 befōn: *catch, trap;* suwodon: *were
    silent;* wundrigende: *being amazed*

19 our: *hour*
20 aspieris: *spies;* bitaak: *hand over*
21 witen: *know*

22 leueful: *allowed*
25 ȝelde: *pay*

spoken this similitude agaynst them. 20 And they watched him, and sent forth spies, which shuld fayne them selves perfecte, to take him in his wordes, and to delyvre him vnto the power and auctorite of the debite. 21 And they axed him sayinge: Master, we knowe that thou sayest and teachest ryght, nother considerest thou eny mannes degre, but teachest the waye of God truly. 22 Ys it laufull for vs to geve Cesar tribute or no? 23 He perceaved their craftynes, and sayde vnto them: why tempt ye me? 24 Shewe me a peny. Whose ymage and superscripcion hath it? They answered and sayde: Cesars. 25 And he sayde vnto them: Geve then vnto Cesar, that which belongeth vnto Cesar: and to God, that which pertayneth to God. 26 And they coulde not reprove his sayinge before the people. But they marvayled at his answer, and helde their peace.

King James

19 And the chiefe Priests and the Scribes the same houre sought to lay hands on him, and they feared the people: for they perceiued that he had spoken this parable against them. 20 And they watched him, and sent foorth spies, which should faine themselues iust men, that they might take holde of his words, that so they might deliuer him vnto the power and authoritie of the gouernour. 21 And they asked him, saying, Master, we know that thou sayest and teachest rightly, neither acceptest thou the person of any, but teachest the way of God truely. 22 Is it lawfull for vs to giue tribute vnto Cesar, or no? 23 But he perceiued their craftines, and said vnto them, Why tempt ye me? 24 Shew me a peny: whose image and superscription hath it? They answered, and said, Cesars. 25 And he said vnto them, Render therefore vnto Cesar the things which be Cesars, and vnto God the things which be Gods. 26 And they could not take holde of his wordes before the people, and they marueiled at his answere, and helde their peace.

New English Bible

19 The lawyers and chief priests wanted to lay hands on him there and then, for they saw that this parable was aimed at them; but they were afraid of the people. 20 So they watched their opportunity and sent secret agents in the guise of honest men, to seize upon some word of his as a pretext for

---

20 debite: *deputy*

handing him over to the authority and jurisdiction of the Governor. 21 They put a question to him: "Master," they said, "we know that what you speak and teach is sound; you pay deference to no one, but teach in all honesty the way of life that God requires. 22 Are we or are we not permitted to pay taxes to the Roman Emperor?" 23 He saw through their trick and said, 24 "Show me a silver piece. Whose head does it bear, and whose inscription?" "Caesar's", they replied. 25 "Very well then," he said, "pay Caesar what is due to Caesar, and pay God what is due to God." 26 Thus their attempt to catch him out in public failed, and, astonished by his reply, they fell silent.

NOTES

19   Vulgate *et timuerunt populum* 'and they feared the people' is parenthetic; not all versions make this clear.

20   OE *mid searwum* 'with cunning' implies the underhand methods of the authorities present in Vulgate *observantes* 'watching' and *insidiatores* 'spies, ambushers.'

The OE words for 'take,' *læccan*, *niman*, lack the sense 'catch out, trap' of *capere(nt)*, so *gescyldgudun* 'find fault with' is a good translation. OE incorrectly takes *principatui* 'authority' as though it were a separate official. Tyndale *debite* is a form of 'deputy,' last recorded by OED for 1549.

23   The NEB omits *Why tempt ye me*. For OE *fandī . . . mīn*, compare X, 25 *n*.

26   OE *befōn* 'seize on' is very literal for *reprehendere* 'catch out.'

XII

JOHN 18

ღღღღღღღღღ

The Betrayal and Audience with Pilate

Vulgate

1 Haec cum dixisset Jesus, egressus est cum discipulis suis trans torrentem
Cedron, ubi erat hortus, in quem introivit ipse, et discipuli eius. 2 Sciebat
autem et Judas, qui tradebat eum, locum, quia frequenter Jesus convenerat
illuc cum discipulis suis. 3 Judas ergo cum accepisset cohortem, et a
pontificibus et pharisaeis ministros, venit illuc cum lanternis, et facibus, et
armis. 4 Jesus itaque sciens omnia quae ventura erant super eum, processit,
et dixit eis: Quem quaeritis? 5 Responderunt ei: Jesum Nazarenum. Dicit
eis Jesus: Ego sum. Stabat autem et Judas, qui tradebat eum, cum ipsis.
6 Ut ergo dixit eis: Ego sum, abierunt retrorsum, et ceciderunt in terram.
7 Iterum ergo interrogavit eos: Quem quaeritis? Illi autem dixerunt: Jesum
Nazarenum. 8 Respondit Jesus: Dixi vobis quia ego sum; si ergo me
quaeritis, sinite hos abire; 9 Ut impleretur sermo, quem dixit: Quia quos
dedisti mihi, non perdidi ex eis quemquam. 10 Simon ergo Petrus habens
gladium eduxit eum, et percussit pontificis servum, et abscidit auriculam
eius dexteram. Erat autem nomen servo Malchus. 11 Dixit ergo Jesus
Petro: Mitte gladium tuum in vaginam. Calicem, quem dedit mihi Pater,
non bibam illum? 12 Cohors ergo, et tribunus, et ministri Judaeorum
comprehenderunt Jesum, et ligaverunt eum: 13 Et adduxerunt eum ad
Annam primum; erat enim socer Caiphae, qui erat pontifex anni illius.
14 Erat autem Caiphas, qui consilium dederat Judaeis: Quia expedit unum
hominem mori pro populo. 15 Sequebatur autem Jesum Simon Petrus, et
alius discipulus. Discipulus autem ille erat notus pontifici, et introivit cum
Jesu in atrium pontificis. 16 Petrus autem stabat ad ostium foris. Exivit
ergo discipulus alius, qui erat notus pontifici, et dixit ostiariae, et introduxit
Petrum. 17 Dicit ergo Petro ancilla ostiaria: Numquid et tu ex discipulis es
hominis istius? Dicit ille: Non sum. 18 Stabant autem servi et ministri ad
prunas, quia frigus erat, et calefaciebant se; erat autem cum eis et Petrus
stans, et calefaciens se. 19 Pontifex ergo interrogavit Jesum de discipulis
suis, et de doctrina eius. 20 Respondit ei Jesus: Ego palam locutus sum

mundo; ego semper docui in synagoga, et in templo, quo omnes Judaei conveniunt; et in occulto locutus sum nihil. 21 Quid me interrogas? interroga eos, qui audierunt quid locutus sim ipsis; ecce hi sciunt quae dixerim ego. 22 Haec autem cum dixisset, unus assistens ministrorum dedit alapam Jesu, dicens: Sic respondes pontifici? 23 Respondit ei Jesus: Si male locutus sum, testimonium perhibe de malo; si autem bene, quid me caedis? 24 Et misit eum Annas ligatum ad Caipham pontificem. 25 Erat autem Simon Petrus stans, et calefaciens se. Dixerunt ergo ei: Numquid et tu ex discipulis eius es? Negavit ille, et dixit: Non sum. 26 Dicit ei unus ex servis pontificis, cognatus eius, cuius abscidit Petrus auriculam: Nonne ego te vidi in horto cum illo? 27 Iterum ergo negavit Petrus; et statim gallus cantavit. 28 Adducunt ergo Jesum a Caipha in praetorium. Erat autem mane; et ipsi non introierunt in praetorium, ut non contaminarentur, sed ut manducarent pascha. 29 Exivit ergo Pilatus ad eos foras, et dixit: Quam accusationem affertis adversus hominem hunc? 30 Responderunt, et dixerunt ei: Si non esset hic malefactor, non tibi tradidissemus eum. 31 Dixit ergo eis Pilatus: Accipite eum vos, et secundum legem vestram judicate eum. Dixerunt ergo ei Judaei: Nobis non licet interficere quemquam; 32 Ut sermo Jesu impleretur, quem dixit, significans qua morte esset moriturus. 33 Introivit ergo iterum in praetorium Pilatus, et vocavit Jesum, et dixit ei: Tu es rex Judaeorum? 34 Respondit Jesus: A temet ipso hoc dicis, an alii dixerunt tibi de me? 35 Respondit Pilatus: Numquid ego Judaeus sum? Gens tua et pontifices tradiderunt te mihi; quid fecisti? 36 Respondit Jesus: Regnum meum non est de hoc mundo; si ex hoc mundo esset regnum meum, ministri mei utique decertarent ut non traderer Judaeis; nunc autem regnum meum non est hinc. 37 Dixit itaque ei Pilatus: Ergo rex es tu? Respondit Jesus: Tu dicis quia rex sum ego. Ego in hoc natus sum, et ad hoc veni in mundum, ut testimonium perhibeam veritati; omnis qui est ex veritate, audit vocem meam. 38 Dicit ei Pilatus: Quid est veritas? Et cum hoc dixisset, iterum exivit ad Judaeos, et dicit eis: Ego nullam invenio in eo causam. 39 Est autem consuetudo vobis ut unum dimittam vobis in Pascha; vultis ergo dimittam vobis regem Judaeorum? 40 Clamaverunt ergo rursum omnes, dicentes: Non hunc, sed Barabbam. Erat autem Barabbas latro.

Old English

1 Þā sē Hǣlend þās þing cwæð, þā ēode hē ofer ðā burnan Cedron, ðǣr wæs ān wyrtūn, intō þām hē ēode and his leorningcnihtas. 2 Witodlīce Iudas,

---

1　Hǣlend [healer]: *Savior;* burna(n):   *disciples*
　　brook; wyrtūn [wort-town]: *orchard;*   2　belǣwde: *betrayed;* wiste (witan):
　　leorningcnihtas　[learning-knights]:   *knew;* oftrǣdlīce: *often;* ðyder: *thither*

þe hyne belǣwde, wiste þā stōwe; for þām þe sē Hǣlend oftrǣdlīce cōm
ðyder mid his leorningcnihton. 3 Þā underfēng Iudas þæt folc and þā
þegnas æt þām bisceopum and æt ðām Phariseon, and cōm þyder mid
lēohtfatum and mid blasum and mid wǣpnum. 4 Witodlīce sē Hǣlend
wiste ealle þā þing þe him tōwearde wǣron; hē ēode ðā forð, and cwæð tō
him, "Hwǣne sēce gē?" 5 Hig andswaredon him and cwǣdon, "Ðone
Nazareniscean Hǣlend." Sē Hǣlend cwæð, "Ic hit eom." Sōðlīce Iudas þe
hine belǣwde stōd mid him. 6 Ðā hē openlīce sǣde "Ic hit eom," ðā ēodon
hig under bæc and fēollon on ðā eorþan. 7 Eft hē hī āxode, "Hwǣne sēce
gē?" Hī cwǣdon, "Þone Nazareniscean Hǣlend." 8 Sē Hǣlend him
andswarode, "Ic sǣde ēow þæt ic hit eom. Gif gē witodlīce mē sēceað,
lǣtað þās faran": 9 þæt sēo sprǣc wǣre gefylled þe hē cwæð, þæt "ic
nānne þæra ne forspille þe ðū mē sealdest." 10 Witodlīce Simon Petrus
ātēah his swurd, and slōh ðæs bisceopes þēowan, and ācerf him of þæt
swȳðre ēare. Þæs þēowan nama wæs Malchus. 11 Ðā cwæð sē Hǣlend tō
Petre, "Dō þīn swurd on scēaðe; þone calic þe mīn Fæder mē sealde, ne drince
ic hine?" 12 Ðæt folc and sē ealdor and þæra Iūdēa ðegnas nāmon þone
Hǣlend and bundon hine, 13 and lǣddon hine ǣrest tō Annan, sē wæs
Caiphas swēor, and sē Caiphas wæs ðæs gēares bisceop. 14 Witodlīce
Kaiphas dihte ðām Iūdēon and cwæð þæt hyt wǣre betere þæt ān man
swulte for folc. 15 Simon Petrus fylide þām Hǣlende, and ōðer leorningcniht.
Sē ōðer leorningcniht wæs ðām bisceope cūð, and hē ēode inn mid þām
Hǣlende on ðæs bisceopes cafertūn. 16 Petrus stōd æt ðǣre dura þǣr ūte.
Þā ēode sē leorningcniht ūt þe wæs ðæs bisceopes cūða, and cwæð tō ðǣre
dureþīnene, and lǣdde Petrum inn. 17 Ðā cwæð sēo duruðīnen tō Petre,
"Cwyst ðū eart ðū of ðyses leorningcnihtum?" Ðā cwæð hē, "Nicc, ne
eom ic." 18 Ðā þēowas and ðā þegnas stōdon æt ðām glēdon and wyrmdon
hig, for þām hit wæs ceald; witodlīce Petrus stōd mid him and wyrmde
hyne. 19 Sē bisceop āxode þone Hǣlend embe his leorningcnihtas, and embe
his lāre. 20 Ðā andswarode sē Hǣlend and cwæð, "Ic sprǣc openlīce tō

---

3 underfēng (-fōn): *obtained;* þegnas:
  servants; æt: *from;* lēohtfat(um) [light-
  vats]: *lanterns;* blas(um) [blaze]:
  torches

4 toweard(e) [toward]: *future;* Hwǣne:
  whom

6 under bæc: *backwards;* fēollon (feallan):
  pt. 3 pl., fell

8 lǣtað: *imper. let;* faran [fare]: *go*

9 sprǣc: *saying;* gefylled: *fulfilled;* forspille: *pr. 1 sg., destroy;* sealdest [sold]:
  gave

10 ātēah (ātēon): *drew;* slōh (slēan)
  [slay]: *struck;* þēowa(n): *servant;* ācerf
  [carve]: *pt. 3 sg., cut;* swȳðre: *right*

11 Dō: *put;* calic: *cup*

12 ealdor: *leader;* nāmon (niman): *pt. 3
  pl., took;* bundon (bindan): *bound*

13 ǣrest: *first;* gēar(es): *gen., year's*

14 dihte: *directed;* swulte: *pt. 3 sg. subj.,
  die*

15 fylide: *followed;* cūð: *known;* cafertūn:
  courtyard

16 cūða [kith]: *acquaintance;* dureþīnen-
  (e): *door-servant*

17 Nicc: *not I*

18 glēdon: *embers;* wyrmdon: *warmed*

19 lār(e) [lore]: *teaching*

20 middaneard(e) [middle-yard]: *the middle enclosure, earth;* symble: *always;*
  gesomnung(e): *gathering;* tōgædere:
  together; dīgelīce: *secretly*

middanearde, and ic lǣrde symble on gesomnunge, and on temple, þār
ealle Iūdēas tōgædere cōmon; and ic ne spæc nān þing dīgelīce. 21 Hwī
āxast ðū mē? āxa þā þe gehȳrdon hwæt ic tō him spræc; hī witon þā ðing
þe ic him sǣde." 22 Ðā hē þis cwæð, þā slōh ān ðǣra þēna þe ðār stōdon
ðone Hǣlend mid his handa, and cwæð, "Andswarast ðū swā þām bisceope?"
23 Sē Hǣlend andswarode him and cwæð, 'Gif ic yfele spræc, cȳð gewittnysse
be yfele; gif ic wel spræc, hwī bēatst þū mē?" 24 Ðā sende Annas hine tō
þām bisceope gebundene. 25 And Symon Petrus stōd and wyrmde hyne.
Ðā cwǣdon hī tō him, "Cwyst þū eart þū of his leorningcnihton?" Hē
wiðsōc, and cwæð, "Ic ne eom." 26 Ðā cwæð ān ðæs bisceopas þēowena,
hys cūða þæs ēare slōh Petrus of, "Hū ne geseah ic ðē on ðām wyrtūne mid
hym?" 27 Petrus þā eft wiðsōc; and sōna sē cocc crēow. 28 Ðā gelæddon hī
þone Hǣlend tō Caiphan on þæt dōmern; hit wæs þā morgen; and hig sylue
ne ēodon intō ðām dōmerne, þæt hyg nǣron besmitene, ac þæt hī ǣton
hyra ēastron. 29 Þā ēode Pilatus ūt tō him, and cwæð, "Hwylce wrōhte
bringe gē ongēan þysne man?" 30 Hig answaredon and cwǣdon tō him,
"Gif hē nǣre yfeldǣde, ne sealde wē hine ðē." 31 Þā cwæð Pilatus tō him,
"Nimað hine, and dēmað him be ēowre ǣ." Ðā cwǣdon þā Iūdēas tō him,
"Ūs nis nā ālȳfed þæt wē ǣnigne mann ofslēan;" 32 þæt þæs Hǣlendes
sprǣc wǣre gefylled þe hē cwæð þā hē geswutelode hwylcon dēaðe hē
swulte. 33 Ðā ēode Pilatus eft intō þām dōmerne, and clypode ðone Hǣlend
and cwæð tō him, "Eart ðū Iūdēa Cining?" 34 Ðā andswarode sē Hǣlend
him and cwæð, "Cwyst þū þis of ðē sylfum, hwæðer ðe hyt þē ōðre sǣdon?"
35 Pilatus him andswarode and cwæð, "Cwyst þū eom ic Iūdēisc? Þīn þēod
and þīne bisceopas ðē sealdon mē; hwæt dydest ðū?" 36 Ðā cwæð sē
Hǣlend, "Mīn rīce nys of ðyson middanearde; gif mīn rīce wǣre of ðyson
middanearde, witodlīce mīne þegnas fuhton þæt ic nǣre geseald Iūdēon;
nis mīn rīce of ðyson middanearde." 37 Ðā cwæð Pilatus tō him, "Eart
ðū witodlīce cyning?" Sē Hǣlend him andswarode and cwæð, "Ðū hit
segst þæt ic eom cyng. On ðām ic eom geboren, and tō þām ic cōm on
middaneard, þæt ic cȳðe sōþfæstnysse. Ælc þǣra þe ys on sōðfæstnysse

---

21 gehȳrdon: *heard*
22 þēn(a): *gen., servants*
23 cȳð: *imper., make known;* bēatst: *beat*
24 sende: *sent;* gebunden(e) (bindan):
    pt. pp., bound
25 wiðsōc (wiðsacan) [*cp.* forsake]: *denied*
27 sōna [soon]: *immediately;* crēow
    (crāwan): *crowed*
28 dōmern [doom-]: *judgment hall;*
    morgen: *morning;* sylue: *selves;* nǣron:
    pt. 3 pl. subj., might not be; besmiten(e)
    [smitten]: *defiled;* ǣton: *pt. 3 pl. subj.,*
    eat; ēastron: *Easter (see Notes)*
29 wrōht(e): *charge*

30 nǣre: *pt. 3 sg. subj.: were not;* sealde
    [sold]: *pt. 1 pl. subj., would give*
31 Nimað: *imper., take;* dēmað [deem]:
    judge; ǣ: *law;* ālȳfed [leave]: *allowed;*
    ofslēan: *kill*
32 geswutelode: *made clear*
33 Cining: *king*
34 hwæðer ðe: *or*
35 þēod: *people*
36 rīce: *kingdom;* fuhton (feohtan): *pt. 3*
    pl. subj., would fight; geseald: *pt. pp.,*
    given
37 On ðām: *for this;* sōþfæstnyss(e):
    truth; gehȳrð: *hears;* stefn(e): *voice*

gehȳrð mīne stefne." 38 Ðā cwæð Pilatus tō him, "Hwæt ys sōðfæstnyss?"
And þā hē ðis cwæð, þā ēode hē eft ūt tō þām Iūdēon, and cwæð tō him,
"Ne funde ic nānne gylt on ðyson menn. 39 Hit ys ēowor gewuna þæt ic
forgyfe ēow ānne mann on ēastron; wylle gē þæt ic forgyfe ēow Iūdēa
Cyning?" 40 Hig clypodon ealle and cwædon, "Nā ðysne, ac Barrabban."
Witodlīce Barrabbas wæs þēof.

Wycliffite (Purvey)

1 Whanne Jhesus hadde seid these thingis, he wente out with hise disciplis
ouer the strond of Cedron, where was a ȝerd, in to which he entride, and hise
disciplis. 2 And Judas, that bitrayede hym, knew the place, for ofte Jhesus
cam thidur with hise disciplis. 3 Therfor whanne Judas hadde takun a
cumpany of knyȝtis, and mynystris of the bischopis and of the Fariseis, he
cam thidur with lanternys, and brondis, and armeris. 4 And so Jhesus
witynge alle thingis that weren to come on hym, wente forth, and seide
to hem, "Whom seken ȝe?" 5 Thei answeriden to hym, "Jhesu of Nazareth."
Jhesus seith to hem, "Y am." And Judas that bitraiede hym, stood with
hem. 6 And whanne he seide to hem, "Y am," thei wenten abak, and fellen
doun on the erthe. 7 And eft he axide hem, "Whom seken ȝe?" And thei
seiden, "Jhesu of Nazareth." 8 He answeride to hem, "Y seide to ȝou, that
Y am; therfor if ȝe seken me, suffre ȝe these to go awei." 9 That the word
which he seide schulde be fulfillid, For "Y loste not ony of hem, whiche
thou hast ȝouun to me." 10 Therfor Symount Petre hadde a swerd, and
drow it out, and smoot the seruaunt of the bischop, and kittide of his riȝt
eer. And the name of the seruaunt was Malcus. 11 Therfor Jhesus seide to
Petre, "Putte thou thi swerd in to thi schethe; wolt thou not, that Y drynke
the cuppe, that my fadir ȝaf to me?" 12 Therfor the cumpenye of knyȝtis,
and the tribune, and the mynystris of the Jewis, token Jhesu, and bounden
hym, 13 and ledden hym first to Annas; for he was fadir of Caifas wijf, that
was bischop of that ȝeer. 14 And it was Caifas, that ȝaf counsel to the
Jewis, that it spedith, that o man die for the puple. 15 But Symount Petre
suede Jhesu, and another disciple; and thilke disciple was knowun to the
bischop. And he entride with Jhesu, in to the halle of the bischop; 16 but
Petre stood at the dore with outforth. Therfor the tother disciple, that was

---

38 funde: *pt. 1 sg., found;* menn: *dat. sg.,*
    man

1   ȝerd: *yard*
4   witynge: *knowing*
9   ȝouun: *given*

39 gewuna: *custom;* forgyfe: *hand over*
40 þēof: *thief*

10 kittide: *cut*
14 spedith: *is beneficial;* o: *one*
15 suede [sue]: *followed*

knowun to the bischop, wente out, and seide to the womman that kepte the dore, and brou3te in Petre. 17 And the damysel, kepere of the dore, seide to Petre, "Whether thou art also of this mannys disciplis?" He seide, "Y am not." 18 And the seruantis and mynystris stooden at the coolis, for it was coold, and thei warmyden hem; and Petre was with hem, stondynge and warmynge hym. 19 And the bischop axide Jhesu of hise disciplis, and of his techyng. 20 Jhesus answerde to hym, "Y haue spokun opynli to the world; Y tau3te euermore in the synagoge, and in the temple, whider alle the Jewis camen togidere, and in hiddlis Y spak no thing. 21 What axist thou me? axe hem that herden, what Y haue spokun to hem; lo! thei witen, what thingis Y haue seid." 22 Whanne he hadde seid these thingis, oon of the mynystris stondynge ni3, 3af a buffat to Jhesu, and seide, "Answerist thou so to the bischop?" 23 Jhesus answeride to hym, "If Y haue spokun yuel, bere thou witnessyng of yuel; but if Y seide wel, whi smytist thou me?" 24 And Annas sente hym boundun to Caifas, the bischop. 25 And Symount Petre stood, and warmyde him; and thei seiden to hym, "Whether also thou art his disciple?" He denyede, and seide, "Y am not." 26 Oon of the bischops seruantis, cosyn of hym, whos eere Petre kitte of, seide, "Sa3 Y thee not in the 3erd with hym?" 27 And Petre eftsoone denyede, and anoon the cok crew. 28 Thanne thei ledden Jhesu to Cayfas, in to the moot halle; and it was eerli, and thei entriden not in to the moot halle, that thei schulden not be defoulid, but that thei schulden ete pask. 29 Therfor Pilat wente out with outforth to hem, and seide, "What accusyng brynge 3e a3ens this man?" 30 Thei answeriden, and seiden to hym, "If this were not a mysdoere, we hadden not bitakun hym to thee." 31 Thanne Pilat seith to hem, "Take 3e hym, and deme 3e him, after 3oure lawe." And the Jewis seiden to hym, "It is not leueful to vs to sle ony man;" 32 that the word of Jhesu schulde be fulfillid, whiche he seide, signifiynge bi what deth he schulde die. 33 Therfor eftsoone Pilat entride in to the moot halle, and clepide Jhesu, and seide to hym, "Art thou kyng of Jewis?" 34 Jhesus answerde, and seide to hym, "Seist thou this thing of thi silf, ether othere han seid to thee of me?" 35 Pilat answeride, "Whether Y am a Jewe? Thi folc and bischops bitoken thee to me; what hast thou don?" 36 Jhesus answeride, "My kingdom is not of this world; if my kingdom were of this world, my mynystris schulden stryue, that Y schulde not be takun to the Jewis; but now my kingdom is not here." 37 And so Pilat seide to hym, "Thanne thou art a king." Jhesus answeride, "Thou seist, that Y am a king. To this thing Y am borun, and to this Y am comun in to the world, to bere witnessing to treuthe. Eche that is of treuthe, herith my vois." 38 Pilat seith to hym, "What is treuthe?" And whanne he hadde seid this

---

20	euermore: *always*	31	leueful: *allowed*
26	sa3: *saw*	33	clepide: *called*
28	moot: *meeting*	34	ether: *or*
30	bitakun: *handed over*		

thing, eft he wente out to the Jewis, and seide to hem, "Y fynde no cause in hym. 39 But it is a custom to ʒou, that Y delyuere oon to ʒou in pask; therfor wole ʒe that Y delyuere to ʒou the kyng of Jewis?" 40 Alle crieden eftsoone, and seiden, "Not this, but Baraban." And Barabas was a theef.

Tyndale

1 When Iesus had spoken these wordes, he went forth with his disciples over the broke Cedron, where was a garden, into the which he entred with his disciples. 2 Iudas also which betrayed him, knewe the place: for Iesus ofte tymes resorted thyther with his disciples. 3 Iudas then after he had receaved a bonde of men, and ministres of the hye Prestes and Pharises, came thyther with lanterns and fyerbrondes and wepens. 4 Then Iesus knowynge all thinges that shuld come on him, went forth and sayde vnto them: whom seke ye? 5 They answered him: Iesus of Nazareth. Iesus sayde vnto them: I am he. Iudas also which betrayed him, stode with them. 6 But assone as he had sayd vnto them, I am he, they went backe wardes and fell to the grounde. 7 And he axed them agayne: whome seke ye? They sayde: Iesus of Nazareth. 8 Iesus answered, I sayde vnto you, I am he. If ye seke me, let these goo their waye. 9 That the sayinge might be fulfilled which he spake: of them which thou gavest me, have I not lost one. 10 Simon Peter had a swearde, and drue it, and smote the hye prestes servaunt, and cut of his ryght eare. The servauntes name was Malchas. 11 Then sayde Iesus vnto Peter: put vp thy swearde into the sheath: shall I not drinke of the cup which my father hath geven me? 12 Then the company and the captayne, and the ministres of the Iewes, toke Iesus and bounde him, 13 and led him awaye to Anna fyrst: For he was fatherelawe vnto Cayphas, which was the hye preste that same yeare. 14 Cayphas was he that gave counsell to the Iewes, that it was expedient that one man shuld dye for the people. 15 And Simon Peter folowed Iesus and another disciple: that disciple was knowen of the hye preste, and went in with Iesus into the pallys of the hye preste. 16 But Peter stode at the dore with out. Then went out that other disciple which was knowen vnto the hye preste, and spake to the damsell that kept the dore, and brought in Peter. 17 Then sayde the damsell that kept the dore, vnto Peter: Arte not thou one of this mannes disciples? He sayde: I am not. 18 The servauntes and the ministres stode there, and had made a fyre of coles: for it was colde: and they warmed them selves. Peter also stode amonge them and warmed him selfe. 19 The hye preste axed Iesus of his disciples and of his doctrine. 20 Iesus answered him: I spake openly in the worlde. I ever taught in the synagoge and in the temple whyther all the Iewes resorted, and in secrete have I sayde nothynge: 21 Why axest thou me? Axe them whiche hearde me, what I sayde vnto

them. Beholde they can tell what I sayde. 22 When he had thus spoken, one of the ministres which stode by, smote Iesus on the face sayinge: answerest thou the hyepreste so? 23 Iesus answered him. If I have evyll spoken, beare witnes of the evyll: yf I have well spoken, why smytest thou me? 24 And Annas sent him bounde vnto Caiphas the hye preste. 25 Simon Peter stode and warmed him selfe. And they sayde vnto him: arte not thou also one of his disciples? He denyed it, and sayde: I am not. 26 One of the servauntes of the hye preste (his cosyn whose eare Peter smote of) sayde vnto him: dyd not I se the in the garden with him? 27 Peter denyed it agayne: and immediatly the cocke crewe. 28 Then led they Iesus from Cayphas into the hall of iudgement. It was in the mornynge, and they them selves went not into the iudgement hall lest they shuld be defyled, but that they myght eate the paschall lambe. 29 Pylate then went out vnto them and sayde: what accusacion bringe ye agaynste this man? 30 They answered and sayd vnto him. If he were not an evyll doar, we wolde not have delyvered him vnto the. 31 Then sayd Pylate vnto them: take ye him, and iudge him after youre awne lawe. Then the Iewes sayde vnto him. It is not lawfull for vs to put eny man to deeth. 32 That the wordes of Iesus myght be fulfilled which he spake, signifyinge what deeth he shuld dye. 33 Then Pylate entred into the iudgement hall agayne, and called Iesus, and sayd vnto him: arte thou the kynge of the Iewes? 34 Iesus answered: sayst thou that of thy selfe, or dyd other tell it the of me? 35 Pylate answered: Am I a Iewe? Thyne awne nacion and hye prestes have delyvered the vnto me. What hast thou done? 36 Iesus answered: my kyngdome is not of this worlde. Yf my kyngdome were of this worlde, then wolde my ministres suerly fight, that I shuld not be delyvered to the Iewes, but now is my kyngdome not from hence. 37 Pylate sayde vnto him: Arte thou a kynge then? Iesus answered: Thou sayst that I am a kynge. For this cause was I borne, and for this cause came I into the worlde, that I shuld beare witnes vnto the trueth. And all that are of the trueth heare my voyce. 38 Pilate sayde vnto him: what thinge is trueth? And when he had sayd that, he went out agayne vnto the Iewes, and sayde vnto them: I fynde in him no cause at all. 39 Ye have a custome, that I shuld delyver you one lowsse at ester. Will ye that I lowse vnto you the kynge of the Iewes. 40 Then cryed they all agayne sayinge: Not him, but Barrabas, that Barrabas was a robber.

King James

1 When Jesus had spoken these wordes, hee went foorth with his disciples ouer the Brooke Cedron, where was a garden, into the which hee entred and his disciples. 2 And Judas also which betrayed him, knew the place:

for Jesus oft times resorted thither with his disciples. 3 Judas then hauing receiued a band of men, and officers from the chiefe Priests and Pharisees, commeth thither with lanternes and torches, and weapons. 4 Jesus therefore knowing all things that should come vpon him, went foorth, and sayde vnto them, Whom seeke ye? 5 They answered him, Jesus of Nazareth. Jesus saith vnto them, I am hee. And Judas also which betraied him, stood with them. 6 Assoone then as he had said vnto them, I am he, they went backeward, and fell to the ground. 7 Then asked hee them againe, Whom seeke ye? And they said, Jesus of Nazareth. 8 Jesus answered, I haue tolde you that I am he: If therefore ye seeke me, let these goe their way: 9 That the saying might be fulfilled, which he spake, Of them which thou gauest me, haue I lost none. 10 Then Simon Peter hauing a sword, drewe it, and smote the high Priests seruant, & cut off his right eare: The seruants name was Malchus. 11 Then said Jesus vnto Peter, Put vp thy sword into the sheath: the cup which my father hath giuen me, shall I not drinke it? 12 Then the band and the captaine, and officers of the Jewes, tooke Jesus, and bound him, 13 And led him away to Annas first, (for he was father in law to Caiaphas) which was the high Priest that same yeere. 14 Now Caiaphas was he which gaue counsell to the Jewes, that it was expedient that one man should die for the people. 15 And Simon Peter followed Jesus, and so did another disciple: that disciple was knowen vnto the high Priest, and went in with Jesus into the palace of the high Priest. 16 But Peter stood at the doore without. Then went out that other disciple, which was knowen vnto the high Priest, and spake vnto her that kept the doore, and brought in Peter. 17 Then saith the damosell that kept the doore vnto Peter, Art not thou also one of this mans disciples? He sayth, I am not. 18 And the seruants and officers stood there, who had made a fire of coales, (for it was colde) and they warmed themselues: and Peter stood with them, and warmed himselfe. 19 The high Priest then asked Jesus of his disciples, and of his doctrine. 20 Jesus answered him, I spake openly to the world, I euer taught in the Synagogue, and in the Temple, whither the Jewes alwayes resort, and in secret haue I said nothing: 21 Why askest thou me? Aske them which heard me, what I haue said vnto them: behold, they know what I said. 22 And when hee had thus spoken, one of the officers which stood by, stroke Jesus with the palme of his hand, saying, Answerest thou the hie priest so? 23 Jesus answered him, If I haue spoken euill, beare witnesse of the euill: but if well, why smitest thou me? 24 Now Annas had sent him bound vnto Caiaphas the high Priest. 25 And Simon Peter stood and warmed himselfe: They said therefore vnto him, Art not thou also one of his disciples? Hee denied it, and said, I am not. 26 One of the seruants of the high Priests (being his kinsman whose eare Peter cut off) saith, Did not I see thee in the garden with him? 27 Peter then denied againe, and immediatly the cocke crew. 28 Then led they Jesus from Caiaphas vnto the hall of Judgement: And it was earely, and they themselues went not into the Judgement hall, lest they should be defiled: but that they might eat the Passeouer. 29 Pilate then went out vnto them, and said, What accusation bring you against this man? 30 They answered, & said vnto him, If he were not a malefactor, we would not haue deliuered him vp vnto thee. 31 Then saide Pilate vnto them, Take ye him, and iudge him according to your law. The Jewes therefore said vnto him, It is not lawfull for vs to put any man to death: 32 That the saying of Jesus might be fulfilled, which hee spake, signifying what death he should die. 33 Then Pilate entred into the Judgement hall againe, and called Jesus, and saide vnto him, Art thou the King of the Jewes? 34 Jesus answered him, Sayest thou this thing of thy selfe? or did others tell it thee of me? 35 Pilate answered, Am I a Jew? Thine owne nation, and the chiefe Priests haue deliuered thee vnto mee: What hast thou done? 36 Jesus answered, My kingdome is not of this world: if my kingdome were of this world, then would my seruants fight, that I should not be deliuered to the Jewes: but now is my kingdome not from hence. 37 Pilate therefore saide vnto him, Art thou a King then? Jesus answered, Thou saiest that I am a King. To this end was I borne, and for this cause came I into the world, that I should beare witnesse vnto the trueth: euery one that is of the trueth heareth my voice. 38 Pilate saith vnto him, What is trueth? And when hee had said this, he went out againe vnto the Jewes, and saith vnto them, I find in him no fault at all. 39 But yee haue a custome that I should release vnto you one at the Passeouer: will ye therefore that I release vnto you the King of the Jewes? 40 Then cried they all againe, saying, Not this man, but Barabbas. Now Barabbas was a robber.

New English Bible

1 After these words, Jesus went out with his disciples, and crossed the Kedron ravine. There was a garden there, and he and his disciples went into it. 2 The place was known to Judas, his betrayer, because Jesus had often met there with his disciples. 3 So Judas took a detachment of soldiers, and police provided by the chief priests and the Pharisees, equipped with lanterns, torches, and weapons, and made his way to the garden. 4 Jesus, knowing all that was coming upon him, went out to them and asked, 'Who is it you want?' 5 'Jesus of Nazareth', they answered. Jesus said, 'I am he.' And there stood Judas the traitor with them. 6 When he said, 'I am he', they drew back and fell to the ground. 7 Again Jesus asked, 'Who is it you want?' 'Jesus of Nazareth', they answered. 8 Then Jesus said, 'I have told you that I am he. If I am the man you want, let these others go.' 9 (This was to make good his words, 'I have not lost one of those whom thou gavest

me.') 10 Thereupon Simon Peter drew the sword he was wearing and struck at the High Priest's servant, cutting off his right ear. (The servant's name was Malchus.) 11 Jesus said to Peter, 'Sheathe your sword. This is the cup my Father has given me; shall I not drink it?'

12 The troops with their commander, and the Jewish police, now arrested Jesus and secured him. 13 They took him first to Annas. Annas was father-in-law of Caiaphas, the High Priest for that year — the same Caiaphas who had advised the Jews that it would be to their interest if one man died for the whole people. 15 Jesus was followed by Simon Peter and another disciple. This disciple, who was acquainted with the High Priest, went with Jesus into the High Priest's courtyard, 16 but Peter halted at the door outside. So the other disciple, the High Priest's acquaintance, went out again and spoke to the woman at the door, and brought Peter in. 17 The maid on duty at the door said to Peter, 'Are you another of this man's disciples?' 'I am not', he said. 18 The servants and the police had made a charcoal fire, because it was cold, and were standing round it warming themselves. And Peter too was standing with them, sharing the warmth. 19 The High Priest questioned Jesus about his disciples and about what he taught. 20 Jesus replied, 'I have spoken openly to all the world; I have always taught in synagogue and in the temple, where all Jews congregate; I have said nothing in secret. 21 Why question me? Ask my hearers what I told them; they know what I said.' 22 When he said this, one of the police struck him on the face, exclaiming, 'Is that the way to answer the High Priest?' 23 Jesus replied, 'If I spoke amiss, state it in evidence; if I spoke well, why strike me?' 24 So Annas sent him bound to Caiaphas the High Priest. 25 Meanwhile Peter stood warming himself. The others asked, 'Are you another of his disciples?' But he denied it: 'I am not', he said. 26 One of the High Priest's servants, a relation of the man whose ear Peter had cut off, insisted, 'Did I not see you with him in the garden?' 27 Peter denied again; and just then a cock crew.

28 From Caiaphas Jesus was led into the Governor's headquarters. It was now early morning, and the Jews themselves stayed outside the headquarters to avoid defilement, so that they could eat the Passover meal. 29 So Pilate went out to them and asked, 'What charge do you bring against this man?' 30 'If he were not a criminal,' they replied, 'we should not have brought him before you.' 31 Pilate said, 'Take him away and try him by your own law.' The Jews answered, 'We are not allowed to put any man to death.' 32 Thus they ensured the fulfilment of the words by which Jesus had indicated the manner of his death. 33 Pilate then went back into his headquarters and summoned Jesus. 'Are you the king of the Jews?' he asked. 34 Jesus said, 'Is that your own idea, or have others suggested it to you?' 35 'What! am I a Jew?' said Pilate. 'Your own nation and their chief priests have brought you before me. What have you done?' 36 Jesus replied, 'My kingdom does not belong to this world. If it did, my

followers would be fighting to save me from arrest by the Jews. My kingly authority comes from elsewhere.' 37 'You are a king, then?' said Pilate. Jesus answered, ' "King" is your word. My task is to bear witness to the truth. For this was I born; for this I came into the world, and all who are not deaf to truth listen to my voice.' 38 Pilate said, 'What is truth?', and with those words went out again to the Jews. 'For my part,' he said, 'I find no case against him. 39 But you have a custom that I release one prisoner for you at Passover. Would you like me to release the king of the Jews?' 40 Again the clamour rose: 'Not him; we want Barabbas!' (Barabbas was a bandit.)

NOTES

1 Here, and frequently, OE has *Hǣlend* 'healer' for *Jesus*.
2 The dative plural ending *-on* in *leorningcnihton* illustrates the late OE weakening of inflexions.
5 The "historic present" of Vulgate *dicit* 'says' is also in the King James.
9 Latin *quia*, *quoniam* and *quod*, all originally 'because,' are often used in the Vulgate to introduce indirect or quoted speech. Purvey *For* is therefore an error.
   All MSS of the OE appear (according to Bright's edition) to have the present *forspille* 'I destroy' for Vulgate preterite *perdidi*.
10 OE *slōh* (infinitive *slēan*) here has its original sense 'strike,' as in 22, rather than its later development 'slay, kill.'
   Vulgate *ergo* is a loose connective — Purvey *Therfor* is too literal.
13 The punctuation of KJ is against the sense.
14 OE *for* + acc. = 'on behalf of' occurs more than once in the *West-Saxon Gospels;* see Bright's note on John 27: 19.
16 Purvey *the tother*: ME *tone* and *tother* result from incorrect word division of OE *þæt ān, þæt ōðer*.
17 OE *Cwyst* and Purvey *Whether* translate *Numquid*, as in 25; compare IV, 12 *n*. *Numquid* does not here imply disbelief, and is closer to *Nonne* 'surely you are.'
   OE *nicc* 'not I' (*ne* + *ic*) survives in the ME verb *nikke;* compare *Sir Gawain and the Green Knight* 706 'al nykked hym wyth nay.'
18 Texts not dependent on the Vulgate refer to making a fire.
24 Note the word order in KJ, *had sent him bound*. It seems evident from the other versions that the meaning is 'had him sent . . .'
27 The modern senses of OE *sōna* and ME *anon* (Vulgate *statim* 'immediately') illustrate the tendency of words meaning 'immediately' to weaken to 'in a short time'; compare also MnE *presently* with the same history.

28   MSS of the Vulgate have both *a* 'from' and *ad* 'to,' accounting for the
     OE and Purvey *to*.
     OE regularly translates *pascha* into the Anglo-Saxon pagan festival of
     Easter, which occasionally produces such absurdities as 'eating Easter.'
29   Note KJ *bring you*, with *you* a nominative (for expected *ye*).
30   OE *sealde* present plural subjunctive: Campbell § 473.
36   Note Tyndale and KJ (pleonastic) *from hence*.
37   NEB *all who are not deaf to truth* is in no other version.
38   OE *funde* first person singular past, analogically from the past plural
     fundon (Campbell § 741), but all other versions here have the present
     tense, including the Vulgate. Vulgate *causam* 'case to answer' (compare
     OE *gylt*) rather than 'cause.'

XIII - XV

≈≈≈≈≈≈≈≈≈≈≈≈≈≈≈≈≈≈≈≈≈≈≈≈≈≈≈≈≈≈≈≈≈≈

BOETHIUS
CONSOLATION OF PHILOSOPHY

Boethius was one of the principal agents in the transmission of classical philosophy, particularly that of Aristotle, to the Middle Ages. He was a leading Roman statesman under the Emperor Theodoric the Goth, but shortly after 522 he was suspected of treason, was imprisoned, and was executed in 524. During his imprisonment he wrote the *Consolation of Philosophy* in five books. Philosophy visits the lamenting Boethius, and convinces him of the worthlessness of earthly prosperity, and of the rewards of the virtuous life. The work is not at any point specifically Christian, but it is now generally agreed that Boethius was the author of other Christian tracts (such as the treatise *De Trinitate*), and wrote the *Consolation* without specific Christian reference in order to justify Christian ethics by the principles of pagan philosophy. The *Consolation* is written in prose and verse. Each passage of prose is followed by a *metrum* (verse passage) that summarizes or illustrates the previous argument. There is an illuminating essay on "Boethius: the first of the scholastics" in E. K. Rand, *The Founders of the Middle Ages* (1928; New York: Dover Books, 1957), pp. 135–180. The work was, after the Bible, one of the most influential in the Middle Ages.

The OE prose extracts here are taken from the edition by W. J. Sedgefield, *King Alfred's Old English version of Boethius* (Oxford: Clarendon Press, 1899), which presents a composite text from the two principal OE MSS. Bodley MS 180 translates the whole of the *Consolation* into prose, while the damaged British Museum MS Cotton Otho A.vi has passages of alliterative verse corresponding to the Boethian *metra*. These verses are not, however, fresh translations of the Latin, but are versifications of the OE prose translation — one example is given below. These "Cotton meters" were edited separately by G. P. Krapp, *The Paris Psalter and the Meters of Boethius* (Anglo-Saxon Poetic Records, V. New York: Columbia University Press, 1932). Alfred's translation — there is no good reason to doubt his authorship — is far from literal. He made it explicitly Christian, and with the aid of various commentaries expanded the original where he felt further elucidation or information was necessary. Frequently the technical terms of classical philosophy are rephrased by Alfred to make sense in English.

Chaucer's translation may be dated about 1380. The extracts given here are from *The Oxford Chaucer*, edited by W. W. Skeat in seven volumes (Oxford, 1894–1897); it is entirely in prose. Chaucer also used the French translation and commentary by Nicholas Trivet. Much of Chaucer's poetry is steeped in the ideas of the *Consolation*. In XIV I have printed a passage from *Troilus and Criseyde* in which a piece of logic which was less successfully rendered in his earlier prose is expressed succinctly.

In XV the translation by John Walton (1410) is taken from E. P. Hammond, *English Verse between Chaucer and Surrey* (1927; New York: Octagon Books, 1965), p. 48. Walton knew the Chaucerian translation, and has verbal echoes of it.

Queen Elizabeth I made her translation of the *Consolation* in 1593; it is edited by C. Pemberton, *Queen Elizabeth's Englishings of Boethius 'De Consolatione Philosophiae'* . . . ., EETS o.s. 113 (1899). The Queen rendered prose into prose, and *metra* into rhyming verse.

The modern translation is by R. H. Green (New York: Bobbs Merrill, 1962).

XIII

CONSOLATION OF PHILOSOPHY: II, prose 1

୬ଡ଼ୄ୬ଡ଼ୄ୬ଡ଼ୄ୬ଡ଼ୄ୬ଡ଼ୄ୬ଡ଼ୄ୬ଡ଼ୄ୬ଡ଼ୄ୬ଡ଼ୄ୬ଡ଼ୄ୬ଡ଼ୄ୬ଡ଼ୄ୬ଡ଼ୄ୬ଡ଼ୄ୬

The Instability of Fortune

Boethius

(1) Quid est igitur, o homo, quod te in maestitiam luctumque deiecit?
(2) Novum, credo, aliquid inusitatumque vidisti. (3) Tu fortunam putas
erga te esse mutatam; erras. (4) Hi semper eius mores sunt, ista natura.
(5) Servavit circa te propriam potius in ipsa sui mutabilitate constantiam.
(6) Talis erat cum blandiebatur, cum tibi falsae inlecebris felicitatis al-
luderet. (7) Deprehendisti caeci numinis ambiguos vultus. (8) Quae sese
adhuc velat aliis, tota tibi prorsus innotuit. (9) Si probas, utere moribus;
ne queraris. (10) Si perfidiam perhorrescis, sperne atque abice perniciosa
ludentem. (11) Nam quae nunc tibi est tanti causa maeroris, haec eadem
tranquillitatis esse debuisset. (12) Reliquit enim te quam non relicturam
nemo umquam poterit esse securus.

King Alfred

(1) Ēala, Mōd, hwæt bewearp þē on ðās care ond on þās gnornunga?
(2) Wēnst þū þæt hit hwæt nīwes sīe oþþe hwæthwugu ungewunelīces þe
þē on becumen is, swelce ōþrum monnum ǣr þæt ilce ne eglede? (3) Gif
þū þonne wēnst þæt hit on þē gelong sīe þæt ðā woruldsǣlða on ðē swā
onwenda sint, þonne eart ðū on gedwolan, (4) ac swylce hiora þēawas sint;
(5) hī behēoldon on ðē hiora āgen gecynd, ond on hiora wandlunga hȳ

Some words are glossed in the Notes.
1 bewearp (beweorpan): *threw;* gnor-
nung(a): *sorrow*
2 *See Notes.* Wēnst [ween]: *suppose;*
nīwes: *gen., new;* hwæthwugu: *something*

3 *See Notes.* onwend(a): *changeable*
4 þēawas: *habits*
5 behēoldon (behealdan): *pt. 3 pl., kept;*
āgen: *own;* wandlung(a): *changing;*
gecȳðdon: *made known;* unfæstrǣd-
ness(e): *inconstancy*

gecȳðdon hiora unfæstrædnesse. (6) Swylce hī wǣron rihte ðā hī ðē mǣst geōlectan swilce hī nū sindon, þēah ðe hī ðē līolcen on þā lēasan sǣlða. (7) Nū ðū hæfst ongiten ðā wanclan trūwa þæs blindan lustes. (8) Þā trīowa þe þē nū sindon opene hī sindon gīt mid manegum ōðrum behelede. Nū þū wāst hwelce þēawas þā woruldsǣlða habbað ond hū hī hwearfiað. (9) Gif þū þonne heora þegen bēon wilt ond þē heora þēawas līciað, tō hwon myrnst þū swā swīðe? Hwī ne hwearfost þū ēac mid him? (10) Gif þū þonne heora untrīowa onscunige, oferhoga hī þonne ond ādrīf hī fram þē; hī spanað þē tō þīnre unðearefe. (11) Ðā ilcan þe þē gedydon nū þās gnornunga forðǣm þe þū hī hæfdest, þā ilcan þē wǣren on stilnesse gif þū hī nā ne underfēnge. (12) Ðā ilcan þē habbað nū heora āgnes ðonces forlǣten, nāles ðīnes, ðā ðe nǣfre nānne mon būton sorge ne forlǣtað.

Chaucer

(1) What eyleth thee, man? What is it that hath cast thee in to morninge and in to wepinge? (2) I trowe that thou hast seyn som newe thing and uncouth. (3) Thou wenest that Fortune be chaunged ayein thee; but thou wenest wrong, yif thou that wene. (4) Alwey tho ben hir maneres; (5) she hath rather kept, as to thee-ward, hir propre stablenesse in the chaunginge of hirself. (6) Right swich was she whan she flatered thee, and deceived thee with unleveful lykinges of fals welefulnesse. (7) Thou hast now knowen and ataynt the doutous or double visage of thilke blinde goddesse Fortune. (8) She, that yit covereth hir and wimpleth hir to other folk, hath shewed hir every-del to thee. (9) Yif thou aprovest hir and thenkest that she is good, use hir maneres and pleyne thee nat. (10) And yif thou agrysest hir false trecherye, despyse and cast awey hir that pleyeth so harmfully; (11) for she, that is now cause of so muche sorwe to thee, sholde ben cause to thee of pees and of Ioye. (12) She hath forsaken thee, forsothe, the whiche that never man may ben siker that she ne shal forsake him.

6 *See Notes.* geōlectan: *flattered;* līolcen (lācan): *pt. 3 pl. subj., deluded;* lēasa(n): *false*
7 ongiten: *pt. pp., understood;* wancl(an): *fickle;* trūwa: *promises*
8 *See Notes.* behelede: *concealed*
9 þegen: *servant;* līciað [like]: *please;* tō hwon: *to what purpose;* myrnst (murnan): *mourn;* hwearfost: *turn*

10 untrīowa: *faithlessness(es);* onscunige [shun]: *fear;* oferhoga: *imper., despise;* ādrīf: *imper., drive away;* spanað: *seduce;* unðearef(e): *detriment*
11 *See Notes.* gedydon: *pt. 3 pl., did, caused;* wǣren: *pt. 3 pl. subj., were, would have been;* underfēnge (-fōn): *pt. 2 sg., received*
12 *See Notes.*

2 uncouth: *strange*
5 to thee-ward: *in your direction*
6 unleveful: *illicit;* lykinges: *pleasures*

10 agrysest: *fear*
12 siker: *certain*

Queen Elizabeth

(1) What is it, therfore, O man, that hath throwne the down to wo and wayle? (2) Thou hast seene, I beleue, som new vnwonted thing. (3) Thou, yf thou thinkest that toward the fortune be changed, art deceaud. (4) This was euer her manner, this was her nature. (5) She hath euer kept toward the rather her own constancy in her mutabilitie. (6) Such one was she, whan she beguild the, and did deceaue with allurementes of false felicitie. (7) Thou hast vnderstode now, the doutfull face of the blynde Goddesse, (8) which though she hyde her self to others, hath made her self to the manifest. (9) Yf thou allow her vse her fashon, complayne not therof; (10) yf thou hatest her treason, skorne her and cast her of, that so falsely beguylde the; (11) for she that now is cause of thy woe, the self same ought be of thy quyett. (12) She hath left the, whom no man can be sure that will not leave him.

Green*

(1) What is it, my friend, that has thrown you into grief and sorrow? (2) Do you think that you have encountered something new and different? (3) You are wrong if you think that Fortune has changed toward you. (4) This is her nature, the way she always behaves. (5) She is changeable, and so in her relations with you she has merely done what she always does. (6) This is the way she was when she flattered you and led you on with the pleasures of false happiness. (7) You have merely discovered the two-faced nature of this blind goddess. (8) Although she still hides herself from others, she is now wholly known to you. (9) If you like her, abide by her conditions and do not complain. (10) But if you hate her treachery, ignore her and her deceitful antics. (11) Really, the misfortunes which are now such a cause of grief ought to be reasons for tranquility. (12) For now she has deserted you, and no man can ever be secure until he has been forsaken by Fortune.

NOTES

1   OE *Mōd* 'mind, heart': Alfred represents the *Consolation* as a dialogue between Wisdom (=Philosophy) and Mind.

* From Boethius: *The Consolation of Philosophy*, translated by Richard Green, copyright ©, 1962, by The Bobbs-Merrill Company, Inc., reprinted by permission of the Liberal Arts Press Division.

2 Alfred: 'do you suppose that it is something new, or something unpre-
cedented, which has happened to you, as though the like never afflicted
other men before?' *ēglede* is impersonal.

3 Alfred: 'if, then, you suppose that it is something private to you (*on
þē gelong* — compare MnE *belonging*) that worldly fortunes are so
changeable towards you, then you are in error.' Alfred renders *Fortuna*
by the plural *ðā woruldsǣlða* 'the fortunes of this world'; the effect is
to destroy entirely the personification of the goddess Fortune. In XV
sīo wyrd 'Fate, Destiny' is used to denote the agency by which men's
prosperity is altered. Moreover, *(woruld)sǣlð* in OE implies good
fortune, and this necessitates some elaboration of the argument by
Alfred. The use of the plural also affects the grammar of the OE.
Compare also 7 *n.*

5 Chaucer *as to thee-ward* indicates that *-ward* could still be used as a
formative suffix in ME; contrast Elizabeth *toward the* (3).

6 Alfred: 'at that very moment (*rihte ðā*) when they most flattered you,
they were just such as they are now, although they enticed you towards
false fortunes.'

7 OE *lustes* 'pleasure' again avoids personification of the blind goddess.

8 OE *þā triowa* 'good faith(s),' ironically, i.e., 'deceits.' *Nū þū wāst . . .
hwearfiað* 'Now you know what habits the fortunes of this world have,
and how they change,' is an addition by Alfred.

11 All versions before Green's incorrectly assume that *Fortuna* is the
antecedent of *quae*; in fact *quae* and *causa* go together — 'that which
is the cause of . . .' The OE is a complete misinterpretation: 'the same
things which recently brought you to sorrow, because you used to
have them, would have brought peace to you (literally, would have
been towards peace for you) if you had never received them.' The error
affects the next line.

12 Alfred: 'these same things have now abandoned you of their own will,
not yours (your will), (these things) which never leave anyone without
causing sorrow.' The original Latin means that Boethius has been
shown the true nature of Fortune; he ought to be glad to have lost
what one must always lose, since he now enjoys the security of misfortune. The OE simply says that the loss of fortune normally brings
sorrow; *heora āgnes ðonces . . . nāles ðīnes* (adverbial genitive) 'of
their own will, not yours' is therefore meaningless. Green gives a
paraphrase rather than a translation.

XIV

CONSOLATION OF PHILOSOPHY: II, prose 4

৻৳

Fortune's Gifts Do Not Bring Happiness

Boethius

(1) Quid igitur, o mortales, extra petitis intra vos positam felicitatem? (2) Error vos inscitiaque confundit. (3) Ostendam breviter tibi summae cardinem felicitatis. (4) Estne aliquid tibi te ipso pretiosius? (5) Nihil, inquies. (6) Igitur si tui compos fueris, possidebis quod nec tu amittere umquam velis, nec fortuna possit auferre. (7) Atque ut agnoscas in his fortuitis rebus beatitudinem constare non posse, sic collige. (8) Si beatitudo est summum naturae bonum ratione degentis, nec est summum bonum quod eripi ullo modo potest, quoniam praecellit id quod nequeat auferri, manifestum est quoniam ad beatitudinem percipiendam fortunae instabilitas adspirare non possit. (9) Ad haec quem caduca ista felicitas vehit vel scit eam, vel nescit, esse mutabilem. (10) Si nescit, quaenam beata sors esse potest ignorantiae caecitate? (11) Si scit, metuat necesse est, ne amittat quod amitti posse non dubitat; quare continuus timor non sinit esse felicem. (12) An vel si amiserit, neglegendum putat? (13) Sic quoque perexile bonum est quod aequo animo feratur amissum.

King Alfred

(1) Hwȳ sēce gē þonne ymbūtan ēow þā gesǣlða þe gē oninnan īow habbað þurh þā godcundan mieht geset? (2) Ac gē nyton hwæt gē dōð; gē sint on gedwolan. (3) Ac ic ēow mæg mid fēawum wordum gereccan hwæt sē hrōf is ealra gesǣlða; wið þās ic wāt þū wilt higian þon ǣr þe ðū hine ongitest;

---

1 sēce: *seek;* ymbūtan: *outside;* gesǣlð-
(a):*happiness;* oninnan:*within;* geset:
pt. pp., placed

2 nyton: *know not;* gedwola(n): *error*
3 fēaw(um): *few;* gereccan: *explain;*
hrōf:*roof;* wið þās . . . gōōd: *see Notes*

þæt is þonne gōod. (4) Meaht þū nū ongitan hwæðer þū auht þē dēorwyrðre hæbbe þonne þē selfne? (5) Ic wēne þeah þæt ðū wille cweþan þæt þū nauht dēorwyrðre næbbe. (6) Ic wāt, gif þū nū hæfde fulne anweald þīnes selfes, þonne hæfde þū hwæthwugu on ðē selfum þæs ðe þū næfre þīnum willum ālǣtan noldes, nē sīo wyrd þē on geniman ne meahte. (7–8) Forðǣm ic ðē mindgige þæt þū ongite þætte nān gesǣlð nis on þis andweardan līfe ðonne sēo gescēadwīsnes, forðǣm hīo þurh nān þing ne mæg þǣm men losian; forðȳ is betere þæt feoh þætte nǣfre losian ne mæg ðonne þætte mæg ond sceal. Hū ne is þē nū genōh sweotole gesǣd þæt sīo wyrd þē ne mæg nāne gesǣlða sellan? forþǣmþe ǣgþer is unfæst, gē sēo wyrd gē sēo gesǣlð; forþām sint swīðe tēdre ond swīðre hrēosende þās gesǣlþa. (9) Hwæt, ǣlc þāra þe þās woruldgesǣlþa hæfð ōþer twēga: oððe hē wāt þæt hī him fromwearde bēoð, oððe hē hit þonne nāt. (10) Gif hē hit þonne nāt, hwelce gesǣlþa hæfð hē æt þām welan gif hē bið swā dysig ond swā ungewiss þæt hē þæt witan ne mæg? (11) Gif hē hit þonne wāt, þonne ondrǣt hē him þæt hī losien, ond ēac geara wāt þæt hē hī ālǣtan sceal. Sē singāla ege ne lǣt nōnne mon gesǣlin ne bīon. (12) Gif þonne hwā ne recð hwæðer hē þā gesǣlþa hæbbe þe næbbe þe hē þonne hæfð, hwæt, (13) þæt þonne bēoð for lȳtla sǣlða oþþe nāne, þæt mon swā ēaðe forlǣtan mæg.

Chaucer

(1) O ye mortal folk, what seke ye thanne blisfulnesse out of yourself, whiche that is put in yourself? (2) Errour and folye confoundeth yow. (3) I shal shewe thee shortely the poynt of sovereyne blisfulnesse. (4) Is ther anything more precious to thee than thyself? (5) Thou wolt answere, "nay". (6) Thanne, yif it so be that thou art mighty over thyself, *that is to seyn, by tranquillitee of thy sowle*, than hast thou thing in thy power that thou

---

4 ongitan: *understand;* auht: *anything;* dēorwyrð(re): *more precious*

5 wēne: *suppose*

6 *See Notes.* anweald: *control;* hwæthwugu: *something;* þīnum willum: *by your own will;* ālǣtan: *abandon;* wyrd: *fate;* geniman: *take away*

7–8 *See Notes.* mindgige: *remind;* gescēadwīsnes: *wisdom;* þǣm men: *dat. sg.,* man; losian: *be lost to;* feoh [*cf.* fee]: *property;* genōh [enough]: *sufficiently;* sweotole: *clearly;* sellan [sell]: *give;* tēdre: *infirm;* hrēosende: *falling,*

transitory

9 *See Notes.* fromweard(e): *sure to depart*

10 wela(n): *prosperity;* dysig [dizzy]: *foolish;* ungewiss: *foolish*

11 ondrǣt (ondrǣdan): *pr. 3 sg., fears;* geara: *readily;* singāla: *continual;* ege: *fear;* gesǣli(n): *happy*

12 hwā [who]: *anyone;* recð: *cares;* hæbbe þe næbbe: *pr. 3 sg. subj., has or has not;* hwæt: *indeed*

13 ēaðe: *easily;* forlǣtan: *abandon*

noldest never lesen, ne Fortune ne may nat beneme it thee. (7) And that thou mayst knowe that blisfulnesse ne may nat standen in thinges that ben fortunous and temporel, now understonde and gader it togidere thus: (8) Yif blisfulnesse be the sovereyn good of nature that liveth by resoun, ne thilke thing nis nat sovereyn good that may be taken awey in any wyse, (for more worthy thing and more digne is thilke thing that may nat ben taken awey), than sheweth it wel, that the unstablenesse of fortune may nat atayne to receiven verray blisfulnesse. (9) And yit moreover, what man that this toumbling welefulnesse ledeth, either he woot that it is chaungeable, or elles he woot it nat. (10) And yif he woot it nat, what blisful fortune may ther be in the blindnesse of ignorance? (11) And yif he woot that it is chaungeable, he moot alwey ben adrad that he ne lese that thing that he ne doubteth nat but that he may lesen it; *as who seith, he mot ben alwey agast lest he lese that he wot wel he may lese it.* For which, the continuel dreed that he hath ne suffreth him nat to ben weleful. (12) Or yif he lese it, he weneth to be dispysed and forleten. (13) Certes eek, that is a ful litel good that is born with evene herte whan it is lost; *that is to seyn, that men do no more fors of the lost than of the havinge.*

Troilus and Criseyde, III, 820–33

O brotel wele of mannes Ioye unstable!
With what wight so thou be, or how thou pleye,
(9)   Either he woot that thou, Ioye, art muable,
Or woot it not, it moot ben oon of tweye;
(10)   Now if he woot it not, how may he seye
That he hath verray Ioye and selinesse,
That is of ignoraunce ay in derknesse?

(11)   Now if he woot that Ioye is transitorie,
As every Ioye of worldly thing mot flee,
Than every tyme he that hath in memorie,
The drede of lesing maketh him that he
May in no parfit selinesse be.
(12–13) And if to lese his Ioye he set a myte,
Than semeth it that Ioye is worth ful lyte.

---

6 lesen; *lose;* beneme: *take away*   11 moot: *must*
8 digne: *worthy;* verray: *true*   12 forleten: *abandoned*
9 woot: *knows*

Queen Elizabeth

(1) "Why do ye mortall men seeke outwardly your felicitie within you? (2) Error and blyndnes confoundes you. (3) I will shew the shortly the thressholl of thy felicitie. (4) Is there to the ought more precious than thy selfe?" (5) "Nothing", quoth I. (6) "Then if thou be wise, thou shalt possesse that nether thou canst lose, nor fortune take away. (7) And that thou mayste knowe felicitie not to stand in happing chaunces, considir it this. (8) Yf happynes be the greatest good of nature lyuing by reason, nor hit the greatest good that may be taken away, the cause hit doth exceede that may not so, It is manifest, that fortunes change can not attayn to the getting of bliss. (9) Besydes, whom falling felicitie caryes, eyther knowith her, or seeth her mutabilitie. (10) Yf he be ignorant, what happy luck can blynde felicitie haue? (11) Yf he know it, he must needes feare to lose that he is sure can not be kepte. His contynuall feare then, depriuith his happynes. (12) Or if he haue lost, will he not care for it? (13) for hit should be a slender good that a man wold easely lose.

Green*

(1) Why then do men look outside themselves for happiness which is within? (2) You are confused by error and ignorance (3) and so I will point out to you the source of perfect happiness. (4) Is anything more precious to you than yourself? (5) You will agree that there is nothing. (6) Then if you possess yourself, you have something you will never want to give up and something which Fortune cannot take from you. (7) If you will consider carefully the following argument, you will have to admit that happiness cannot depend on things which are uncertain. (8) If happiness is the highest good of rational natures, and if nothing which can be lost can be a supreme good (because it is obviously less good than that which cannot be lost), then clearly unstable Fortune cannot pretend to bring happiness. (9) The man who enjoys fleeting happiness either knows that it is perishable, or he doesn't. (10) If he does not know it, his condition is unhappy because it rests on blind ignorance; (11) if he knows his happiness is perishable, he must live in fear of losing what he knows can be easily lost — and such constant fears will not let him be happy. (12) And if he should lose it, would he think that a trivial matter? (13) Whatever can be given up without regret is indeed a thing of little worth.

NOTES

1   Note the OE Christian addition *þurh þā godcundan mieht* 'by divine power.'

2   Chaucer *folye* is not quite correct for *inscitia* 'ignorance, lack of knowledge.'

3   All versions translate *cardinem* differently; literally it means 'hinge, as of a door' — hence Elizabeth *thressholl* — and so 'that on which something depends.' Chaucer may have been thinking of *cardo* in its sense of an astronomical point. OE *hrōf* 'roof' — i.e., highest point — is incorrect. Alfred's addition seems to mean: 'I know you will think of these things· (*gesǣlða*, fortunes) before you attain it (*sē hrōf*), that is the Good' — *þonne* is difficult.

5   Elizabeth *quoth I*: she is treating the dialogue as a real one between Boethius and Fortune, rather than a hypothetical one posed by Philosophy.

6   *tui compos:* 'in possession of yourself' — Elizabeth *wise* misses the point. Alfred's 'if you now had full control of yourself (which you have not)' is also incorrect.

7–8   The logical sequence is this: (a) the highest good is happiness; (b) that which can be taken away is not the highest good, because (c) that which can *not* be taken away is necessarily better than that which can; therefore (d) the instability of Fortune cannot confer happiness. By taking the highest good to be wisdom (*gescēadwīsnes*), Alfred destroys the syllogism: 'therefore I remind you so that you may understand that there is no fortune in this present life (better) than wisdom, for wisdom cannot be lost to any man by any means: for that property is better that cannot be lost than that which can and must (be lost). Surely it has now been stated clearly enough that Fortune (Fate, *wyrd*) cannot confer any prosperity? For both Fate and prosperity are unstable, for these fortunes are very frail and transitory.'
Note OE *losian* with the dative, 'be lost (to someone).'

8   All versions take *naturae* and *ratione degentis* together, but it is possible that it means 'the highest good of Nature for a man living by reason.' It is this phrase that has led Alfred to assume the highest good to be wisdom or reason. Elizabeth *the cause . . . may not so* is parenthetic: 'the reason (being that) that which may not (be taken away) surpasses (that which may).'

9   The passage from the *Troilus* begins here. Elizabeth misses the sense entirely. In the OE *ōðer twēga* introduces the alternatives and causes what in MnE would be an anacoluthon: 'every man who has these worldly fortunes, — one of two things: either . . . etc.'

10 Note Elizabeth *happy* in the modern sense: in ME *happy luck* would have been a tautology, meaning simply 'chance'; in MnE it is equally tautologous, meaning 'good fortune.'

11 OE *losien*: see on 7–8 above; the subject is *þā gesælða* understood. Chaucer *that he ne lese* 'lest he lose' is a French construction. In Chaucer's parenthetic gloss, *as who seith* = 'as one might say'; *it* is redundant — 'he must always be afraid lest he lose what he well knows he may lose (it).'

12 OE has made the last two sentences into one, by making (12) a conditional clause. Chaucer *to be dispysed and forleten* is clearly an error; in the *Troilus* the error has been corrected.

13 Elizabeth *should be* 'certainly is.'

XV

CONSOLATION OF PHILOSOPHY: II, meter 5

The Glories of the Former Age

Boethius

Felix nimium prior aetas
Contenta fidelibus arvis
Nec inerti perdita luxu,
Facili quae sera solebat
5 Ieiunia solvere glande.
Non Bacchica munera norant
Liquido confundere melle,
Nec lucida vellera Serum
Tyrio miscere veneno.
10 Somnos dabat herba salubres,
Potum quoque lubricus amnis,
Umbras altissima pinus.
Nondum maris alta secabat,
Nec mercibus undique lectis
15 Nova litora viderat hospes.
Tunc classica saeva tacebant,
Odiis neque fusus acerbis
Cruor horrida tinxerat arva.
Quid enim furor hosticus ulla
20 Vellet prior arma movere,
Cum vulnera saeva viderent
Nec praemia sanguinis ulla?
Utinam modo nostra redirent
In mores tempora priscos!
25 Sed saevior ignibus Aetnae
Fervens amor ardet habendi.
Heu primus quis fuit ille

Auri qui pondera tecti
Gemmasque latere volentes
30 Pretiosa pericula fodit?

King Alfred

(1) Ēala, hū gesǣlig sēo forme eld was þises midangeardes, (2) ðā ǣlcum men þūhte genōg on þǣre eorþan wǣstmum. Nǣron þā welige hāmas, nē mistlīce swōtmettas, nē drincas, nē dīorwyrðra hrǣgla hī ne girndan, forþām hī þā gīt nǣran, nē hīo nānwuht ne gesāwon, nē ne gehērdon. (3) Nē gēmdon hīe nānes fyrenlustes, būton swīðe gemetlīce þā gecynd beēodan; (4) ealne weg hī ǣton ǣne on dæg, ond þæt was tō ǣfennes. Trēowa wǣstmas hī ǣton ond wyrta, (6) nálles scīr wīn hī ne druncan, nē nānne wǣtan hī ne cūþon wið hunige mengan; (8) nē seolecenra hrǣgla mid mistlīcum blēowum hī ne gīmdon. (10) Ealne weg hī slēpon ūte on trīowa sceadum; (11) hlūterra wella wǣter hī druncon. (13) Nē geseah nān cēpa ēaland nē weroð, (16) nē gehērde nōn mon þā gēt nānne sciphere, nē furþon ymbe nān gefeoht sprecan. (17) Nē sēo eorðe þā gēt besmiten mid ofslǣgenes monnes blōde, nē mon furðum gewundod; nē monn ne geseah þā gīt yfelwillende men; nǣnne weorðscipe nǣfdon, nē hī nōn mon ne lufude. (23) Ēala þæt ūre tīda nū ne mihtan weorþan swilce. (25) Ac nū manna gītsung is swā byrnende swā þæt fȳr on þǣre helle, sēo is on þām munte þe Ætne hātte, on þām īeglande þe Sicilia hātte; sē munt bið simle swefle birnende, ond ealla þā nēahstōwa þǣrymbūtan forbærnð. (27) Ǣala, hwæt sē forma gītsere wǣre, (28) þe ǣrest þā eorþan ongan delfan æfter golde, ond æfter gimmum, (29–30) ond þā frēcnan dēorwyrðnesse funde þe ǣr behȳd wæs ond beheolod mid ðǣre eorþan.

---

1 gesǣlig [silly]: *blessed;* forme: *first;* midangeardes [middle-yard]: *earth*

2 *See Notes.* þūhte: *seemed;* genōg: *enough;* wǣstm(um): *fruits;* mistlīc(e): *various;* girndan: *longed for;* nǣran: *were not*

3 *See Notes.* gēmdon: *cared for;* gemetlīce: *moderately;* gecynd: *natures;* beēodan: *performed*

4 ealne weg [always]: *lit., in every way, throughout;* ǣton (etan): *pt. 3 pl., ate;* ǣnne: *once;* ǣfennes: *evening;* Trēow(a): *gen. pl., trees;* wyrt(a) [worts]: *plants*

6 *See Notes.* nálles: *not;* scīr [sheer]: *bright;* wǣta(n) [wet]: *liquid*

8 seolecen(ra): *silken;* hrǣgl(a): *garments;* blēow(um): *colors;* gīmdon = gēmdon

10 slēpon: *pt. 3 pl., slept;* scead(um): *shades*

11 hlūter(ra): *bright*

13 cēpa: *merchant;* ēaland: *island*

16 sciphere: *invading fleet;* gefeoht: *fight*

17 *See Notes.* besmiten (besmītan) [smitten]: *struck;* ofslǣgen(es) (ofslēan) [slain]: *killed;* gewundod: *wounded;* yfelwillende [evil-willing]: *of evil intention;* weorðscipe [worship]: *glory*

23 tīd(a) [tide]: *times;* weorþan: *become*

25 *See Notes.* gītsung: *greed;* hātte (hātan): *is called;* simle: *always;* nēahstōw(a): *neighboring places;* forbærnð: *burns up*

28 ǣrest: *first;* ongan (onginnan): *began;* gimm(um): *jewels*

29-30 frēcn(an): *dangerous;* behȳd: *pt. pp., hidden;* beheolod: *covered*

Old English: Cotton Meter 8

(1) Hwæt, sīo forme eld   foldbūendum
     geond eorðan scēat   æghwām dōhte,

(2) þā þā ānra gehwǣm   on eorðwæstmum
     genōh ðūhte. Nis hit nū ðā swelc!
     Nǣron þā geond weorulde   welige hāmas,
     nē mislīce   mettas nē drincas,
     nē hī þāra hrægla   hūru ne gēmdon
     þe nū drihtguman   dīorost lǣtað.
     Forðǣm hiora nǣnig   næs þā gīeta,
     nē hī ne gesāwon   sundbūende,
     nē ymbutan hī   āwer ne hērdon.

(3) Hwæt, hī firenlusta   frēce ne wǣron,
     būton swā hī meahton   gemetlīcost
     ðā gecynd begān   þe him Crist gesceōp,

(4) and hī ǣne on dæge   ǣton symle
     on ǣfentīd   eorðan wæstmas,
     wudes and wyrta,   (6) nālles wīn druncon
     scīr of stēape. Næs þā scealca nān
     þe mete oððe drinc   mængan cūðe,
     wæter wið hunige,   (8) nē heora wǣda þon mā
     sioloce siowian,   nē hī siarocræftum
     godweb giredon,   nē hī gimreced
     setton searolīce,   (10) ac hī simle him
     eallum tīdum   ūte slēpon
     under bēamsceade,   (11) druncon burnan wæter,
     calde wyllan.   (13) Nǣnig cēpa ne seah
     ofer eargeblond   ellendne wearod,

(16) nē hūru ymbe sciphergas   scealcas ne hērdon,
     nē furðum fīra nān   ymb gefeoht sprecan.

Words that occur in the OE prose are not glossed here.

1 foldbūend(um): *land-dwellers, men;* scēat: *surface;* æghwām: *dat., everyone;* dōhte (dugan): *pt. 3 sg., was good for*

2 ānra gehwǣm: *to everyone;* drihtguma-(n): *warriors;* lǣtað: *consider;* sundbūende: *sea-dwellers, men;* āwer: *anywhere*

3 frēce: *greedy;* būton swā: *lit., except as;* begān: *perform;* gesceōp (scapan) [shape]: *created*

4 ǣfentīd: *eventide*

6 stēap(e): *flagon;* scealca: *man*

8 wǣd(a) [weeds]: *clothes;* þon mā: *any the more;* siowian: *sew;* siarocræft(um): *by ingenious skills;* godweb: *fine cloth;* giredon: *prepared;* gimreced: *jewel-hall, palace*

10 bēamscead(e) [beam-]: *tree-shade*

11 burna(n): *gen., stream;* wyll(an) [well]: *springs*

13 eargeblond: *wave-blend, sea;* ellend(ne): *foreign*

(17) Næs ðēos eorðe besmiten āwer þā gēta
beornes blōde þe hine bill rude,
nē furðum wundne wer weoruldbūende
gesāwan under sunnan. Nǣnig siððan wæs
weorð on weorulde, gif mon his willan ongeat
yfelne mid eldum; hē wæs æghwǣm lāð.

(23) Ēala, þǣr hit wurde, oððe wolde God,
þæt on eorðan nū ūssa tīda
geond þās wīdan weoruld wǣren æghwæs
swelce under sunnan. (25) Ac hit is sǣmre nū,
þæt ðēos gītsunc hafað gumena gehwelces
mōd āmerred, þæt hē māran ne recð,
ac hit on witte weallende byrnð.
Efne sīo gītsung þe nǣnne grund hafað
swearte swǣfeð sumes onlīce
efne þām munte þe nū monna bearn
Etne hātað. Sē on īglonde
Sicilia swēfle byrneð,
þæt mon helle fȳr hāteð wīde,
forþǣm hit symle bið sinbyrnende,
and ymbūtan hit ōðra stōwa
blāte forbærnð biteran lēge.

(27) Ēala, hwæt sē forma feohgītsere
wǣre on worulde, (28) sē þās wongstedas
grōf æfter golde and æfter gimcynnum.

(29–30) Hwæt, hē frēcnu gestrēon funde mænegum
bewrigen on weorulde, wætere oððe eorðan.

---

17 beorn(es): *gen., warrior;* rude (rēodan) [red]: *pt. 3 sg. subj., reddened with blood;* wund(ne): *wounded;* weoruldbūende: *world-dwellers, men;* Nǣnig . . . lāð: *see Notes;* weorð [worth]: *honored;* ongeat (ongitan): *pt. 3 sg., perceived;* eld(um): *men;* lāð [loath]: *hateful*

23 wurde (weorðan): *pt. 3 sg. subj., might become;* oððe wolde God: *or God might be willing;* æghwæs: *in every way*

25 sǣmre: *worse;* gum(ena): *gen. pl.,*

men; mōd [mood]: *heart;* āmerred [mar]: *harmed;* recð: *cares;* on witt(e): *in his mind;* weallende: *boiling;* Efne . . . efne: *just so . . . as;* grund: *bottom;* swearte: *blackly, evilly;* swǣfeð: *burns;* sumes onlīce: *somewhat like;* bearn [bairn]: *children;* hātað: *call;* blāte: *pallidly;* lēg(e): *flame*

27 feohgītsere: *miser*

28 wongstedas: *plains;* grōf (grafan) [grave]: *excavated*

29–30 gestrēon: *treasure;* bewrigen (bewrēon): *covered*

Chaucer

(1) Blisful was the first age of men! (2) They helden hem apayed with the metes that the trewe feldes broughten forth. (3) They ne distroyede nor deceivede nat hem-self with outrage. (4) They weren wont lightly to slaken hir hunger at even with acornes of okes. (6) They ne coude nat medly the yifte of Bachus to the cleer hony; *that is to seyn, they coude make no piment nor clarree;* (8) ne they coude nat medle the brighte fleeses of the contree of Seriens with the venim of Tyrie; *this is to seyn, they coude nat deyen whyte fleeses of Serien contree with the blode of a maner shelfisshe that men finden in Tyrie, with whiche blood men deyen purpur.* (10) They slepen hoolsom slepes up-on the gras, (11) and dronken of the renninge wateres; (12) and layen under the shadwes of the heye pyn-trees. (13) Ne no gest ne straungere ne carf yit the heye see with ores or with shippes; (14-15) ne they ne hadde seyn yit none newe strondes, to leden marchaundyse in-to dyverse contrees. (16) Tho weren the cruel clariouns ful hust and ful stille, (17) ne blood y-shad by egre hate ne hadde nat deyed yit armures. (19) For wher-to or which woodnesse of enemys (20) wolde first moeven armes, (21) whan they seyen cruel woundes, (22) ne none medes be of blood y-shad?

(23) I wolde that oure tymes sholde torne ayein to the olde maneres! (25) But the anguissous love of havinge brenneth in folk more cruely than the fyr of the mountaigne Ethna, that ay brenneth. (27) Allas! what was he that first dalf up the gobetes or the weightes of gold covered under erthe, (29) and the precious stones that wolden han ben hid? (30) He dalf up precious perils. *That is to seyn, that he that hem first up dalf, he dalf up a precious peril; for-why, for the preciousnesse of swiche thinge hath many man ben in peril.*

Walton

(1)   Full wonder blisseful was þat raþer age,
(2)   When mortal men couthe holde hymself payed
      To fede þeym self with oute suche outerage,
      Wiþ mete þat trewe feeldes haue arrayed;

---

  2   apayed: *pleased*   21   seyen: *saw*
  6   piment: *spiced wine*   22   medes: *rewards*
 19   woodnesse: *madness*   29   han: *infin., have*

  1   raþer: *former* (*see Notes*)

(4)   Wiþ acorne þaire hunger was alayed,
       And so þei couthe sese þaire talent.
(6)   Thei had yit no queynt craft assayed
       As clarry for to make ne pyment.

(8)   To deen purpure couthe þei noght beþynke,
       The white flees wyþ venym tyryen.
(11) Þe rennyng ryuer yaf hem lusty drynke,
(10) And holsom sleep þei took vpon þe grene.
(12) The pynes þat so full of braunches been,
       þat was þaire hous to kepe vnder schade.
(13) The see to kerue no schippes were þere seen;
(14) þer was no man þat marchaundise made.

(15) Thay liked not to sailen vp and doun,
       But kepe hem self where þei weren bred.
(16) Tho was ful huscht þe cruel clarioun;
(17) For eger hate þer was no blood isched,
       Ne þer with was non armour yit bebled;
(19) For in þat tyme who durst haue be so wood
       Suche bitter woundes þat he nold haue dred
       Wiþ outen reward forto lese his blood?

(23) I wold oure tyme myght lerne certanly,
       And þise maneres alwey with vs dwelle;
(25) But loue of hauyng brenneþ feruently
       More fersere þan þe verray fuyre of helle.
(27) Allas! who was þat man þat wold him melle
       This gold and gemmes, þat were keuered þus,
       þat first began to myne I can not telle —
(30) Bot þat he fond a parelous precious.

Queen Elizabeth

      Happy to muche the formar Age
        With faithful fild content,
        Not Lost by sluggy Lust,

---

4   talent: *appetite*   11   lusty: *pleasant*
6   queynt [quaint]: *clever;* assayed: *attempted*

    (4)   that wontz the Long fastz
          To Louse by son-got Acorne.
            that knew not Baccus giftz
          With molten hony mixed
            Nor Serike shining flise
          With tirius venom die.
    (10)   Sound slipes Gaue the grasse
          ther drink the running streme
            Shades gaue the hiest pine.
          The depth of sea they fadomd not
            Nor wares chosen from fur
    (15)   Made Stranger find new shores.
            Than wer Navies Stil,
          Nor bloudshed by Cruel hate
            Had fearful weapons staned.
          What first fury to foes shuld
    (20)   any armes rayse,
          Whan Cruel woundz he Saw
            and no reward for bloude?
          Wold God agane Our formar time
            to wonted maners fel!
    (25)   But Gridy getting Loue burnes
            Sorar than Etna with her flames.
          O who the first man was
            of hiden Gold the waight
          Or Gemmes that willing lurkt
    (30)   The deare danger digd?

Green*

(1) Men were most happy in former ages, (2) content with the yield of fertile fields, (3) and not yet ruined by indolent luxury. (4–5) Their hunger was easily satisfied by acorns. (6) They did not know the potent mixture of wine and honey; (8) they had not learned to color fine silk of Syria with Tyrian dye. (10) They slept soundly on the soft grass, (11) drank from the running streams, (12) and rested in the shade of the high pines. (13) Travelers had not yet sailed the high seas to visit foreign ports with their merchandise. (16) Trumpets of war were silent, (17) and blood had

---

* From Boethius: *The Consolation of Philosophy*, translated by Richard Green, copyright ©, 1962, by The Bobbs-Merrill Company, Inc., reprinted by permission of the Liberal Arts Press Division.

not with fierce hate dyed red the gory fields. (19) For how could hostile fury drive men to take up arms (21) when war offered no rewards for gaping wounds except the blood that was spilled? (23) Would that our age could return to those ancient virtues; (25) but now man's avarice burns more fiercely than Aetna's fires. (27) Who was he that first dug up the buried gold, the gems that wished to remain hidden, (30) and with them all our costly dangers?

NOTES

The OE verse translation was made from the OE prose, not directly from the Latin. It should be noted that Walton's version was clearly influenced by Chaucer; quotations are also given here from Chaucer's poem "The Former Age," which was based primarily on this Boethian *metrum*. Elizabeth has performed a remarkable tour de force by making each line of her translation correspond exactly with those of the original (except for 25–26); this has frequently strained the syntax of her translation unbearably.

1 Elizabeth *to muche* for *nimium* is too literal. OE *forme* 'first' refers not so much to the classical idea of the Golden Age as to the first of the Six Ages of the World (from Adam to the Flood). Walton *raþer*: OE *hraðe* 'quickly': the comparative therefore comes to mean 'sooner, earlier.'

2 The OE expansion, fully utilized in the verse, reads: 'there were not then wealthy homes nor various sweetmeats or drinks, and men did not long for precious clothes, for they did not yet exist, and men had not seen or heard of any.' In the original the fields were 'faithful' because they could be trusted to pay back the seed put into them, a common classical motif. Note that *mete(s)* in ME means 'food' in general, not necessarily flesh.

3 OE: 'they did not long for any sinful pleasure, but fulfilled their natural desires very moderately.' This is an overinterpretation of *luxus* which refers generally to luxurious living; note *būton*, which has almost developed its MnE sense from contexts such as this ('not . . . except . . .'). Chaucer *nor deceivede* is unnecessary and incorrect; Chaucer also clearly takes the reference to be to sexual luxury, unlike Walton who has compressed this line with (2) and assumed that Chaucer *outrage* referred to overindulgence in eating — he can hardly have derived his interpretation from *inerti . . . luxu*.

4 *Sera* 'late,' i.e., they allowed their hunger to remain unsatisfied a long time. Walton and Green omit it, but other versions interpret correctly.

6   Boethius is referring to the use of honey in fermenting grapes (the gifts of Bacchus); Green's 'mixture of wine and honey' is therefore wrong. Alfred has taken the use of honey to refer to the making of mead (mixed from water and honey): 'they did not drink bright wine, and did not know how to mix water with honey.' Walton's use of Chaucer is clear in this line. Elizabeth has destroyed the syntax by using the participle *mixed* instead of the infinitive.

8   *Serum* genitive plural 'the Chinese'; both Chaucer (perhaps misled by the French *les toisons de Sirians*) and Green have misunderstood this as 'Syrian.'

9   *venenum* is common in Latin for 'dye'; 'venom' is too literal a translation.

10   OE has combined (10) and (12).

13–15   OE *weroð = waroð* 'shore.' Chaucer's somewhat long-winded version is better expressed in "The Former Age":

> No ship yit karf the wawes grene and blewe;
> No marchaunt yit ne fette outlandish ware.

Elizabeth *depth* for *alta* is probably wrong — the phrase 'high seas' is common in Latin.

16   *classica* 'trumpets': Alfred and Elizabeth, both monarchs preoccupied with the threat of naval invasion, have translated this as though it were *classes* 'fleets.'

17   In the OE either understand *wæs*, or read *Næs* 'was not' for *Ne*. Versions differ according to whether they read in 18 *arva* 'fields' (OE, Green) or *arma* 'arms' (Chaucer, Elizabeth, Walton). The OE interpolation means: 'no one had yet seen men of evil intention; they had no glory, and no one loved it (glory).' It is also possible, however, to assume that the subject of *næfdon* 'did not have' is 'men of evil intention' rather than 'men in those days' (who had no concept of martial glory), and that *hī* is not feminine singular accusative (*weorðscipe*) but accusative plural (*yfelwillende men*). This is how the author of the OE metrical version took it: 'No one was afterwards honored in the world, if his intention was known to be evil among men; he was hated by everyone.'

19–22   Compare "The Former Age":

> What sholde it han avayled to werreye?
> Ther lay no profit, ther was no richesse.

23–24   Elizabeth *formar* is wrong in this position; her translation is very strained.

25–26   The OE expansion reads: 'But now the greed of men burns like the fire in the hell [compare Walton] which is in the mountain called Ætne on the island called Sicily; the mountain always burns with fire, and scorches all the neighboring places round it.' The

double comparative in Walton *More fersere* is common in ME
(Mustanoja, p. 281).

27ff.   The OE has turned the rhetorical question into an exclamation.
The construction in Walton 'that first concerned himself with . . .,
that first mined . . .' is confused.

XVI · XVII

భిబి

BEDE
THE HISTORY OF THE ENGLISH CHURCH

The two passages here are from Book I, ch. 1, of Bede's *Historia Ecclesiastica*, "The History of the English Church," completed A.D. 731, ed. C. Plummer, 2 vols. (Oxford: Clarendon Press, 1896). The Old English translation was made in the late ninth century; it is not now attributed directly to King Alfred, but clearly formed part of his massive program and was probably produced under his aegis. It was edited by T. Miller, EETS o.s. 95, 96 (1890–1891).

There is no Middle English translation of the *Historia Ecclesiastica*, but by an indirect route we can use as a parallel the work of the Cornishman John Trevisa, whose work is also represented below (XXIX). In 1387 John Trevisa translated into English the Latin *Polychronicon* of Ralph Higden (d. 1364), which was to a large extent a compilation from many earlier histories, that of Bede included. Trevisa's translation is printed alongside the original in the edition of the *Polychronicon* by C. Babington, 9 vols., Rolls Series, 41 (1865–86). The present extracts are from Vol. II (1869) as follows: XVI(a), 1–9 = Trevisa, p. 13; 10 = p. 17; 11 = p. 53; 12–13 = p. 9; XVI(b) = Trevisa, pp. 143–145.

The third translation is that of Thomas Stapleton, *History of the Church of England* (Antwerp, 1565), (Oxford: Basil Blackwell, 1930).

The modern version is by Leo Sherley-Price (Harmondsworth: Penguin Books, 1955).

XVI

THE HISTORY OF THE ENGLISH CHURCH

৩৩৩

Description of Britain

Bede

(1) Opima frugibus atque arboribus insula, et alendis apta pecoribus ac
iumentis; (2) vineas etiam quibusdam in locis germinans; sed et avium
ferax terra marique generis diversi; (3) fluviis quoque multum piscosis ac
fontibus praeclara copiosis, et quidem praecipue issicio abundat et anguilla.
(4) Capiuntur autem saepissime et vituli marini et delphines, necnon et
balenae; (5) exceptis variorum generibus concyliorum, in quibus sunt et
musculae, quibus inclusam saepe margaritam omnis quidem coloris optimam
inveniunt, id est et rubicundi, et purpurei, et iacintini, et prasini, sed
maxime candidi. (6) Sunt et cocleae satis superque abundantes, quibus
tinctura coccinei coloris conficitur, cuius rubor pulcherrimus nullo umquam
solis ardore, nulla valet pluviarum iniuria pallescere, sed quo vetustior, eo
solet esse venustior. (7) Habet fontes salinarum, habet et fontes calidos,
et ex eis fluvios balnearum calidarum omni aetati et sexui per distincta
loca iuxta suum cuique modum accommodos. (8) Aqua enim, ut sanctus
Basilius dicit, fervidam qualitatem recipit, cum per certa quaedam metalla
transcurrit, et fit non solum calida, sed et ardens. (9) Quae etiam venis
metallorum, aeris, ferri, et plumbi, et argenti, fecunda, (10) gignit et
lapidem gagatem plurimum optimumque; est autem nigrogemmeus, et
ardens igni admotus, incensus serpentes fugat, adtritu calefactus adplicita
detinet, aeque ut sucinum. (11) Erat et civitatibus quondam xx et viii
nobilissimis insignita, praeter castella innumera, quae et ipsa muris,
turribus, portis ac seris erant instructa firmissimis. (12) Et quia prope sub
ipso septentrionali vertice mundi iacet, lucidas aestate noctes habet;
(13) ita ut medio saepe tempore noctis in quaestionem veniat intuentibus,
utrum crepusculum adhuc permaneat vespertinum, an iam advenerit
matutinum.

Old English (? Alfred)

(1) Hit is welig þis ēalond on wæstmum and on trēowum misenlīcra cynna; and hit is gescrǣpe on lǣswe scēapa and nēata; (2) and on sumum stōwum wīngeardas grōwaþ. Swylce ēac þēos eorþe is berende missenlīcra fugela and sǣwihta, (3) and fiscumwyllum wæterum and wyllgespryngum. (4) And hēr bēoþ oft fangene sēolas and hronas and mereswȳn; (5) and hēr bēoþ oft numene missenlīcra cynna weolcscylle and muscule, and on þām bēoð oft gemētte þā betstan meregrotan ǣlces hīwes. (6) And hēr bēoð swȳþe genihtsume weolocas, of þām bið geweorht sē weolocreada tælgh, þone ne mæg sunne blǣcan nē ne regn wyrdan; ac swā hē biþ yldra, swā hē fægerra biþ. (7) Hit hafað ēac þis land sealtsēaþas; and hit hafaþ hāt wæter, and hāt baðo ǣlcere yldo and hāde ðurh tōdǣlede stōwe gescrǣpe. (9) Swylce hit is ēac berende on wecga ōrum āres and īsernes, lēades and seolfres. (10) Hēr biþ ēac gemeted gagātes: sē stān bið blæc gym; gif mon hine on fȳr dēþ, þonne flēoþ þǣr nēddran onweg. (11) Wæs þis ēalond ēac gēo gewurðad mid þām æðelestum ceastrum, ānes wana þrittigum, ðā þe wǣron mid weallum and torrum and geatum and þām trumestum locum getimbrade, būtan ōðrum lǣssan unrīm ceastra. (12) And forðan ðe ðis ēalond under þām sylfum norððǣle middangeardes nȳhst ligeþ, and lēohte nihte on sumera hafað, — (13) swā þæt oft on middre nihte geflit cymeð þām behealdendum, hwæðer hit sī þe ǣfenglommung ðe on morgen deagung. . . .

Trevisa

(1) For þis ilond is beest and bringeþ forþ trees and fruyt and reþeren and oþer bestes, (2) and wyn groweþ þere in som place. Þe lond haþ plente of foules and of bestes of dyuers manere kynde; þe lond is plentevous and þe

---

1   welig: *wealthy;* ēalond: *island;* wæstm-(um): *fruits;* misenlīc(ra): *various;* cynn(a): *kinds;* gescrǣpe: *advantageous;* lǣs(we): *pasture;* nēat(a): *animals*

2   stōw(um): *places;* wīngeardas: *vineyards;* berende: *bearing, productive;* fugel(a) [fowl]: *birds;* sǣwiht(a): *sea creatures*

3   fisc(um)wyll(um): *rich in fish;* wyllgespryng(um): *wellsprings*

4   fangen(e) (fōn): *pt. pp., taken*

5   numene (niman): *pt. pp., taken;* weolcscyll(e): *whelk shells;* meregrotan: *see Notes;* hīw(es): *gen., color*

6   genihtsum(e): *abundant;* geweorht [wrought]: *pt. pp., made;* tælgh: *dye;*

blǣcan: *bleach;* wyrdan: *destroy*

7   sealtsēaþas: *salt springs;* yldo: *age;* hād(e): *rank;* tōdǣlede: *divided*

9   wecg(a): *gen. pl., wedges;* ōr(um): *metals*

10 gagātes: *jet;* dēþ (dōn): *places;* flēoþ: *flee;* onweg: *away*

11 See Notes. gewurðad: *made splendid;* æðelest(um): *most noble;* torr(um): *towers;* trumest(um): *firmest;* būtan: *apart from;* unrīm: *countless number*

12 norððǣl(e): *north part;* middangeard-(es) [middle-yard]: *earth;* ligeþ: *lies*

13 geflit: *debate;* cymeð (cuman): *comes;* behealdend(um): *beholders;* ǣfenglommung: *evening twilight*

1   reþeren: *cows*

see also. (3) Þe lond is noble, copious, and riche of nobil welles and of nobil ryueres wiþ plente of fische; þere is grete plente of small fische, of samon, and of elys...... (4) Þere beeþ ofte i-take dolphyns, and see calues, and baleynes, grete fisches as hit were of whales kynde, (5) and dyuers manere schelfische. Among þe schelfisch beeþ muskles þat haueþ wiþ ynne hem margery perles of alle manere colour and hewe, of rody and rede, of purpur and of blew, and specialliche and moste of whyte. (6) Þere is also plente of schellefische þat me dyeþ wiþ reed fyn; þe redenesse þerof is wonder fyn and stable, and steyneþ neuere wiþ colde ne with hete, wiþ wete ne wiþ drie; but euere þe eldere þe hewe is þe fairer. (7) Þere beeþ also salt welles and hote welles; þer of renneþ stremes of hote bathes i-deled in dyuers places, acordynge for man and womman, and for alle manere age, olde and ȝonge. (8) Basilius seiþ þat þe water þat renneþ and passeþ by veynes of certayn metal takiþ in his cours grete hete. (9) Þis ilond is plentevous of veynes of metals, of bras, of iren, of leed, of tyn, of siluer also ... (10) In þis ilond groweþ a stoon þat hatte gagates; ȝif me axeþ of his fairenesse, he is blak as gemmes beeþ. ... I-tend in þe fire hit feseþ awey serpentes; if hit is hotter, hit holdeþ what hym neigheþ, as succinis, a stoon þat so hatte. (11) The kyngdom of Bretayne was somtyme i-hight wiþ eiȝte and twenty noble citees, wiþ oute welle many castelles þat were wiþ walles, wiþ toures, wiþ ȝates, wiþ barres, stalworþliche i-buld. (12) And for þis lond lieþ vnder þe norþ nolle of þe world, þey haþ liȝt and briȝt nyȝtes in þe somertyme, (13) so þat ofte tyme at mydnyȝt men haueþ questiouns and doute where it be euentyde or dawenynge.

Stapleton

(1) It is an Iland very batfull of corne, frute & pasture. (2) In sum places it beareth vines, it hath plentif of fowles of diverse sortes, both by sea and by land, (3) of sprynges also and rivers full of fysh but specially of lampriles and eles. (4) Ther be many times also taken porposes, Dolphyns and whales, (5) beside many kynde of shellfishes, among other of muskles, in whom be founde perles of all coulours as red, purple, crymson, but specially white: (6) ther is also great store of cockles, whereof is made the dye of crymson, whose rudd will be appalled nether with heate of sonne nether with wette of wether, but the oulder it is, the more bright and beutifull glasse it casteth. (7) It hath also sprynges fitt to make salt, and

---

4   baleynes: *whales*

7   ideled: *divided;* acordynge for: *suitable for*

10 hatte: *is called;* me: *men, one;* itend:

kindled; feseþ: *drives;* neigheþ: *approaches*

11 ihight: *see Notes*

12 nolle: *head, top*

others of whott waters, where ar buylded severall places meete for all ages as well for men as women to bathe them selves. (8) For the water (as saynt Basill writeth) runnyng thowrogh certayne metalles, receiveth therof such vertue of heate, that it is not only made warme therby but also skalding whot. (9) This Iland is stored wyth mynes of sundry metalles, as of brasse, lead, iron, & sylver. (10) It bringeth furth also great plenty of the Geate stone, and that of the best. This stone is blacke and burneth being put to the fire, and then is of vertu good to chase away serpentes. If you rub him till he be warme, he holdeth fast such thinges as ar layd unto him even as Aumber doth. (11) This Iland had in it sumtimes xxviii fayre cities, beside an innumerable sort of castles whiche also wer well and strongly fensyd wyth walles, turrettes, gates, and bullwarkes. (12) And for as much as it is placed right in manner under the north pole, it hath light nightes in the sommer, (13) so that at mydnigt many times men dowteth whether it be yet twylight of the evening past, or breach of the day followyng.

Sherley-Price

(1) Britain is rich in grain and timber; it has good pasturage for cattle and draught animals, (2) and vines are cultivated in various localities. There are many land and sea birds of various species, (3) and it is well known for its plentiful springs and rivers abounding in fish. There are salmon and eel fisheries, (4) while seals, dolphins, and sometimes whales are caught. (5) There are also many varieties of shell-fish, such as mussels, in which are often found excellent pearls of several colours, red, purple, violet, and green, but mainly white. (6) Cockles are abundant, and a beautiful scarlet dye is extracted from them which remains unfaded by sunshine or rain; indeed, the older the cloth, the more beautiful its colour. (7) The country has both salt and hot springs, and the waters flowing from them provide hot baths, in which the people bathe separately according to age and sex. (8) As Saint Basil says: "Water receives its heat when it flows across certain metals, and becomes hot, and even scalding." (9) The land has rich veins of many metals, including copper, iron, lead, and silver. (10) There is also much black jet of fine quality, which sparkles in firelight: when burned, it drives away snakes, and, like amber, when it is warmed by friction, it clings to whatever is applied to it. (11) In old times, the country had twenty-eight noble cities, and innumerable castles, all of which were guarded by walls, towers, and barred gates.

(12) Since Britain lies far north toward the pole, the nights are long in summer, (13) and at midnight it is hard to tell whether the evening twilight still lingers or whether dawn is approaching.

NOTES

1   Trevisa *beest* is translating a text with *optima* 'best' instead of *opima* 'rich,' and has therefore taken *frugibus* . . . 'fruits' with *alendis apta* . . . 'fit for growing.'

2   Trevisa is following a text with *atque bestiarum* 'and beasts' after *avium* 'birds,' but has still produced a complicated version. The original Latin literally means 'but (the island) is also rich in birds (and beasts) of various kinds both by land and by sea.' OE *and sǣwihta* 'and sea-creatures' is incorrect.

3   The OE abbreviates, omitting *praeclara* 'renowned,' *copiosis* 'copious,' and *et quidem . . . anguilla* 'and . . . eels'; Trevisa seems to have taken *copiosis* with (*insula*) *praeclara*. Stapleton's *lampriles* 'lampreys' was probably a guess for *issici*(*um*) 'salmon.'

4   The order of the sea animals in Bede is: seals (literally sea-calves), dolphins, whales; in the OE it is seals, whales, and dolphins (literally sea-pigs); in Trevisa it is dolphins, seals (*see calues*), and whales. Stapleton's *porposes* for *vituli marini* 'sea-calves' is an understandable error. Note Trevisa's Latin borrowing *baleynes* which he has had to gloss.

5   Bede *exceptis* 'set aside,' i.e., to say nothing of: see XXX, 11 *n.* OE *meregrotan* 'sea-pebbles' is an interesting piece of interpretative etymology for *margarita* 'pearl,' as though *mar-* = *mere* and *-garita* = *grot* 'particle.'
Higden's Latin reads *in quibus sunt et musculae inclusam continentes saepe margaritam omnis quidem coloris* 'in which there are also mussels containing frequently pearl of every color'; this is of course the text followed by Trevisa.
The OE omits the list of colors; Trevisa has *rody and rede* for *rubicundi*, but omits *et prasini* 'and green,' as does Stapleton.

6   Trevisa 'with which men dye red cloth' — the position of *wiþ* is typical in ME word order.

7   Stapleton *fitt to make salt* is an interpretation.

8   This line is omitted by the OE, and abbreviated by Trevisa (after Higden).

9   Trevisa *of tyn*, following Higden's addition *stanni*.

10 Bede (see the modern version) lists three qualities of jet; the OE and Trevisa take the first two together. Higden's text omits *adtritu* 'by rubbing' which explains why Trevisa has no reference to friction. The OE word *gagātes* has been taken directly from the Latin, together with its ending.

11 OE 'thirty minus one' must have had a text with *xxviiii*. The OE takes the description of the fortifications to refer to the cities, but in

Bede it is the 'innumerable forts' which are described. Trevisa's *ihight* would normally mean 'named.' Its sense may have been extended to include 'renowned' (*insignita*), but it may be an error for *idight* 'prepared.'

12   The OE sentence runs on after *deagung*, and provides a main verb; in this extract the whole of (12) is subordinate after *forðan ðe* 'because.'

XVII

THE HISTORY OF THE ENGLISH CHURCH

The Arrival of the Picts

Bede

(1) In primis autem haec insula Brettones solum, a quibus nomen accepit, incolas habuit, (2) qui de tractu Armoricano, ut fertur, Brittaniam advecti, australes sibi partes illius vindicarunt. (3) Et cum plurimam insulae partem, incipientes ab Austro, possedissent, (4) contigit gentem Pictorum de Scythia, ut perhibent, longis navibus non multis Oceanum ingressam, circumagente flatu ventorum, extra fines omnes Brittaniae Hiberniam pervenisse, eiusque septentrionales oras intrasse, (5) atque inventa ibi gente Scottorum, sibi quoque in partibus illius sedes petisse, nec inpetrare potuisse . . . (6) Respondebant Scotti, quia non ambos eos caperet insula, (7) 'sed possumus', inquiunt, 'salubre vobis dare consilium, quid agere valeatis. (8) Novimus insulam aliam esse non procul a nostra contra ortum solis, quam saepe lucidioribus diebus de longe aspicere solemus. (9) Hanc adire si vultis, habitabilem vobis facere valetis, vel, siqui restiterit, nobis auxiliariis utimini.' (10) Itaque petentes Brittaniam Picti, habitare per septentrionales insulae partes coeperunt, nam austrina Brettones occupaverant. (11) Cumque uxores Picti non habentes peterent a Scottis, ea solum condicione dare consenserunt, (12) ut ubi res veniret in dubium, magis de feminea regum prosapia quam de masculina regem sibi eligerent, quod usque hodie apud Pictos constat esse servatum.

Old English (? Alfred)

(1) On fruman ǣrest wǣron þysses ēalondes bīgengan Bryttas āne, fram þām hit naman onfēng. (2) Is þæt sǣd, ðæt hī cōmon fram Armoricano þǣre mǣgeþe on Breotone, and þā sūðdǣlas þyses ēalondes him gesǣton and geāhnodon.

---

1 fruma(n): *beginning;* ǣrest: *first;* bīgenga(n): *inhabitants;* onfēng (onfōn): *pt. 3 sg., received*

2 sǣd: *pt. pp., said;* mǣgeþ(e): *tribe;* gesǣton (gesittan): *settled;* geāhnodon [own]: *possessed*

143

(3–4) Þā gelamp æfter þon þætte Peahte ðēod cōm of Scyððia lande on scipum and þā ymbærndon eall Breotone gemæro, þæt hī cōmon on Scotland upp, (5) and þǣr gemētton Sceotta þēode, and him bǣdon setles and eardungstōwe on heora lande betwȳh him. (6) Andswearedon Scottas, þæt heora land ne wǣre tō þæs mycel, þæt hī mihton twā þēode gehabban. (7) Ac cwǣdon: "Wē magon ēow sellan hālwende geþeahte, hwæt gē dōn magon. (8) Wē witan heonan nōht fēor ōðer ēalond ēastrihte, þæt wē magon oft lēohtum dagum gesēon. (9) Gif gē þæt sēcan wyllaþ, þonne magon gē þǣr eardungstōwe habban: oððe gif hwylc ēow wiðstondeð, þonne gefultumiað wē ēow." (10) Ðā fērdon Peohtas in Breotone, and ongunnon eardigan þā norðdǣlas þyses ēalondes; and Bryttas, swā wē ǣr cwǣdon, ðā sūðdǣlas. (11) Mid þȳ Peohtas wīf næfdon, bǣdon him fram Scottum. Ðā geþafedon hī ðǣre ārēdnesse, and him wīf sealdon, (12) þæt ðǣr sēo wīse on twēon cyme, þæt hī ðonne mā of þām wīfcynne him cyning curan þonne of þām wǣpnedcynne: þæt gēt tō dæg is mid Peohtum healden.

Trevisa

(1) (Bretouns wonede first in þis ilond . . .) (2) Þei come hider and took hir cours from Armorik, þat now is þe oþer Bretayne; (3) þey helde long tyme þe souþ contrayes of þe ilond. (3–4) Hit byfelle afterwarde in Vespasianus tyme, duke of Rome, þatt þe Pictes out of Scythia schipped into occean, and were i-dryue aboute wiþ þe wynde, and entrede in to þe norþ costes of Irlond, (5) and founde þere Scottes, and prayed for to haue a place to wonye inne, and myȝte none gete. (6) For Irlond, as Scottes seide, myȝt nouȝt susteyne boþe peple. (7–11) Scottes sente þe Pictes to the norþ side of Bretayne, and behiȝte hem help aȝenst þe Bretouns þat were enemyes, yf þey wolde arise, and took hem to wyfes of here douȝtres vppon suche a condicioun: (12) ȝif doute fel who schulde haue ryȝt for to be kyng, he schulde raþer chese hem a kyng of þe moder side þan of þe fader side, of þe wommen kyn raþer þan of þe men kyn.

3–4 gelamp (gelimpan): *happened;* ðēod: *people;* ymbærndon: *went round;* gemǣr(o): *boundaries*
5 bǣdon (biddan): *asked;* eardungstōw-(e): *dwelling place*
6 tō þæs: *to this extent*
7 hālwende: *useful;* geþeaht(e): *advice*
8 heonan: *from here;* ēastrihte: *due east*
9 sēcan: *seek;* hwylc [which]: *anyone;* gefultumiað: *help*

10 fērdon: *went;* ongunnon (onginnan): *began*
11 Mid þȳ: *because;* næfdon: *had not;* geþafedon: *agreed;* ārēdness(e): *stipulation;* sealdon [sold]: *gave*
12 ðǣr: *if;* wīse: *matter;* cyme (cuman): *pr. 3 sg. subj., came;* curan (cēosan): *pt. 3 pl. subj., choose;* wǣpnedcynn(e) [weaponed-kind]: *male line;* tō dæg: *today*

1 wonede: *dwelt*

7–11 behiȝte: *promised*

Stapleton

(1) At the first this land was inhabited of none other nation but only of the Britannes, of whom it receiveth his name: (2) which Britannes comyng out of *Armorica* (called now litle Britanny) as it is thought, chose unto them selves the sowth parte of this land. (3) And after when they from the sowth forward had in their possession a great parte of the Ile, (4) it chaunced that certaine people of the Pictes coming owt of Scythia, as it is sayd, travailing uppon the seas with a few long shippes, the winde dryving them in cumpasse rounde about the coaste of Britannye, blew them a land on Irelands syde, on the north partes therof. (5) Which they finding inhabited of the Scottes, besought them to allow them some part of the land, where they might plante them selves. But they coulde not obtayne their desire . . . (6) The Scottes aunsered that the Iland was not bigg inowgh to hold them both. (7) But we can geve you good counsel (quoth they) what we thynke best for you to doe. (8) We know well there is another Iland not farre from ours standing easte ward from hence, which we may see owt of this land in a fayer sonnye day. (9) If you will goe thether, you may inhabit ther at will. And if there be any resistance made against you, we wil ayde you. (10) Wherupon the Pictes arriving in Britanny planted them selves in the North partes therof. For as for the sowth partes the Britannes had taken upp before. (11) And wheras the Pictes having no wyves did require of the Scottes to marry their dawghters, the Skottes agreed to graunt them their bone, under condition, (12) that as often as the matter was in dowt, they should choose their kyng rather of the next of the howse of the woman then of the man. Which order, it is well knowen the Pictes kepeth even to this day.

Sherley-Price

(1) The original inhabitants of the island were the Britons, from whom it takes its name, (2) and who, according to tradition, crossed into Britain from Armorica, and occupied the southern parts. (3) When they had spread northwards and possessed the greater part of the island, (4) it is said that some Picts from Scythia put to sea in a few longships, and were driven by storms around the coasts of Britain, arriving at length on the north coast of Ireland. (5) Here they found the nation of the Scots, from whom they asked permission to settle, but their request was refused . . . (6) The Scots replied that there was not room for them both, (7) but said, "We can give you good advice. (8) There is another island not far to the east, which we often see in the distance on clear days. (9) Go and settle there if you wish;

should you meet resistance, we will come to your help." (10) So the Picts crossed into Britain, and began to settle in the north of the island, since the Britons were in possession of the south. (11) Having no women with them, these Picts asked wives of the Scots, who consented on condition that, (12) when any dispute arose, they should choose a king from the female royal line rather than the male. This custom continues among the Picts to this day.

NOTES

Higden is not quoting Bede directly in (1), and his version of (7)–(11) is considerably abbreviated; he is, of course, followed by Trevisa.

1   Note Stapleton *his* 'its' — see I, 15 *n.*

2–3   Trevisa has abbreviated this and the following sentence somewhat, so that it is not clear where (2)–(4) should be divided. 3 *þey helde long tyme* translates Higden *diu tenerunt* (for which Bede has *sibi . . . vindicarunt* 'claimed for themselves'). The OE also has abbreviated (3).

4   The OE omits *longis* 'long,' *non multis* 'not many,' the driving of the wind, and the North shores as the site of the landing. Trevisa omits all reference to the ships; his reference to Vespasian is derived from Higden.

OE *Scotland* (Bede *Hibernia*): the normal OE name for Ireland, which was inhabited by the tribe known as the Scots (so Bede).

5   The OE appears to omit *nec inpetrare potuisse* 'could not bring it about,' but may have been translating the end of the sentence in Bede which both the OE and this text omit. The sentence described Ireland.

7–11   As noted above, these lines are abbreviated by Higden, and thus by Trevisa — lines (9) and (11) appear in part.

12   The remark that the custom is observed *usque hodie* 'till today' is omitted by Higden and Trevisa.

XVIII-XXI

᪥᪥᪥᪥᪥᪥᪥᪥᪥᪥᪥

VERGIL
THE AENEID

English translations of Books II and IV of *The Aeneid* have been selected from several sources. Gavin Douglas's translations into Scots riming couplets, completed in 1513, are taken from D. F. C. Coldwell, *Selections from Gavin Douglas* (Oxford: Clarendon Press, 1964). Coldwell shows that Douglas sometimes made use of the commentary on *The Aeneid* by the Dutchman Ascensius (ca. 1500). Henry Howard, Earl of Surrey, translated Books II and IV only in 1554 and 1557; the text here is from Emrys Jones, *Surrey: Poems* (Oxford: Clarendon Press, 1964). Surrey knew and made full use of Douglas's version; Jones gives an illuminating comparison of the methods of the two translators. The version by Dryden (1697) is edited by J. Kinsley, *Poems of John Dryden* (Oxford: Clarendon Press, 1958); Dryden's translation is the furthest from the original. The modern version is by C. Day Lewis, *The Aeneid of Vergil* (London, 1952; re-issued by Four Square Classics, London, 1962). This modern version is very close to the original, and makes the lines of the translation correspond to those of the original as far as possible.

XVIII

THE AENEID II, 199-233

&&&&&&&&&&&&&&&&&&&&&&&&&

The Death of Laocoön

Vergil

Hic aliud maius miseris multoque tremendum
obicitur, magis atque improvida pectora turbat.
Laocoon, ductus Neptuno sorte sacerdos,
sollemnis taurum ingentem mactabat ad aras.
5 Ecce autem gemini a Tenedo tranquilla per alta
(horresco referens) immensis orbibus angues
incumbunt pelago pariterque ad litora tendunt;
pectora quorum inter fluctus arrecta iubaeque
sanguineae superant undas; pars cetera pontum
10 pone legit sinuatque immensa volumine terga.
Fit sonitus spumante salo; iamque arva tenebant
ardentisque oculos suffecti sanguine et igni
sibila lambebant linguis vibrantibus ora.
Diffugimus visu exsangues. Illi agmine certo
15 Laocoonta petunt; et primum parva duorum
corpora natorum serpens amplexus uterque
implicat et miseros morsu depascitur artus;
post ipsum auxilio subeuntem ac tela ferentem
corripiunt spirisque ligant ingentibus; et iam
20 bis medium amplexi, bis collo squamea circum
terga dati superant capite et cervicibus altis.
Ille simul manibus tendit divellere nodos
perfusus sanie vittas atroque veneno,
clamores simul horrendos ad sidera tollit:
25 qualis mugitus, fugit cum saucius aram
taurus et incertam excussit cervice securim.
At gemini lapsu delubra ad summa dracones
effugiunt saevaeque petunt Tritonidis arcem,
sub pedibusque deae clipeique sub orbe teguntur.

148

30   Tum vero tremefacta novus per pectora cunctis
insinuat pavor, et scelus expendisse merentem
Laocoonta ferunt, sacrum qui cuspide robur
laeserit et tergo sceleratam intorserit hastam.
ducendum ad sedes simulacrum orandaque divae
35   numina conclamant.

Gavin Douglas

(1)   Betyd, the ilke tyde, a fer grettar woundir
And mair dreidful to catyvis be sik hunder,

(2)   Quhilk of Trojanys trublit mony onwarnyt breste.

(3)   As Laocon, that was Neptunus prest
And chosyn by kavill onto that ilk office,
A fair gret bull offerit in sacrifyce
Solemnytly befor the haly alteir,

(5)   Throw the styl sey from Tenedos infeir,
Lo, twa gret lowpit edderis, with mony thraw,
Fast throu the flude towart the land gan draw.
My spreit abhorris this mater to declare:

(8)   Abufe the watir thar hals stude evermare,
With bludy crestis owtwith the wallis hie;
The remanent swam always under see,
With grysly bodeis lynkit mony fald;

(11)   The salt fame stowris from the fard thai hald.
Onto the grund thai glaid with glowand eyn
Stuffit ful of vennom, fyre and fellon teyn,
Wyth tongis quhislyng in thar mowthis rede
Thai lyk the twynkland stangis in thar hed.

(14)   We fled away al bludeles for affeir,
Bot, wyth a braid, to Laocon infeir
Thai stert atanys, and hys twa sonnys ying
First athir serpent lappit lyke a ryng,
And, with thar cruell byt and stangis fell,
Of tendir membris tuke mony sary morcell.

(18)   Syne thai the prest invadit, baith twane,
Quhilk with hys wapynnys dyd hys byssy pane
His childryng forto helpyn and reskew.

---

1 Betyd: *happened*

3 kavill: *lot*

5 infeir: *together;* thraw: *twist*

8 hals: *necks;* wallis: *see Notes*

11 *See Notes.* glaid: *glided;* fellon:*fierce;*
teyn: *anger;* stangis: *stings*

14 braid: *swift movement*

18 Syne: *afterwards*

(20)   Bot thai about hym lowpit in wympillis threw
 And twys cyrkyllit his myddil rownd about
 And twys faldis thar sprutlit skynnys but dowt
 About hys hals — bath nek and hede thai schent.

(22)   As he etlys thar hankis to have rent
 Of with his handis, and thame away have draw,
 Hys hed bendis and garlandis all war blaw
 Ful of vennom and rank poyson atanys,
 Quhilk infekkis the flesch, blude and banys.

(24)   And tharwith eik sa horribilly schowtis he,
 His cryis dynnyt to the sternys on hie;

(25)   Lyke as a bull doith rummysing and rayr
 Quhen he eschapis hurt from the altair,
 And charris by the ax with his nek wight,
 Gif on his forhed the dynt hyttis nocht rycht.

(27)   Syne thir twa serpentis hastely glaid away,
 Onto the cheif tempil fled ar thai
 Of stern Pallas to the hallowit place

(29)   And crap in under the feit of the goddes,
 Hyd thame behynd the boys of hir bukleir.

(30)   Than trymlit thar mony stowt hart for feir,
 The onkowth dreid into thar brestis crap.

(31)   All said, "Laocon justly, sik was his hap,
 Has deir ybocht his wikkit and schrewit deid,
 For he the haly hors or stalwart steid
 With violente strake presumyt forto deir
 And tharintil to fessyn his cursit speir.

(34)   Onto the hallowit sted bryng in," thai cry,
 "The gret fygur! And lat us sacryfy
 The haly goddes, and magnyfy hyr mycht
 With orysonys and offerandis day and nycht!"

Surrey

(1)   Us caitifes then a far more dredful chaunce
(2)   Befell, that trobled our unarmed brestes.

---

20 wympillis: *folds;* threw: *twisted;*
 sprutlit: *speckled*
22 etlys: *attempts*
24 sternys: *stars*
25 *See Notes.*

29 boys: *boss*
30 onkowth: *strange*
31 schrewit: *cursed;* deir: *harm*
34 orysonys: *prayers*

(3)   Whiles Laocon, that chosen was by lot
       Neptunus priest, did sacrifice a bull
       Before the holy altar, sodenly

(5)   From Tenedon, behold, in circles great
       By the calme seas come fletyng adders twaine
       Which plied towardes the shore (I lothe to tell)

(8)   With rered brest lift up above the seas,
       Whoes bloody crestes aloft the waves were seen.
       The hinder parte swamme hidden in the flood;
       Their grisly backes were linked manifold.

(11)   With sound of broken waves they gate the strand,
       With gloing eyen, tainted with blood and fire;
       Whoes waltring tongs did lick their hissing
         mouthes.

(14)   We fled away, our face the blood forsoke.
       But they with gate direct to Lacon ran.
       And first of all eche serpent doth enwrap
       The bodies small of his two tender sonnes,
       Whoes wretched limmes they byt, and fed theron.

(18)   Then raught they hym, who had his wepon caught
       To rescue them; twise winding him about,
       With folded knottes and circled tailes, his wast.
       Their scaled backes did compasse twise his neck,
       Wyth rered heddes aloft and stretched throtes.

(22)   He with his handes strave to unloose the knottes;
       Whose sacred fillettes all besprinkled were
       With filth of gory blod and venim rank.

(24)   And to the sterres such dredfull shoutes he sent,

(25)   Like to the sound the roring bull fourth loowes
       Which from the altar wounded doth astart,
       The swarving axe when he shakes from his neck.

(27)   The serpentes twain with hasted trail they glide
       To Pallas temple and her towres of heighte;

(29)   Under the feete of which the goddesse stern,
       Hidden behinde her targettes bosse, they crept.

(30)   New gripes of dred then pearse our trembling
         brestes.

(31)   They sayd Lacons desertes had derely bought
       His hainous dede, that pearced had with stele
       The sacred bulk, and throwen the wicked launce.

(34)   The people cried with sondry greeing shoutes
       To bring the horse to Pallas temple blive,
       In hope thereby the goddesse wrath t'appease.

Dryden

(1) A greater Omen, and of worse portent,
(2) Did our unwary Minds with fear torment:
Concurring to produce the dire Event.
(3) *Laocoon*, *Neptune*'s Priest by Lot that Year,
With solemn pomp then sacrific'd a Steer.
(5) When, dreadful to behold, from Sea we spy'd
Two Serpents rank'd abreast, the Seas divide,
And smoothly sweep along the swelling Tide.
(8) Their flaming Crests above the Waves they show,
Their Bellies seem to burn the Seas below:
Their speckled Tails advance to steer their Course,
(11) And on the sounding Shoar the flying Billows
force.
And now the Strand, and now the Plain they held,
Their ardent Eyes with bloody streaks were fill'd:
Their nimble Tongues they brandish'd as they
came,
And lick'd their hissing Jaws, that sputter'd
Flame.
(14) We fled amaz'd; their destin'd Way they take,
And to *Laocoon* and his Children make:
And first around the tender Boys they wind,
Then with their sharpen'd Fangs their Limbs and
Bodies grind.
(18) The wretched Father, running to their Aid
With pious Haste, but vain, they next invade:
(20) Twice round his waste their winding Volumes
rowl'd,
And twice about his gasping Throat they fold.
The Priest, thus doubly choak'd, their Crests
divide,
And tow'ring o're his Head, in Triumph ride.
(22) With both his Hands he labours at the Knots,
His Holy Fillets the blue Venom blots:
(24) His roaring fills the flitting Air around.
(25) Thus, when an Oxe receives a glancing Wound,
He breaks his Bands, the fatal Altar flies,
And with loud Bellowings breaks the yielding
Skies.
(27) Their Tasks perform'd, the Serpents quit their
prey,

And to the Tow'r of *Pallas* make their way:
(29) Couch'd at her Feet, they lie protected there,
By her large Buckler, and protended Spear.
(30) Amazement seizes all; the gen'ral Cry
Proclaims *Laocoon* justly doom'd to die,
Whose hand the Will of *Pallas* had withstood,
And dar'd to violate the Sacred Wood.
(34) All vote t'admit the Steed, that Vows be paid,
And Incense offer'd to th'offended Maid.

C. Day Lewis

Just then another event, the most alarming yet,
Befell us wretches, muddling still further our hooded
    minds.
Laocoon, whom we'd elected by lot as Neptune's priest,
Was sacrificing a great bull at the official altar,
(5) When over the tranquil deep, from Tenedos, we saw —
Telling it makes me shudder — twin snakes with immense
    coils
Thrusting the sea and together streaking towards the shore:
Rampant they were among the waves, their blood-red
    crests
Reared up over the water; the rest of them slithered along
(10) The surface, coil after coil sinuously trailing behind them.
We heard a hiss of salt spray. Next, they were on dry land,
In the same field — a glare and blaze of bloodshot eyes,
Tongues flickering like flame from their mouths, and the
    mouths hissing.
Our blood drained away at the sight; we broke and ran. The
    serpents
(15) Went straight for Laocoon. First, each snake knotted itself
Round the body of one of Laocoon's small sons, hugging
    him tight
In its coils, and cropped the piteous flesh with its fangs.
    Next thing,
They fastened upon Laocoon, as he hurried, weapon in
    hand,
To help the boys, and lashed him up in their giant whorls.
(20) With a double grip round his waist and his neck, the scaly
    creatures

Embrace him, their heads and throats powerfully poised
above him.
All the while his hands are struggling to break their knots,
His priestly headband is spattered with blood and pitchy
venom;
All the while, his appalling cries go up to heaven —
(25)   A bellowing, such as you hear when a wounded bull escapes
from
The altar, after it's shrugged off an ill-aimed blow at its
neck.
But now the twin monsters are gliding away and escaping
towards
The shrine of relentless Minerva, high up on our citadel,
Disappearing behind the round of the goddess' shield, at
her feet there.
(30)   Then, my god! a strange panic crept into our people's
fluttering
Hearts: they argued Laocoon had got what he deserved
For the crime, the sacrilege of throwing his spear at the
wooden
Horse and so profaning its holiness with the stroke.
'Bring the horse to Minerva's shrine! Pray for her
goodwill!'

NOTES

1   Douglas *be sik hunder* 'a hundred times,' is a common expression in
Middle Scots.
5   Douglas *edderis:* the MnE form here is derived from OE *næddre* (I, 1)
by incorrect division of *a nadder;* the converse is seen in words like
nickname < *an eke-name* 'an additional name.'
8   Douglas *wallis* (Vergil *fluctus*): the word may be associated with the
verb *well* (OE *wiellan*) 'surge, boil,' and perhaps also influenced by ME
wawe 'wave.' Surrey's *Their grisly backes were linked manifold* is
derived almost exactly from Douglas.
10   Vergil *pone legit* 'skims (the sea) behind' — both Douglas and Surrey
incorrectly translate *pone* 'underneath.'
11   Douglas: 'the salt-foam rises in a cloud from the journey (*fard*) they
make (*hald*)' — note the omission of the object relative pronoun.
Note Dryden's rhyme *held: fill'd.*
13   Douglas has expanded the line considerably.

18 Dryden omits the reference to Laocoon's weapons.

20 Douglas *bath nek and hede thai schent* 'they wounded both head and neck' is a mistranslation of *superant* which here = not 'conquer' but 'tower above.' Dryden's version is not close to the original.

23 Douglas *Quhilk infekkis . . . etc.* is not in Vergil.

25 Douglas *charris by the ax* 'turns the axe aside' — *by* is adverbial. Douglas *rummysing* 'roaring' may be either present participle — a poor parallel to *rayr* 'roar' infinitive — or verbal noun, in which case *rayr* must also be a noun; neither is very satisfactory. Douglas has rendered *incertam* 'uncertain' (compare Surrey *swarving*) by a whole sentence.

27 Vergil *lapsu* 'gliding, slithering.'

29 Dryden's *protended Spear* is not in Vergil.

30 Douglas dramatically uses direct speech twice, where Vergil has indirect speech. His expansion of 34–35 is probably derived, as Cold-well shows, from Ascensius.

XIX

THE AENEID IV, 1-30

Dido's Growing Love

Vergil

At regina gravi iamdudum saucia cura
vulnus alit venis et caeco carpitur igni.
Multa viri virtus animo multusque recursat
gentis honos: haerent infixi pectore vultus
5   verbaque, nec placidam membris dat cura quietem.
Postera Phoebea lustrabat lampade terras
umentemque Aurora polo dimoverat umbram,
cum sic unanimam adloquitur male sana sororem:
'Anna soror, quae me suspensam insomnia terrent!
10 Quis novus hic nostris successit sedibus hospes,
quem sese ore ferens, quam forti pectore et armis!
credo equidem, nec vana fides, genus esse deorum.
Degeneres animos timor arguit. Heu, quibus ille
iactatus fatis! Quae bella exhausta canebat!
15 Si mihi non animo fixum immotumque sederet
ne cui me vinclo vellem sociare iugali,
postquam primus amor deceptam morte fefellit;
si non pertaesum thalami taedaeque fuisset,
huic uni forsan potui succumbere culpae.
20 Anna, fatebor enim, miseri post fata Sychaei
coniugis et sparsos fraterna caede penatis
solus hic inflexit sensus animumque labantem
impulit. Agnosco veteris vestigia flammae.
Sed mihi vel tellus optem prius ima dehiscat
25 vel pater omnipotens abigat me fulmine ad umbras,
pallentis umbras Erebo noctemque profundam,
ante, pudor, quam te violo aut tua iura resolvo.
Ille meos, primus qui me sibi iunxit, amores
abstulit; ille habeat secum servetque sepulcro.'
30 Sic effata sinum lacrimis implevit obortis.

Gavin Douglas

(1)   Be this the queyn, throw hevy thochtis onsound,
In every vayn nurysys the greyn wound,
Smytyn so deip with the blynd fyre of lufe
Hir trublyt mynd gan fra all rest remufe.

(3)   Compasing the gret prowes of Ene,
The large wirschip feill sys remembris sche
Of his lynnage and folkis; for ay present
Deip in hir breist so was hys figur prent
And all hys wordis fixt, that, for bissy thocht,
Noyn eys hir membris nor quyet suffir mocht.

(6)   The nyxt day following, with hys lamp brycht
As Phebus dyd the grund or erth alycht,
Eftir the dawing heth the donk nychtis clowd
Chasyt from the sky and the ayr new schrowd,

(8)   Ful evil at eys Queyn Dido on this kynd
Spak to hir systir, wes of the sammyn mynd:

(9)   "My sistir An, quhat swevynnys beyn thir,"
    quod sche,
"Quhilk me affrays in sik proplexite?

(10) Quhat be he, this gret new gest or stranger,
Onto our realm laitly is drevyn heir?

(11) Quhou wys in speche and in his commonyng
He schawys hym self! O God, quhat wondir thing!
Quhou stout in curage, in weir quhou vailyeand!

(12) I trow, sistir, and, as I undirstand,
Myne opinion is nane oncertane thing,
Thai beyn sum lynnage of verray goddis of-
    spring,

(13) For dreid always and schaymful kowardys
Degeneryt wightis and bowbartis notyfys.
Allace, quhat wondir fatale aventuris
Hes hym bywaif! quhat travel, pane and curis,
How huge batellis, be hym eschevit, tald he!

(15) Now certis, war it not determyt with me
And fixit in my mynd onmovabilly

---

3 feill sys: *see Notes*
6 schrowd: *dressed*
9 swevynnys: *dreams;* thir: *these;* affrays: *terrify*
11 commonyng: *talking;* weir: *war*

12 verray: *true*
13 wightis: *creatures;* bowbartis: *peasants;* bywaif: *blown;* travel: *sorrow;* curis: *anxieties*

That to no wyght in wedlok me list I
Cuppil nor knyt, sen my first luf is gane,
By deth dissoverit, and left me alane;
(18)   War not alsso to me is displesant
Genyus chalmyr or matrymone to hant;
(19)   Perchans I mycht be venquist in this rage,
Throu this a cryme of secund mariage.
(20)   Annes, I grant to the, sen the deces
Of my sory husband Syche, but les,
Quhar that our hows with brodyrris ded wes
    sprent,
Only this man hes movit myne entent,
And heth my mynd inducyt to forvay:
(23)   I knaw and felis the wemmys and the way
Of the ald fyre and flambe of luffis heit.
(24)   Bot rather I desyre baith cors and spreit
Of me the erth swelly law adown,
Or than almychty Jove with thundris soun
Me smyte ful deip onto the schaddoys dern,
Amang pail gastis of hellis holl cavern,
In the profond pot of deth and dyrk nycht,
Or I becum so schamful wrachit wyght
That I myne honeste fyle or womanhed,
Or brek your lawis — na, quhil I be ded!
(28)   He that me first to hym in wedlok knyt
My first flowr of amouris tuke, and yit
For evermair with hym he sal thame have,
And he most keip thame with hym in his grave."
(30)   Thus sayand, the brycht teris onon owtbrist
And fillyt all hir bosum or scho wist.

Surrey

(1)   But now the wounded quene with hevy care,
Throughout the veines she norisheth the playe,
Surprised with blind flame; (3) and to hir mind
Gan eke resort the prowesse of the man
And honour of his race; while in her brest

---

15 dissoverit: *see Notes*
20 but les: *in truth;* sprent: *sprinkled;*
forvay: *wander*

23 wemmys: *see Notes*
24 dern: *secret;* holl: *hollow;* Or I: *before
I;* fyle: *defile;* quhil: *until*

Imprinted stack his wordes and pictures forme;
Ne to her limmes care graunteth quiet rest.

(6) The next morow with Phebus laump the earth
Alightned clere, and eke the dawning day
The shadowes dank gan from the poale remove,

(8) When all unsound her sister of like minde
Thus spake she to: (9) "O sister Ann, what dreames
Be these, that me tormented thus afray?

(10) What new guest is this that to our realm is come?

(11) What one of chere! how stout of hart in armes!

(12) Truly I think (ne vain is my belefe)
Of goddish race some offspring shold he be:

(13) Cowardry notes hartes swarved out of kind.
He driven, Lord, with how hard destiny!
What battailes eke atchived did he recount!

(15) But that my mind is fixt unmoveably
Never with wight in wedlock ay to joyne
Sith my first love me left by death dissevered,

(18) If geniall brands and bed me lothed not,

(19) To this one gilt perchaunce yet might I yeld.

(20) Anne, for I graunt, sith wretched Sichees death
My spouse, and house with brothers slaughter staind,
This onely man hath made my sences bend
And pricked foorth the mind that gan to slide.

(23) Now feelingly I tast the steppes of mine old flame.

(24) But first I wish the earth me swalow down,
Or with thunder the mighty Lord me send
To the pale gostes of hel and darknes deepe,
Ere I thee staine, shamefastnes, or thy lawes.

(28) He that with me first coppled, tooke away
My love with him; enjoy it in his grave."

(30) Thus did she say, and with supprised teares
Bained her brest.

Dryden

(1) But anxious Cares already seiz'd the Queen:
She fed within her Veins a Flame unseen:

(3) The Heroe's Valour, Acts, and Birth inspire
Her Soul with Love, and fann the secret Fire.
His Words, his Looks imprinted in her Heart,

Improve the Passion, and increase the Smart.
(6)   Now, when the Purple Morn had chas'd away
The dewy Shadows, and restor'd the Day;
(8)   Her Sister first, with early Care she sought,
And thus in mournful Accents eas'd her Thought.
(9)   My dearest *Anna*, what new Dreams affright
My lab'ring Soul; what Visions of the Night
Disturb my Quiet, and distract my Breast,
(10)   With strange Ideas of our *Trojan* Guest?
His Worth, his Actions, and Majestick Air,
A Man descended from the Gods declare:
(13)   Fear ever argues a degenerate kind,
His Birth is well asserted by his Mind.
Then, what he suffer'd, when by Fate betray'd,
What brave Attempts for falling *Troy* he made!
Such were his Looks, so gracefully he spoke,
(15)   That were I not resolv'd against the Yoke
Of hapless Marriage; never to be curs'd
With second Love, so fatal was my first;
(19)   To this one Error I might yield again:
(20)   For since *Sichæus* was untimely slain,
This onely Man, is able to subvert
The fix'd Foundations of my stubborn Heart.
(23)   And to confess my Frailty, to my shame,
Somewhat I find within, if not the same,
Too like the Sparkles of my former Flame.
(24)   But first let yawning Earth a Passage rend;
And let me through the dark Abyss descend;
First let avenging *Jove*, with Flames from high,
Drive down this Body, to the neather Sky,
Condemn'd with Ghosts in endless Night to lye;
Before I break the plighted Faith I gave;
(28)   No; he who had my Vows, shall ever have;
For whom I lov'd on Earth, I worship in the Grave.
(30)   She said; the Tears ran gushing from her Eyes,
And stop'd her Speech.

C. Day Lewis

But now for some while the queen had been growing more
   grievously love-sick,
Feeding the wound with her life-blood, the fire biting
   within her.

Much did she muse on the hero's nobility, and much
On his family's fame. His look, his words had gone to her
heart

(5)   And lodged there: she could get no peace from love's
disquiet.
The morrow's morn had chased from heaven the dewy
darkness,
Was carrying the sun's torch far and wide over earth,
When, almost beside herself, she spoke to her sister, her
confidante: —
'Anna, sister, why do these nerve-racking dreams haunt
me?

(10) This man, this stranger I've welcomed in my house —
what of him?
How gallantly he looks, how powerful in chest and
shoulders!
I really do think, and have reason to think, that he is
heaven-born.
Mean souls convict themselves by cowardice. Oh, imagine
The fates that have harried him, the fight to a finish he
told of!

(15) Were it not that my purpose is fixed irrevocably
Never to tie myself in wedlock again to anyone,
Since that first love of mine proved false and let death
cheat me;
Had I not taken a loathing for the idea of marriage,
For him, for this one man, I could perhaps have weakened.

(20) Anna, I will confess it, since poor Sychaeus, my husband,
Was killed and our home broken up by my brother's
murderous act,
This man is the only one who has stirred my senses and
sapped
My will. I feel once more the scars of the old flame.
But no, I would rather the earth should open and swallow
me

(25) Or the Father of heaven strike me with lightning down to
the shades —
The pale shades and deep night of the Underworld —
before
I violate or deny pure widowhood's claim upon me.
He who first wedded me took with him, when he died,
My right to love: let him keep it, there in the tomb, for
ever.'

(30) So Dido spoke, and the rising tears flooded her bosom.

NOTES

1 Douglas *greyn* 'green,' i.e., fresh. Surrey *playe* 'wound' (French *plaie*, Latin *plaga*), now obsolete.

3 Douglas *feill sys* 'many times,' ME *fele sithes*, OE *fela sīðas* (or *-es*).

4 Surrey *pictures forme* 'the form of his appearance,' Vergil *vultus* 'face.'

6 In Vergil *Postera Aurora* 'the next dawn' is subject of *lustrabat* 'visited'; it is not clear that Douglas and Surrey have understood this.

7 Douglas *and the ayr new schrowd* 'and newly clothed the air' is an addition.

11 Vergil *sese ore ferens* 'bearing himself, with his look' is fully expanded by Douglas. Lewis has omitted *armis* 'arms.'

15 This passage has been much abbreviated by Dryden.

17 Vergil (*me*) *deceptam morte fefellit* 'tricked me, having been deceived, by death.' Surrey has followed Douglas (*By deth dissoverit* 'separated by death') in what appears to be an error; see Jones's note.

18 Douglas: 'were it not (that) the marriage-bed is unpleasing to me.' Coldwell suggests that *Genyus chalmyr* (Vergil *thalami* 'marriage-chamber') is a misunderstanding of Ascensius's gloss *'thori genialis' * 'nuptial couch,' but the association of the deity Genius with Love is a common medieval one — compare Gower's *Confessio Amantis*.

19 Vergil *huic uni . . . culpae* 'to this one sin (fault)' is obscured by Lewis's 'for this one man.' Douglas *secund mariage* derives from Ascensius (Coldwell).

20 Dryden omits the reference to the brother's murderous acts.

23 Vergil 'the traces of the old flame' — *vestigia* has lost its original sense 'footprints, tracks'; Surrey's *steppes* is therefore unnecessarily literal; Douglas tries to have it both ways by *wemmys and the way* 'scars and the path,' somewhat clumsily.

27 Dryden *the plighted Faith* obscures the point that Dido is addressing Pudor, a sense of shame (compare Lewis's *widowhood's claim*).

29 Surrey *enjoy* is jussive subjunctive, 'let him enjoy.' Dryden's rendering is an interpretation rather than a translation.

XX

THE AENEID IV, 173-194

The Monster Fame

Vergil

Extemplo Libyae magnas it Fama per urbes,
Fama, malum qua non aliud velocius ullum:
mobilitate viget virisque adquirit eundo,
parva metu primo, mox sese attollit in auras
5 ingrediturque solo et caput inter nubila condit.
Illam Terra parens ira inritata deorum
extremam, ut perhibent, Coeo Enceladoque
  sororem
progenuit pedibus celerem et pernicibus alis,
monstrum horrendum, ingens, cui quot sunt
  corpore plumae,
10 tot vigiles oculi subter (mirabile dictu),
tot linguae, totidem ora sonant, tot subrigit auris.
Nocte volat caeli medio terraeque per umbram
stridens, nec dulci declinat lumina somno;
luce sedet custos aut summi culmine tecti
15 turribus aut altis, et magnas territat urbes,
tam ficti pravique tenax quam nuntia veri.
Haec tum multiplici populos sermone replebat
gaudens, et pariter facta atque infecta canebat;
venisse Aenean Troiano sanguine cretum,
20 cui se pulchra viro dignetur iungere Dido;
nunc hiemem inter se luxu, quam longa, fovere
regnorum immemores turpique cupidine captos.

Gavin Douglas

(1) The fame heirof, belyve, gan walx and spreid
Throu cheif citeis of all Affrik on breid:

(2) Fame is myscheif, quham na harm undyr the lyft
In motioun nor sterage is mair swyft.

(3) Movand scho growis, and, passand our alquhar,
Hir strenth encressis and walxis mair and mayr.

(4) Lytil, for feir, the fyrst tyme semys sche,
Sone eftir rysys to the starnys on hie;
Apon the grond scho walkis fra sted to sted,
And up amang the clowdis hydis hyr hed.

(6) Throu greif of goddis commovyt, and nocht glaid,
Erth, the gret moder, bayr this child, as is said,

(7) Last systir to Ceyos and Enchelades,

(9) Ane huge, horribill and strange monstre, but les,

(8) Spedy of fut, and on weyngis swyft as wynd.

(9) Quhou mony fedderis bene on hir body fynd,
Als mony walkryfe eyn lurkis thar undir,
Als feil tongis, that for totell is wondir,
With als feil mouthis carpis sche and beris,
Als mony hes scho prik upstandand eris.

(12) By nycht scho fleys amyd the hevyn throu owt,
Circuland the schaddow of the erth about
With huge fard, nother cuyr gevand nor keip
Hir eyn anys to rest nor tak a sleip;

(14) Al day scho syttis, wachand byssely,
Apon the top of nobillis howsis, to spy,
Or on thir princis palyce with towris hie,
And with hir noys gret citeis affrays sche —

(16) Als weil ramembring fenyeit and schrewit sawys
As scho the treuth and verite furth schawis.

(17) Thys ilke wensch, that tyme, with mony a taill,
Glaidly this rumour gan throu the pepill skaill,
Telland the thing wrocht, and not wrocht, togiddir;

(19) Quhou of the Trojane blude wes cummyn thiddir

---

1 belyve: *quickly;* walx: *increase;* breid: *breadth*
2 lyft: *sky;* sterage: *movement*
3 our alquhar: *over everywhere*
4 starnys: *stars;* sted: *place*
6 commovyt: *moved*

9 but les: *in truth;* walkryfe: *sleepless;* feil: *many;* carpis: *speaks*
12 fard: *journey;* cuyr: *care;* keip: *care*
14 affrays: *terrifies*
16 schrewit: *cursed;* sawys: *sayings*
17 skaill: *spread*

Ene, with quham the fair Dido be wed
Dedenyt, and as husband go to bed;
(21) And how the wyntir sesson betwix thame tway
Thai spend in lang reffell, lust and play,
Of thar realmys na thing remembring,
In fowle delyte ybond by Cupyd kyng.

Surrey

(1) Forthwith Fame flieth through the great Libian
    towns:
(2) A mischefe Fame, there is none els so swift:
(3) That moving growes, and flitting gathers force;
(4) First small for dred, sone after climes the skies,
    Stayeth on earth, and hides her hed in cloudes.
(6) Whom our mother the earth, tempted by wrath
    Of gods, begat: the last sister (they write)
    To Caeus, and to Enceladus eke;
(8) Spedie of foote, of wyng likewise as swift;
(9) A monster huge, and dredfull to descrive.
    In every plume that on her body sticks
    (A thing in dede much marvelous to heare)
    As many waker eyes lurk underneath,
    So many mouthes to speake, and listning eares.
(12) By night she flies amid the cloudie skie,
    Shriking by the dark shadow of the earth,
    Ne doth decline to the swete sleepe her eyes.
(14) By day she sits to mark on the house top,
    Or turretts hye, and the great towns afraies,
(16) As mindefull of yll and lyes as blasing truth.
(17) This monster blithe with many a tale gan sow
    This rumor then into the common eares,
    As well things don as that was never wrought:
(19) As, that there comen is to Tyrians court
    Aeneas, one outsprong of Troyan blood,
(20) To whom fair Dido wold her self be wed,
(21) And that the while the winter long they passe
    In foule delight, forgetting charge of reigne,
    Led against honour with unhonest lust.

19 Dedenyt: *disdained*

Dryden

(1)   The loud Report through *Lybian* Cities goes;
(2)   Fame, the great Ill, from small beginnings grows.
      Swift from the first; and ev'ry Moment brings
      New Vigour to her flights, new Pinions to her
        wings.
      Soon grows the Pygmee to Gygantic size;
      Her Feet on Earth, her Forehead in the Skies:
(6)   Inrag'd against the Gods, revengeful Earth
      Produc'd her last of the *Titanian* birth.
      Swift is her walk, more swift her winged hast:
(9)   A monstrous Fantom, horrible and vast;
      As many Plumes as raise her lofty flight,
      So many piercing Eyes inlarge her sight:
      Millions of opening Mouths to Fame belong;
      And ev'ry Mouth is furnish'd with a Tongue:
      And round with listning Ears the flying Plague is
        hung.
(12) She fills the peaceful Universe with Cries;
      No Slumbers ever close her wakeful Eyes.
(14) By Day from lofty Towr's her Head she shews;
      And spreads through trembling Crowds disastrous
        News.
      With Court Informers haunts, and Royal Spies,
(16) Things done relates, not done she feigns; and
        mingles Truth with Lyes.
      Talk is her business; and her chief delight
      To tell of Prodigies, and cause affright.
(19) She fills the Peoples Ears with *Dido*'s Name;
      Who, lost to Honour, and the sense of Shame,
      Admits into her Throne and Nuptial Bed
      A wandring Guest, who from his Country fled:
(21) Whole days with him she passes in delights;
      And wasts in Luxury long Winter Nights.
      Forgetful of her Fame, and Royal Trust;
      Dissolv'd in Ease, abandon'd to her Lust.

C. Day Lewis

Straightaway went Rumour through the great cities of
   Libya —

Rumour, the swiftest traveller of all the ills on earth,
Thriving on movement, gathering strength as it goes; at
    the start
A small and cowardly thing, it soon puffs itself up,
(5) And walking upon the ground, buries its head in the
    cloud-base.
The legend is that, enraged with the gods, Mother Earth
    produced
This creature, her last child, as a sister to Enceladus
And Coeus — a swift-footed creature, a winged angel of
    ruin,
A terrible, grotesque monster, each feather upon whose
    body —
(10) Incredible though it sounds — has a sleepless eye beneath
    it,
And for every eye she has also a tongue, a voice and a
    pricked ear.
At night she flits midway between earth and sky, through
    the gloom
Screeching, and never closes her eyelids in sweet slumber:
By day she is perched like a look-out either upon a roof-top
(15) Or some high turret; so she terrorises whole cities
Loud-speaker of truth, hoarder of mischievous falsehood,
    equally.
This creature was now regaling the people with various
    scandal
In great glee, announcing fact and fiction indiscriminately:
Item, Aeneas has come here, a prince of Trojan blood,
(20) And the beauteous Dido deigns to have her name linked
    with his;
The couple are spending the winter in debauchery, the
    whole long
Winter, forgetting their kingdoms, rapt in a trance of lust.

NOTES

2 Dryden has abbreviated this passage considerably.

4 Vergil *metu* 'by fear': Rumour is small at first because people are afraid of it; Lewis indicates this by *cowardly*.

5 Surrey *stayeth on earth* represents Vergil's sense, but is not an exact translation of *ingreditur* 'walks'; the other two texts of Surrey read *Per(e)cing*, which Jones suggests is an error for *Pacing*.

6   Jones notes that Surrey's *tempted* 'provoked' arises from the phrase 'tempt God.'

8   Dryden's rhyme *hast*: *vast* indicates a long vowel in *vast*.

9   Douglas *fynd* is either an analogous past participle or a passive infinitive 'are to be found.' Note Dryden's rhyme *belong*: *Tongue*.

12   Vergil 'between heaven and earth, in a shade'; both Douglas and Surrey incorrectly take *terrae* 'earth' with *umbram* 'shade.' Dryden almost wholly omits the line.

14   Dryden's *Court Informers* . . . etc. is his own interpolation.

16ff.   Dryden is not very close to Vergil in this passage; his use of the historic present tense obscures the change in 17 from the general description of Rumour to this specific instance in Carthage.

20   Lewis *to have her name linked with* is coy for *se iungere* 'join herself.'

XXI

THE AENEID IV, 642-662

࿓࿓࿓࿓࿓࿓࿓࿓࿓࿓࿓࿓࿓࿓࿓࿓࿓࿓࿓࿓࿓࿓࿓

Dido's Final Lament

Vergil

At trepida et coeptis immanibus effera Dido
sanguineam volvens aciem, maculisque trementis
interfusa genas et pallida morte futura,
interiora domus inrumpit limina et altos
5   conscendit furibunda gradus ensemque recludit
Dardanium, non hos quaesitum munus in usus.
Hic, postquam Iliacas vestis notumque cubile
conspexit, paulum lacrimis et mente morata
incubuitque toro dixitque novissima verba:
10 'Dulces exuviae, dum fata deusque sinebat,
accipite hanc animam meque his exsolvite curis.
Vixi et quem dederat cursum fortuna peregi,
et nunc magna mei sub terras ibit imago.
Urbem praeclaram statui, mea moenia vidi,
15 ulta virum poenas inimico a fratre recepi,
felix, heu nimium felix, si litora tantum
numquam Dardaniae tetigissent nostra carinae.'
Dixit, et os impressa toro, 'Moriemur inultae,
sed moriamur' ait. 'Sic, sic iuvat ire sub umbras.
20 Hauriat hunc oculis ignem crudelis ab alto
Dardanus, et nostrae secum ferat omina mortis.'

Gavin Douglas

(1) Bot now the hasty, egyr and wild Dydo,
Into hyr cruell purpos enragyt so,

(2)   The bludy eyn rollyng in hir hed,
Wan and ful paill for feir of the neir ded,
With chekis freklyt, and al of tychirris bysprent,
Quakyng throu dreid, (4) ruschit furth, or scho
    wald stent,
Onto the innar wardis of hyr place,

(5)   As wod woman clam on the byng, allace!
And furth scho drew the Trojane swerd, fute hait,

(6)   A wapyn was never wrocht for syk a nate.

(7)   And sone as sche beheld Eneas clething,
And eik the bed bekend, a quhile wepyng,
Stude musyng in hir mynd, and syne, but baid,
Fel in the bed, and thir last wordis said:

(10)   "O sweit habyte, and lykand bed," quod sche,
"So lang as God lyst suffir and destane,
Ressave my blude, and this sawle that on flocht is,
And me delyvir from thir hevy thochtis.

(12)   Thus lang I levyt have, and now is spent
The term of lyfe that forton heth me lent;

(13)   For now my gret gost undir erth mon go.

(14)   A richt fair cite have I beild alsso,
Myne awyn wark and wallys behald have I,

(15)   My spows wrokyn of my brothir ennemy,
Fra hym byreft hys tressour, and quyt hym weill.

(16)   Happy, allace! our happy, and ful of seyll,
Had I beyn, only gyf that never nane
At our cost had arryvit schip Trojane."

(18)   And sayand this, hir mouth fast thristis sche
Doun in the bed: "Onwrokyn sal we de?
De us behufis," scho said, "and quhou behald!"
And gan the scharp sword to hir breist uphald;
"Ya, thus, thus lykis us starve and to depart!"
And with that word, rave hir self to the hart.

(20)   "Now lat yon cruel Trojane swelly and se
This our fyre funerale from the deip see,

(21)   And of our deth turs with hym fra Cartage
Thys takyn of myscheif in hys vayage."

---

2 eyn: *eyes;* ded: *death;* bysprent: *sprinkled*	10 lykand: *pleasing;* flocht: *flight*
4 or: *before;* stent: *cease*	13 mon: *must*
5 wod: *mad;* byng: *bench*	15 wrokyn: *avenged*
6 nate: *purpose*	16 seyll: *happiness*
7 bekend: *known;* syne but baid: *afterwards without delay*	18 *See Notes;* lykis: *pleases*
	20 swally: *swallow, see Notes*
	21 turs: *carry*

Surrey

(1) But trembling Dido egerly now bent
    Upon her sterne determinacion,
(2) Her bloodshot eyes roling within her head,
    Her quivering chekes flecked with deadly staine,
    Both pale and wan to think on death to come,
(4) Into the inward wardes of her palace
    She rusheth in, (5) and clam up as distraught
    The buriall stack, and drew the Troyan swerd,
(6) Her gift sometime, but ment to no such use.
(7) Where when she saw his weed and wel knowen bed,
(8) Weping a while, in study gan she stay,
(9) Fell on the bed, and these last words she said:
(10) "Swete spoiles, whiles God and destenies it wold,
(11) Receve this sprite, and rid me of these cares.
(12) I lived and ranne the course fortune did graunt,
(13) And under earth my great gost now shall wende.
(14) A goodly town I built, and saw my walles,
(16) Happy, alas to happy, if these costes
(17) The Troyan shippes had never touched aye."
(18) This said, she laid her mouth close to the bed.
    "Why then," quoth she, "unwroken shall we die?
    But let us die, for thus and in this sort
    It liketh us to seeke the shadowes darck.
(20) And from the seas the cruel Troyans eyes
    Shall wel discern this flame, (21) and take with him
    Eke these unlucky tokens of my death."

Dryden

(1) But furious *Dido*, with dark Thoughts involv'd,
    Shook at the mighty Mischief she resolv'd.
(2) With livid Spots distinguish'd was her Face,
    Red were her rowling Eyes, and discompos'd her
      Pace:
    Ghastly she gaz'd, with Pain she drew her Breath,
    And Nature shiver'd at approaching Death.
(4)   Then swiftly to the fatal place she pass'd;
    And mounts the Fun'ral Pile, with furious haste.

(6)   Unsheaths the Sword the *Trojan* left behind,
       (Not for so dire an Enterprise design'd,)
(7)   But when she view'd the Garments loosely spred,
       Which once he wore, and saw the conscious Bed,
       She paus'd, and, with a Sigh, the Robes embrac'd;
       Then on the Couch her trembling Body cast,
       Repress'd the ready Tears, and spoke her last.
(10)   Dear Pledges of my Love, while Heav'n so pleas'd,
       Receive a Soul, of Mortal Anguish eas'd:
(12)   My fatal Course is finish'd; and I go
       A glorious Name, among the Ghosts below.
(14)   A lofty City by my Hands is rais'd;
(15)   *Pygmalion* punish'd, and my Lord appeas'd.
(16)   What cou'd my Fortune have afforded more,
       Had the false *Trojan* never touch'd my Shore!
(18)   Then kiss'd the Couch; and must I die, she said;
       And unreveng'd; 'tis doubly to be dead!
       Yet ev'n this Death with Pleasure I receive;
       On any terms, 'tis better than to live.
(20)   These Flames, from far, may the false *Trojan* view;
       These boding Omens his base flight pursue.

C. Day Lewis

But Dido, trembling, distraught by the terrible thing she
    was doing,
Her bloodshot eyes all restless, with hectic blotches upon
Her quivering cheeks, yet pale with the shade of advancing
    death,
Ran to the innermost court of the palace, climbed the lofty
5   Pyre, frantic at heart, and drew Aeneas' sword —
Her present to him, procured once for a far different
    purpose.
Then, after eyeing the clothes he had left behind, and the
    memoried
Bed, pausing to weep and brood on him for a little,
She lay down on the bed and spoke her very last words: —
10 'O relics of him, things dear to me while fate, while heaven
    allowed it,
Receive this life of mine, release me from my troubles!
I have lived, I have run to the finish the course which
    fortune gave me:

And now, a queenly shade, I shall pass to the world below.
I built a famous city, saw my own place stablished,
15 Avenged a husband, exacted a price for a brother's enmity.
Happy I would have been, ah, beyond words happy,
If only the Trojan ships had never come to my shore!'
These words; then, burying her face in the bed: — 'Shall I
   die unavenged?
At least, let me die. Thus, thus! I go to the dark, go gladly.
20 May he look long, from out there on the deep, at my
   flaming pyre,
The heartless! And may my death-fires signal bad luck
   for his voyage!'

NOTES

2 Dryden has expanded this passage.

6 Both Douglas and Dryden omit the fact that the sword was Dido's
gift to Aeneas.

7 Dryden *conscious Bed* implies guilt; Vergil simply means the bed that
Dido remembered for its pleasure. Lewis *memoried* is scarcely modern
idiom.

9 Dryden *the Robes embrac'd* — a touch of his own.

13 Note Dryden's *A glorious Name*, but Dido is referring to her ghost
that is but an image of herself. Surrey follows Douglas's *gret gost*.

15 The line was omitted accidentally by Surrey. Douglas *Fra hym byreft
hys tressour* is not in Vergil — it is possible that Douglas mistook
poenas 'penalties' for some other word.

18 Dryden has expanded the passage and emphasized the paradox of
'double death.' Douglas also has expanded the sentence: *and quhou
behald* seems to mean 'and let anyone look,' or 'even if anyone looks.'
The line beginning *And with that word* was suggested by Ascensius
(Coldwell). Douglas *onwrokyn sal we de?* has been adopted entirely
by Surrey.

20 Vergil *hauriat* 'let him drink in'; Surrey (*shall*) may have had a text
with *hauriet* (future). Douglas has tried to keep the metaphor with
swelly 'swallow.'

PART
TWO

XXII

OLD ENGLISH CHRONICLE

❦❦❦❦❦❦❦❦❦❦❦❦❦❦❦❦❦❦❦❦❦❦❦❦❦❦❦❦❦❦

Cynewulf and Cyneheard

This entry in the *Old English Chronicle* for A.D. 755 ranks as one of the earliest pieces of literary prose in the language. It describes events of some thirty years later, and was perhaps inserted in the early ninth century among the brief annalistic notices of the earlier years by an editor particularly interested in early West Saxon history. The primitive nature of the English is indicated by the confusing use of the third person plural pronoun at the end of the entry; the writer was clearly unaware of the problems of *written* as opposed to spoken English. The text is from C. Plummer and J. Earle, *Two . . . Saxon Chronicles*, 2 vols., (Oxford: Clarendon Press, 1892–99), I, 46–48.

Hēr Cynewulf benam Sigebryht his rīces ond Westseaxna wiotan for unryhtum dǣdum, būton Hāmtūnscīre, ond hē hæfde þā oþ hē ofslōg þone aldormon þe him lengest wunode. Ond hiene þā Cynewulf on Andred ādrǣfde, ond hē þǣr wunade oþ þæt hiene ān swān ofstang æt Pryfetes flōdan, ond hē wrǣc þone aldormon Cumbran. Ond sē Cynewulf oft miclum 5 gefeohtum feaht uuiþ Bretwalum; ond ymb xxxi wintra þæs þe hē rīce hæfde, hē wolde ādrǣfan ānne æþeling sē was Cyneheard hāten — ond sē Cyneheard wæs þæs Sigebryhtes brōþur. Ond þā geāscode hē þone cyning lȳtle werode on wīfcȳþþe on Merantūne, ond hine þǣr berād, ond þone būr ūtan beēode, ǣr hine þā men onfunden þe mid þām kyninge wǣrun. 10

Ond þā ongeat sē cyning þæt, ond hē on þā duru ēode, ond þā unhēanlīce hine werede oþ hē on þone æþeling lōcude, ond þā ūt rǣsde on hine ond hine miclum gewundode; ond hīe alle on þone cyning wǣrun feohtende oþ þæt hīe hine ofslægenne hæfdon. Ond þā on þæs wīfes gebǣrum onfundon þæs cyninges þegnas þā unstilnesse, ond þā þider urnon swā hwelc swā þonne 15 gearo wearþ, ond radost. Ond hiera sē æþeling gehwelcum feoh ond feorh gebēad, ond hiera nǣnig hit geþicgean nolde, ac hīe simle feohtende wǣran oþ hīe alle lǣgon būtan ānum Bryttiscum gīsle, ond sē swīþe gewundad wæs.

20 Đā on morgenne gehīerdun þæt þæs cyninges þegnas, þe him beæftan
wǣrun, þæt sē cyning ofslægen wæs, þā ridon hīe þider, ond his aldormon
Osrīc, ond Wīferþ his þegn, ond þā men þe hē beæftan him lǣfde ǣr, ond
þone æþeling on þǣre byrig mētton þǣr sē cyning ofslægen læg (ond þā
gatu him tō belocen hæfdon) ond þā þǣrtō ēodon. Ond þā gebēad hē him
25 hiera āgenne dōm fēos ond londes, gif hīe him þæs rīces ūþon, ond him
cȳþdon þæt hiera mǣgas him mid wǣron, þā þe him from noldon. Ond þā
cuǣdon hīe þæt him nǣnig mǣg lēofra nǣre þonne hiera hlāford, ond hīe
nǣfre his banan folgian noldon. Ond þā budon hīe hiera mǣgum þæt hīe
gesunde from ēodon; ond hīe cuǣdon þæt tæt ilce hiera gefērum geboden
30 wǣre þe ǣr mid þām cyninge wǣrun. Đā cuǣdon hīe þæt hīe hīe þæs ne
onmunden 'þon mā þe ēowre gefēran þe mid þām cyninge ofslægene
wǣrun.' Ond hīe þā ymb þā gatu feohtende wǣron oþ þæt hīe þǣrinne
fulgon ond þone æþeling ofslōgon, ond þā men þe him mid wǣrun, alle
būtan ānum, sē wæs þæs aldormonnes godsunu, ond hē his feorh generede,
35 ond þēah hē wæs oft gewundad.

Translation

In this year Cynewulf and the West-Saxon parliament deprived Sigebryht
of all of his kingdom except Hampshire, because of his misconduct; he
retained this [Hampshire] until he killed the adviser who had been with him
longer than anyone. Cynewulf then banished him into Andred, where he
lived until he was stabbed to death by a herdsman at Privet's Flood: the
herdsman was avenging the adviser Cumbra. This Cynewulf frequently
fought great battles against the Welsh; thirty-one years after he had come
to the throne, he planned to banish a certain nobleman called Cyneheard —
Cyneheard was Sigebryht's brother. He [Cyneheard] found out that the
king was at Merton visiting a woman, with only a small company; he
overtook him there, and surrounded the king's quarters before the men
who were with the king had a chance to discover him. When the king was
aware of this, he went to the door and defended himself bravely, until he
noticed the nobleman; then he rushed out at him and wounded him severely.
All of them continued to attack the king until they had killed him. Hearing
the woman's screams, the king's men became aware of the disturbance, and
everyone that was ready ran there as quickly as possible. The noblemen
offered each of them his life and money, but none of them would accept his
offer. They continued to fight until all of them lay dead except for a Welsh
hostage (and he was severely wounded).

In the morning, when the king's servants who were following him
learned that he had been killed, they rode there: they included his adviser

Osric, his servant Wiferth, and the men he had left behind. They came on the nobleman in the fort where the king lay dead; the gates had been shut against them, and they rode up to them. Then Cyneheard offered them their own choice in money and land, on condition that they grant him the kingship; they [Cyneheard's men] said that their [Osric's men's] kinsmen were with them, and would not leave. They [Osric's men] replied that no kinsman meant as much to them as their lord: they would never follow his killer; then they offered their kinsmen the chance of coming out unharmed. They [those inside] said that the very same offer had been made to their companions who had been with the king, and said 'we regard the offer no more highly than your companions did, who were killed with the king.' Then they went on fighting around the gates until they broke in and killed the nobleman and all those who were with him except one, who was the adviser's godson: he managed to save his life, but was nevertheless badly wounded.

NOTES

This passage of early West Saxon illustrates many of the general tendencies of OE word order, such as the order verb-subject after an adverb in *Ond þā on þæs wīfes gebǣrum onfundon þæs cyninges þegnas þā unstilnesse*, or the order subject . . . verb in dependent clauses (*gif hīe him þæs rīces ūþon*) and after *ond* (*ond hīe alle on þone cyning wǣrun feohtende*). Two syntactic features should be noted: the use of the verb *be* + present participle to indicate continuous action; and the pluperfect tense in *oþ þæt hīe hine ofslægenne hæfdon*, in which the past participle agrees with the accusative object.

3   *aldormon:* a senior adviser, sometimes (depending on the context) 'general.'

20   *Đā on morgenne* . . .: the word order suggests that this is a main clause rather than a 'when . . .' clause.

23–24   *ond þā gatu* . . .: the gates were shut either against the attackers or 'in on themselves'; in either case the subject is 'Cyneheard's men.'

24ff.   The difficulty in understanding the various offers and counteroffers is partly the result of the extravagant use of pronouns, which suggests a writer unpracticed in the problems of written, as opposed to spoken, English.

XXIII

OLD ENGLISH CHRONICLE

Danish Campaign 895–896

Text from A. H. Smith, *The Parker Chronicle (832–900)*, 3rd ed. (London: Methuen, 1951; New York: Appleton-Century-Crofts, 1966), pp. 49–50.

895. On þȳ ilcan gēre worhte sē foresprecena here geweorc be Lygean xx mīla bufan Lundenbyrig. Þā þæs on sumera fōron micel dæl þāra burgwara ond ēac swā ōþres folces þæt hīe gedydon æt þāra Deniscana geweorce, ond þær wurdon geflīemde ond sume fēower cyninges þegnas ofslægene. Þā

5 þæs on hærfeste þā wīcode sē cyng on nēaweste þǣre byrig, þā hwīle þe hīe hira corn gerȳpon, þæt þā Deniscan him ne mehton þæs rīpes forwiernan. Þā sume dæge rād sē cyng ūp bī þǣre ēæ ond gehāwade hwǣr mon mehte þā ēa forwyrcan, þæt hīe ne mehton þā scipu ūt brengan, ond hīe ðā swā dydon; worhton ðā tū geweorc on twā healfe þǣre ēas. Þā hīe ðā þæt geweorc

10 furþum ongunnen hæfdon ond þǣrtō gewīcod hæfdon, þā onget sē here þæt hīe ne mehton þā scipu ūt brengan. Þā forlēton hīe hīe, ond ēodon ofer land þæt hīe gedydon æt Cwatbrycge be Sæfern ond þær gewerc worhton. Þā rād sēo fird west æfter þǣm herige ond þā men of Lundenbyrig gefetedon þā scipu, ond þā ealle þe hīe ālǣdan ne mehton tōbrǣcon, ond þā þe þǣr

15 stælwyrðe wǣron binnan Lundenbyrig gebrōhton. Ond þā Deniscan hæfdon hira wīf befæst innan Ēast-Engle ǣr hīe ūt of þǣm geweorce fōron. Þā sǣton hīe þone winter æt Cwatbrycge. Þæt wæs ymb þrēo gēr þæs þe hīe on Limene mūðan cōmon hider ofer sǣ.

896. Ðā þæs on sumera on ðysum gēre tōfōr sē here, sum on Ēast-Engle,

20 sum on Norðhymbre, ond þā þe feohlēase wǣron him þǣr scipu begēton, ond sūð ofer sǣ fōron tō Sigene. Næfde sē here, Godes þonces, Angelcyn ealles forswīðe gebrocod. Ac hīe wǣron micle swīþor gebrocede on þǣm þrim gēarum mid cēapes cwilde ond monna, ealles swīþost mid þǣm þæt manige þāra sēlestena cynges þēna þe þǣr on londe wǣron forðfērdon on

25 þǣm þrim gēarum.

180

Translation

895. During this same year the above-mentioned [Danish] army built a fort on the Lea, twenty miles above London. During this summer a great number of the townspeople (and also a number of other people as well) marched out until they reached the Danes' fort, but they were put to flight, and four of the king's servants were killed. During the harvest season, the king camped in the neighborhood of the city, while they were reaping their corn, so that the Danes could not deprive them of their harvest. One day the king rode up along the river, and noticed a place where the river could be blocked so that the Danes could not bring their ships out; they did this, and then built two forts, one on each side of the river. When they had begun the fortification and had made their camp there, the [Danish] army realized that they could not get their ships out. They abandoned them, and went overland until they reached Bridgnorth on the Severn; there they built a fort. The English levy rode west in pursuit of the Danes. The people of London removed their ships [i.e., the Danes' ships], breaking up those that they could not move, and bringing into London all those that were serviceable. The Danes, who had left their women in safety in East Anglia before they left their fort, settled at Bridgnorth throughout the winter. It was now three years since they had come across the sea and landed at the mouth of the Lympne.

896. Then, in the summer of this year, the [Danish] army split up, some going to East Anglia and some to Northumbria; those who had no property got themselves boats and went south over the channel to the Seine. The Danes had not, thank God, entirely destroyed England. However, the English had been more devastated during the three years by the death of cattle and men, most of all in that many of the best of the king's servants in the land died during the three years.

NOTES

4   Note *cyninges* beside the later form *cyng*.

7   *ēa*: this word, which survives only in a few place-names (e.g., *Graveney* in Kent) was replaced in ME by *river*, which originally meant 'bank' (Latin *riparium*).

8   Note the number of *for*- prefixes in OE (*forwiernan, forwyrcan*, etc.).

15   *stælwyrðe:* MnE *stalwort*.

19   *tōfōr:* the prefix *tō* in OE commonly denotes separation, as it does in the common Spenserian *all-to-* prefix.

21 *Godes þonces:* an adverbial genitive (as *ealles*) — compare above XIII,
    12. There are several survivals in MnE (*once* < OE *ānes*, *needs* adv.,
    etc.), and the colloquial *of a night* 'at night, nightly' may be an imita-
    tion of it.

XXIV

PASTORAL CARE: ALFRED'S PREFACE

❧❧

The State of Learning in England

This passage is from the preface to King Alfred's translation, made some time after 893, of Gregory's *Cura Pastoralis* (*Hierdebōc*). The text is from *King Alfred's West-Saxon Version of Gregory's Pastoral Care*, ed. H. Sweet, EETS o.s. 45, 50 (1871–2), 3–5.

Ælfred kyning hāteð grētan Wærferð biscep his wordum luflīce ond frēondlīce; ond ðē cȳðan hāte ðæt mē cōm swīðe oft on gemynd, hwelce wiotan iū wǣron giond Angelcynn, ǣgðer gē godcundra hāda gē woruld-cundra; ond hū gesǣliglīca tīda ðā wǣron giond Angelcynn; ond hū ðā kyningas ðe ðone onwald hæfdon ðæs folces on ðām dagum Gode ond his 5
ǣrendwrecum hērsumedon; ond hīe ǣgðer gē hiora sibbe gē hiora siodo gē hiora onweald innanbordes gehīoldon, ond ēac ūt hiora ēðel gerȳmdon; ond hū him ðā spēow ǣgðer gē mid wīge gē mid wīsdōme; ond ēac ðā godcundan hādas, hū giorne hīe wǣron ǣgðer gē ymb lāre gē ymb liornunga, gē ymb ealle ðā ðīowotdōmas ðe hīe Gode dōn scoldon; ond hū man 10
ūtanbordes wīsdōm ond lāre hieder on lond sōhte, ond hū wē hīe nū sceoldon ūte begietan, gif wē hīe habban sceoldon. Swǣ clǣne hīo wæs oðfeallenu on Angelcynne ðæt swīðe fēawa wǣron behionan Humbre ðe hiora ðēninga cūðen understondan on Englisc oððe furðum ān ǣrendgewrit of Lǣdene on Englisc āreccean; ond ic wēne ðætte nōht monige begiondan Humbre 15
nǣren. Swǣ fēawa hiora wǣron ðæt ic furðum ānne ānlēpne ne mæg geðen-cean be sūðan Temese, ðā ðā ic tō rīce fēng. Gode ælmihtegum sīe ðonc ðætte wē nū ǣnigne onstal habbað lārēowa. Ond for ðon ic ðē bebīode ðæt ðū dō swǣ ic gelīefe ðæt ðū wille, ðæt ðū ðē ðissa woruldðinga tō ðǣm geǣmetige, swǣ ðū oftost mæge, ðæt ðū ðone wīsdōm ðe ðē God sealde, 20
ðǣr ðǣr ðū hiene befæstan mæge, befæste. Geðenc hwelc wītu ūs ðā becōmon for ðisse worulde, ðā ðā wē hit nōhwæðer nē selfe ne lufodon, nē ēac ōðrum monnum ne lēfdon: ðone naman ānne wē lufodon ðætte wē Cristne wǣren, ond swīðe fēawe ðā ðēawas.

Translation

King Alfred sends his greetings to Bishop Werferth in his own words, in love and friendship. I want to let you know that it has often occurred to me to think what wise men there once were throughout England, both of religious orders and secular, and how happy those days were in England, and how in those days the kings who ruled over the people used to obey God and his messengers, and how they managed to preserve peace and morality and control at home, and also to extend the boundaries of their country outside, and how they prospered both in war and in wisdom; and also the religious orders — how eager they were in both teaching and learning, and in all the services which they owed to God; and how people once used to come here to England from abroad in search of wisdom and learning — and how nowadays we would have to get it abroad (if we were to have it at all). Learning had so declined in England that there were very few people this side of the Humber who could understand their service-books in English, let alone translate a letter out of Latin into English — and I don't imagine there were many north of the Humber, either. There were so few of them that I cannot think of even a single one south of the Thames at the time when I came to the throne. Thanks be to almighty God that we now have any supply of teachers! For this reason I suggest to you that you do as I believe you will, namely, that you free yourself of these worldly affairs as often as you can, with this purpose, that you may apply the wisdom which God gave you wherever you can [best] apply it. Consider what punishments have come upon us in this world, because we have neither loved it [wisdom] ourselves in any way nor allowed other men to do so. We loved only the name of being Christians, but very few of the habits.

NOTES

1   The change from third person to first person (*hāteð . . . hāte*) after the formal opening is a mark of epistolary style, and may be an imitation of Latin.

11–12   *hīe . . . hīe:* these could be plural (*wīsdōm ond lāre*), but *hīo* (feminine) refers back only to *lāre*.

20   *geǣmetige:* note that this > MnE *empty*, with an intrusive *p* between *m* and *t:* compare I, 18 *bremelas*, MnE *brambles*, and XXXI, 15.

22ff.   This line provides a good example of OE multiple negatives.

XXV

KING ALFRED'S OROSIUS

ೲೲೲೲೲೲೲೲೲೲೲೲೲೲೲೲೲೲೲೲೲೲೲ

The Voyage of Ohthere

This passage is part of an interpolation by Alfred in his translation of Orosius's *History of the World*. The text (with corrections) is from *King Alfred's Orosius*, ed. H. Sweet, EETS o.s. 79 (1883), 17–18.

Ōhthere sǣde his hlāforde, Ælfrede cyninge, þæt hē ealra Norðmonna norþmest būde. Hē cwæð þæt hē būde on þǣm lande norþweardum wiþ þā Westsǣ. Hē sǣde þēah þæt þæt land sīe swīþe lang norþ þonan; ac hit is eal wēste, būton on fēawum stōwum styccemǣlum wīciað Finnas, on huntoðe on wintra, ond on sumera on fiscaþe be þǣre sǣ. Hē sǣde þæt hē æt sumum 5
cirre wolde fandian hū longe þæt land norþryhte lǣge, oþþe hwæðer ǣnig mon be norðan þǣm wēstenne būde. Þā fōr hē norþryhte be þǣm lande: lēt him ealne weg þæt wēste land on ðæt stēorbord, ond þā wīdsǣ on ðæt bǣcbord þrīe dagas. Þā wæs hē swā fēor norþ swā þā hwælhuntan firrest faraþ. Þā fōr hē þāgīet norþryhte swā fēor swā hē meahte on þǣm ōþrum 10
þrim dagum gesiglan. Þā bēag þæt land þǣr ēastryhte, oþþe sēo sǣ in on ðæt lond, hē nysse hwæðer, būton hē wisse ðæt hē ðǣr bād westanwindes ond hwōn norþan, ond siglde ðā ēast be lande swā swā hē meahte on fēower dagum gesiglan. Þā sceolde hē ðǣr bīdan ryhtnorþanwindes, for ðǣm þæt land bēag þǣr sūþryhte, oþþe sēo sǣ in on ðæt land, hē nysse hwæþer. Þā 15
siglde hē þonan sūðryhte be lande swā swā hē mehte on fīf dagum gesiglan. Ðā læg þǣr ān micel ēa ūp in on þæt land. Þā cirdon hīe ūp in on ðā ēa, for þǣm hīe ne dorston forþ bī þǣre ēa siglan for unfriþe; for þǣm ðæt land wæs eall gebūn on ōþre healfe þǣre ēas. Ne mētte hē ǣr nān gebūn land, siþþan hē from his āgnum hām fōr; ac him wæs ealne weg wēste land on 20
þæt stēorbord, būtan fiscerum ond fugelerum ond huntum, ond þæt wǣron eall Finnas; ond him wæs ā wīdsǣ on ðæt bǣcbord. Þā Beormas hæfdon swīþe wel gebūd hira land: ac hīe ne dorston þǣr on cuman. Ac þāra Terfinna land wæs eal wēste, būton ðǣr huntan gewīcodon, oþþe fisceras, oþþe fugeleras. 25

Fela spella him sǣdon þā Beormas ǣgþer gē of hiera āgnum lande gē of
þǣm landum þe ymb hīe ūtan wǣron; ac hē nyste hwæt þæs sōþes wæs, for
þǣm hē hit self ne geseah. Þā Finnas, him þūhte, ond þā Beormas sprǣcon
nēah ān geþēode. Swīþost hē fōr ðider, tōēacan þæs landes scēawunge, for
30 þǣm horshwælum, for ðǣm hīe habbað swīþe æþele bān on hiora tōþum
(þā tēð hīe brōhton sume þǣm cyninge); ond hiora hȳd bið swīðe gōd tō
sciprāpum. Sē hwæl bið micle lǣssa þonne ōðre hwalas: ne bið hē lengra
ðonne syfan elna lang; ac on his āgnum lande is sē betsta hwælhuntað; þā
bēoð eahta and fēowertiges elna lange, and þā mǣstan fīftiges elna lange;
35 þāra hē sǣde þæt hē syxa sum ofslōge syxtig on twām dagum.

Translation

Ohthere told his lord, King Alfred, that he lived the furthest north of all
the Norsemen; he said that he lived in the northern part of the land,
opposite the North Sea [it was the West Sea to the Scandinavians]. He said,
however, that the land continues far to the north of there, but is entirely
desolate, except that there are Finns living in a few places here and there,
hunting during the winter and fishing in the sea in the summer. Ohthere
said that on one occasion he decided to investigate how far the land continued to the north, and to see if anyone lived north of the wilderness. Then
he sailed due north along the coast; he kept the wilderness on his starboard
and the open sea on his port side all the way for three days. At this point he
was as far north as the whale-hunters go on their furthest trips. Then he
continued to sail due north for as far as he could go, for the next three days.
At that point the land turned due east, or the sea turned in on the land, he
didn't know which, but he did know that there he had the wind from the
west and somewhat from the north. Then he sailed due east along the coast
for as far as he could sail for four days. At that point he had to wait for a
wind from due north [or he said that he had the wind straight from the
north], because there the land turned due south (or the sea turned in on the
land, he didn't know which). From there he sailed due south along the
coast for as far as he could sail for five days. There a big river went up into
the land. They turned up into the river, as they did not dare sail past the
river because of [the danger of] war, for the land on the other side of the
river was all inhabited. He had not come across any inhabited land since
he set out from his own home: all the way he had had nothing on his starboard but wilderness, apart from fishermen, bird-catchers and hunters,
who consisted entirely of Finns; he always had the open sea on his port side.
The Permians had settled their land very well, but they [Ohthere's party]
did not dare land there. The land of the Terfinns, however, was entirely
desolate except for where hunters lived, or fishermen or bird-catchers.

The Permians told him many stories about their own land and the lands surrounding them, but he did not know what was true, as he had not seen it for himself. The Finns and the Permians, it seemed to him, spoke almost the same language. He went there most of all for the walruses [horse-whales], in addition to his desire to see the land, as they have very fine bone in their teeth (they brought some of the teeth to the king); their skins are very good for making ship's ropes. This whale is much smaller than other whales; it does not exceed seven cubits in length, whereas the best whale-hunting is in Ohthere's own land: there they are forty-eight cubits long, and the biggest fifty cubits. He said that he and five others killed sixty of them in two days.

NOTES

3   *Westsǣ:* the West Sea of the Scandinavians is the North Sea to the English.

4   *būton:* this usage illustrates the development of *but* as a pronoun. It is easy to see how the line could almost have been translated 'it is entirely desolate, but in a few places . . .' Compare below l. 12.

   styccemǣlum: the second element is seen in MnE *piecemeal.*

8   *stēorbord*, the 'steering side' still survives; the MnE *larboard* (usually replaced by *port*) may be connected with OE *lād* 'loading' — i.e., the side of the boat on which things were loaded, namely the port side.

12   *hē nysse hwæðer:* the alternatives were that the land turned east, or that he had simply turned into a large bay. In this case, the former was true, as he had reached the Northern limit of Scandinavia; his change of direction to the South, however, (ll. 15–16) was into the bay of the White Sea.

   bād: OE *bīdan* is ambiguous for modern readers, as it can mean both 'wait for' and 'experience'; here and in l. 14 either is possible.

17   *ēa:* see above, XXIII, 7 *n.*

21   *ond þæt wǣron:* in MnE the subject pronoun is normally "attracted" into the number of the predicate.

35   *syxa sum:* a common OE idiom — 'he, one of six.'

   ofslōge: subjunctive, because it is reported speech.

XXVI

WULFSTAN

❧❧❧❧❧❧❧❧❧❧❧❧

On False Gods

Wulfstan's sermon, written at the end of the tenth or beginning of the eleventh century, is an adaptation of one by Ælfric, abbot of Eynsham. The text is from D. Bethurum, *Homilies of Wulfstan* (Oxford: Clarendon Press, 1957), pp. 221–223.

Ēala, gefyrn is þæt ðurh dēofol fela þinga misfōr, and þæt mancynn tō swȳðe Gode mishȳrde, and þæt hæðenscype ealles tō wīde swȳðe gederede and gȳt dereð wīde. Ne rǣde wē þēah āhwār on bōcum þæt man ārǣrde ǣnig hæðengyld āhwār on worulde on eallum þām fyrste þe wæs ǣr Noes flōde.
5 Ac syððan þæt gewearð þæt Nembroð and ðā entas worhton þone wundor- līcan stȳpel æfter Noes flōde, and him ðā swā fela gereorda gelamp, þæs þe bēc secgað, swā ðǣra wyrhtena wæs. Þā syððan tōfērdon hȳ wīde landes, and mancyn þā sōna swȳðe wēox; and ðā æt nȳhstan wurdon hī bepæhte þurh ðone ealdan dēofol þe Adam iū ǣr beswāc swā þæt hī worhton wōlīce
10 and gedwollīce him hæþene godas, and ðone sōðan God and heora āgenne scyppend forsāwon, þe hȳ tō mannum gescōp and geworhte.
Hī nāmon ēac him ðā þæt tō wīsdōme þurh dēofles lāre þæt hȳ wurðedon him for godas þā sunnan and ðone mōnan for heora scīnendan beorhtnesse, and him lāc þā æt nȳhstan þurh dēofles lāre offrodon and forlēton heora
15 Drihten þe hȳ gescōp and geworhte. Sume men ēac sǣdan be ðām scīnendum steorrum þæt hī godas wǣron, and āgunnan hȳ weorðian georne, and sume hȳ gelȳfdon ēac on fȳr for his fǣrlīcum bryne, sume ēac on wæter, and sume hȳ gelȳfdon on ðā eorðan forðan þe hēo ealle þing fēdeð. Ac hȳ mihton georne tōcnāwan, gif hī cūðon þæt gescēad, þæt sē is sōð God þe
20 ealle þās ðing gescōp ūs mannum tō brīce and tō note for his miclan gōdnesse þe hē mancynne geūðe. Ðās gesceafta ēac ealle dōð swā swā him gedihte heora āgen scyppend and ne magon nān þing dōn būtan ūres Drihtnes þafunge, forðām þe nān ōðer scyppend nis būton sē āna sōða God þe wē on gelȳfað, and wē hine ǣnne ofer ealle ōðre þing lufiad and wurðiaþ mid

gewissum gelēafan, cweþende mid mūðe and mid mōdes incundnesse þæt 25
sē ān is sōð God þe ealle ðing gescōp and geworhte.

Gȳt ðā hæþenan noldon bēon gehealdene on swā fēawum godum swā hȳ
ǣr hæfdan, ac fēngon tō wurðienne æt nȳhstan mistlīce entas and strece
woruldmen þe mihtige wurdan on woruldafelum and egesfulle wǣran þā
hwȳle þe hȳ leofedon, and heora āgenum lustum fullīce fullēodan. Ān man 30
wæs on geārdagum eardiende on þām īglande þe Crēata hātte sē wæs
Saturnus gehāten, and sē wæs swā wælhrēow þæt hē fordyde his āgene
bearn ealle būtan ānum and unfæderlīce macode heora līf tō lyre sōna on
geogoðe. Hē lǣfde swāþēah unēaðe ǣnne tō līfe, þēah ðe hē fordyde þā
brōðra elles; and sē wæs Iōvis gehāten, and sē wearð hetol fēond. Hē 35
āflȳmde his āgene fæder eft of ðām ylcan foresǣdan īglande þe Crēta hātte
and wolde hine forfaran georne gif hē mihte; and sē Iovis wearð swā swȳðe
gāl þæt hē on his āgenre swyster gewīfode, sēo wæs genamod Iūno, and hēo
wearð swȳðe hēalīc gyden æfter hæðenscype geteald. Heora twā dōhtra
wǣron Minerva and Vēnus. Þās mānfullan men þe wē ymbe specað wǣron 40
getealde for ðā mǣrostan godas þā on ðām dagum, and þā hæðenan
wurðodon hȳ swȳðe þurh dēofles lāre; ac sē sunu wæs swāþēah swȳðor on
hæðenscype gewurðod þonne sē fæder wǣre, and hē is geteald ēac
ārwurðost ealra þǣra goda þe þā hæðenan on ðām dagum for godas hæfdon
on heora gedwylde. And hē hātte Þor ōðrum naman betwux sumum þēodum; 45
ðone Denisca lēoda lufiað swȳðost and on heora gedwylde weorðiaþ
geornost.

Translation

It is now, alas, a long time since the Devil caused so much to go wrong:
too often men disobeyed God, and all too widespread was the harm done by
heathenism, harm which continues today. However, we do not find it
written in books anywhere that heathen worship was established anywhere
in the world in all the time that preceded Noah's flood. It was later, after
Noah's flood, that Nimrod and the giants built their remarkable tower;
according to what the books say, they were then afflicted by as many
languages as there were workmen. Afterwards they scattered far and wide
throughout the earth, and mankind quickly increased in numbers. Next,
the old Devil who had long before tricked Adam deceived them into making
heathen gods for themselves in their wrongheadedness and folly: they
ignored the true God, their own creator, who had made them and formed
them as men.

Also, through the teaching of the Devil, they then adopted the following
as the course of wisdom: they worshiped the sun and the moon as their gods

because of their shining brightness, and next offered them sacrifices because of the Devil's teaching, abandoning their Lord who shaped and created them. Also some people said of the shining stars that they were gods, and they eagerly began to worship them; some people also believed in fire because of its spontaneous burning, and some in water, and some of them believed in the earth because it feeds everything. However, if they had been aware of the distinction, they could easily have realized that the true god is he that created all these things for the use and enjoyment of us men out of the great goodness which he bestowed on mankind. Moreover, these creations all do exactly as their own creator arranged for them; they can do nothing without the permission of our Lord, because there is no other creator except the one true God in whom all of us believe — we love and honor him alone above all other things with sure faith, and say with our voice and innermost heart that he alone is the true God who made and created everything.

The heathens would still not be restricted to as few gods as they had had before: next they began to worship various giants and violent mortals who had been strong in worldly power and were terrible while they lived, fully indulging themselves in their own pleasures. In former days there was a certain man called Saturn who lived on the island of Crete; he was so cruel that he killed all his children but one, unnaturally cutting off their lives immediately, in their youth. Nevertheless, unintentionally, he left one alive, although he had otherwise killed all his brothers; this one was called Jupiter, and he became a hateful fiend. He later banished his own father from the aforementioned island of Crete (and would have killed him if he could). This Jupiter was so lecherous that he had intercourse with his own sister, whose name was Juno; she was reckoned as a very important goddess among heathens. These sinful men that we are talking about were reckoned in those days as the most renowned gods; through the Devil's teaching, the heathens worshiped them greatly. The son, however, was worshiped by the heathens even more than his father had been; he is also reckoned to be the most worthy of honor of all the gods that the heathens counted as gods in those days in their error. He is given another name among some people, Thor; the Danes love him most, and in their error are most eager to honor him.

NOTES

1-2 *tō swȳðe:* it would be a mistake to assume that 'too often' implies that for Wulfstan there was a reasonable level of disobedience; Wulfstan frequently uses *tō* to denote excess in general. On his style, which is highly individual, see Professor Bethurum's Introduction.

6   *swā fela gereorda gelamp:* 'so many languages befel them' — note that
    fela is a singular in OE, even though it is followed by the genitive plural.
    þæs þe: þæs is an adverbial genitive in this conjunctional phrase.

8   *æt nȳhstan:* etymologically the ancestor of MnE *next.*

13 *þā sunnan and ðone mōnan:* note that in ME the gender of these nouns
    was often reversed. *Sun* became masculine, perhaps under the influence
    of Latin *sol* and the mythological association with Apollo; *moon,*
    however, was frequently feminine, after Latin *luna* and the goddess
    Diana. See Mustanoja, pp. 45–46.

23–24 *þe wē on gelȳfað, and wē hine . . .:* it is common in OE and ME for
    the construction of a relative clause to revert to that of a main clause,
    with a repeated pronoun. Compare XXXIV, 82.

31 *īglande:* the MnE form *island* derives its *s* (which has never been
    pronounced) from French *isle* < Latin *insula.*

33 *unfæderlīce . . .:* literally 'in an unfatherlike fashion made their lives
    for a loss, immediately in their youth.'

35 *fēond:* originally 'enemy' — the sense 'fiend' comes from the phrase
    Hostis antiquus, 'the Old Enemy, the Devil.' Sometimes, as here, it is
    not certain whether OE *fēond* has its original or its transferred sense.

XXVII

PETERBOROUGH CHRONICLE

ぐぐぐぐぐぐぐぐぐぐぐぐぐぐぐぐぐぐぐぐぐぐぐぐぐぐぐぐぐぐ

The Anarchy

This passage is taken from the final continuation (1121–55) of the MS of the Old English Chronicle known as the *Peterborough Chronicle*, because of the clear evidence that it was written at the Benedictine Abbey there. The Peterborough sections and additions, together with the continuations, have been edited by Cecily Clark (Oxford: Clarendon Press, 1958); the text of the present extract is from J. A. W. Bennett and G. V. Smithers, *Early Middle English Verse and Prose* (Oxford: Clarendon Press, 1966), pp. 210–212.

1140. On þis gær wolde þe king Stephne tæcen Rodbert eorl of Gloucestre, þe kinges sune Henries, ac he ne myhte, for he wart it war. Þerefter in þe lengten þestrede þe sunne and te dæi abuton non-tid dæies, þa men eten, ðat me lihtede candles to æten bi, and þat was xiii kalendarum Aprilis.

5 Wæron men suythe ofwundred. Þerefter fordfeorde Willelm ærcebiscop of Cantwarbyri, and te king makede Teodbald ærcebiscop, þe was abbot in the Bec. Þerefter wæx suythe micel uuerre betuyx þe king and Randolf eorl of Cæstre; noht forþi ðat he ne iaf him al ðat he cuthe axen him, alse he dide alle othre, oc æfre þe mare he iaf heom þe wærse hi wæron him. Þe

10 eorl heold Lincol agænes þe king, and benam him al ðat he ahte to hauen; and te king for þider, and besætte him and his brother Willelm de Romare in þe castel. And te æorl stæl ut and ferde efter Rodbert eorl of Gloucestre, and brohte him þider mid micel ferd, and fuhten suythe on Candelmasse dæi agenes heore lauerd, and namen him, for his men him suyken and flugæn;

15 and læd him to Bristowe and diden þar in prisun and in feteres. Þa was al Engleland styred mar þan ær wæs, and al yuel wæs in lande. Þerefter com þe kinges dohter Henries, þe hefde ben emperice in Alamanie and nu wæs cuntesse in Angou, and com to Lundene; and te Lundenissce folc hire wolde tæcen, and scæ fleh, and forles þar micel. Þerefter þe biscop of Wincestre,

20 Henri þe kinges brother Stephnes, spac wid Rodbert eorl and wyd þemperice,

and suor heom athas ðat he neure ma mid te king his brother wolde halden,
and cursede alle þe men þe mid him heoldon, and sæde heom ðat he uuolde
iiuen heom up Wincestre, and dide heom cumen þider. Þa hi þærinne
wæren, þa com þe kinges cuen mid al hire strengthe, and besæt heom, ðat
þer wæs inne micel hungær. Þa hi ne leng ne muhten þolen, þa stalen hi ut   25
and flugen; and hi wurthen war widuten, and folecheden heom, and namen
Rodbert eorl of Gloucestre and ledden him to Rouecestre and diden him
þare in prisun; and te emperice fleh into an minstre.

Þa feorden þe wise men betwyx þe kinges freond and te eorles freond and
sahtlede sua ðat me sculde leten ut þe king of prisun for þe eorl, and te eorl   30
for þe king, and sua diden. Sithen þerefter sathleden þe king and Randolf
eorl at Stanford, and athes suoren and treuthes fæston ðat her nouþer
sculde besuyken other. And it ne forstod naht: for þe king him sithen nam in
Hamtun, þurhc wicci ræd, and dide him in prisun, and efsones he let him ut,
þurhc wærse red, to ðat forewarde ðat he suor on halidom and gysles fand   35
þat he alle his castles sculde iiuen up. Sume he iaf up, and sume ne iaf he
noht; and dide þanne wærse þanne he hær sculde. Þa was Engleland suythe
todeled: sume helden mid te king, and sume mid þemperice. For, þa þe king
was in prisun, þa wenden þe eorles and te rice men þat he neure mare sculde
cumen ut, and sæhtleden wyd þemperice, and brohten hire into Oxenford,   40
and iauen hire þe burch. Þa þe king was ute, þa herde ðat sægen, and toc
his feord and besæt hire in þe tur, and me læt hire dun on niht of þe tur mid
rapes, and stal ut, and scæ fleh and iæde on fote to Walingford. Þærefter
scæ ferde ouer sæ, and hi of Normandi wenden alle fra þe king to þe eorl of
Angæu (sume here þankes and sume here unþankes) for he besæt heom til   45
hi aiauen up here castles, and hi nan helpe ne hæfden of þe king.

Translation

In this year King Stephen planned to seize Robert, Earl of Gloucester,
the son of King Henry (I), but he was unable to do so, for Robert realized
his intention. After this, during Lent the sun and the daylight were eclipsed
at about midday when people were eating, so that they lit candles to eat by:
this was on 20 March; everyone was very amazed. After this, William,
Archbishop of Canterbury, died, and the king appointed Theobald, abbot
of Bec, archbishop. After this there was a great war between the king and
Randolph, Earl of Chester, not because he [Stephen] didn't give him all he
could ask (as he did to everyone else): always, the more he gave them, the
worse they behaved towards him. The Earl held Lincoln against the king,
and deprived him of everything that was rightfully his; the king rode there

and besieged Randolph and his brother William of Roumare in the castle. The earl stole out and went for Robert, Earl of Gloucester, and brought him back there with a big army; they fought a great battle against their lord on Candlemas Day, and captured him, for his own men betrayed him and fled. They took him to Bristol, where they put him in prison in chains. Now the whole of England was in turmoil more than it had ever been before, and there was nothing but evil in the land. After this King Henry's daughter arrived; she had been Empress in Germany and was now Countess of Anjou; she came to London, and the people of London tried to capture her, but she fled, abandoning a great deal [of property]. After this, Henry, Bishop of Winchester and King Stephen's brother, negotiated with Earl Robert and the Empress; he swore oaths to them that he would never again ally himself with his brother the king; he denounced all those who sided with him, and said that he would surrender Winchester to them, and got them to go there. As soon as they were inside, the king's queen arrived with all her force and besieged them, causing great hunger inside. When they could stand it no longer, they stole out and fled; those outside became aware of this and went in pursuit; they captured Robert, Earl of Gloucester, and took him to Rochester where they put him in prison; the Empress fled to a monastery.

Then counsellors negotiated between the king's allies and the earl's allies, and came to an agreement: the king was to be released from prison in exchange for the earl, and the earl for the king; this was done. After this the king and Earl Randolph came to an agreement at Stanford; they swore oaths and pledged solemn promises that neither would betray the other. However, it counted for nothing, as the king later captured the earl at Northampton, on bad advice, and imprisoned him; later, on even worse advice, he released him on this condition: the earl swore by God, producing hostages, that he would surrender all his castles. Some he surrendered, but others he did not surrender, and then behaved worse than he ever should have done [or had done before].

England was now totally divided; some people sided with the king, and some with the Empress. For when the king was in prison the earls and nobles assumed that he would never get out again, and made an agreement with the Empress; they brought her into Oxford and handed the city over to her. Now when the king was released, he heard news of this, and took his army and besieged her in the tower. During the night she was let down from the tower by ropes; she stole out and fled, going on foot to Wallingford. After this, she crossed the Channel, and the people of Normandy all turned from the king to the Earl of Anjou, some willingly, others unwillingly, as he besieged them until they surrendered their castles; they got no assistance from the king.

NOTES

In a passage of such early ME it is important to observe the number of loanwords: e.g., (ON) *tæcen, toc,* (OF) *candles, uuerre, prisun,* etc.

2 *þe kinges sune Henries:* this passage provides several examples of ME word order in inflected genitive constructions.

3 *lengten:* the time when the days lengthened, Lent.

4 *me:* the common ME indefinite pronoun, corresponding approximately to OE *man, mon,* MnE *one, they.*

10 *ahte to hauen:* OE *āgan* 'own, possess' acquires the sense of obligation quite early — compare MnE 'I have my homework to do,' 'I have to do my homework.' The past *āhte* had by late ME acquired present sense, as in MnE *ought,* which is never used of the past — 'you ought to go' but 'you had to go.'

15 *Bristowe,* early *Brycgstow* 'bridge-place,' acquired its final *l* in the ME period but the spelling was not common until early MnE.

19 *scæ:* note this early occurrence of *she* for OE *hēo.* There are several theories of the origin of the word; it is most likely that in OE the stress in the diphthong shifted to produce *heō,* and, with slight assibilation of the consonant, *hjō;* position in the sentence after certain other consonants (particularly dentals and *s*) may have caused this consonant to develop to *sh.* Whatever the explanation, there is little doubt that the word would be under pressure to change pronunciation: as the OE diphthong *ēo* developed to ME *ē,* the feminine pronoun nominative would have become indistinguishable from the masculine *hē.*

23 *dide heom cumen:* on 'causative' *do* in ME, see Mustanoja, pp. 600–605.

45 *here þankes . . .:* compare XXIII, 21 *n.*

XXVIII

SAWLES WARDE

୧ଡ଼ଡ଼ଡ଼ଡ଼ଡ଼ଡ଼ଡ଼ଡ଼ଡ଼ଡ଼ଡ଼ଡ଼ଡ଼

Description of Hell

The *Sawles Warde* ('Guardianship of the Soul') is a West Midland text of the late twelfth century, closely related in language to the famous *Ancrene Wisse* (or *Ancrene Riwle*); it is a vigorous allegory of the soul, in the Old English homiletic tradition. The extract here is from the speech by Death's Messenger. The text is from Bennett and Smithers (who edit the whole of the *Sawles Warde*), pp. 250–251.

Helle is wid wiðute met ant deop wiðute grunde; ful of brune uneuenlich, for ne mei nan eorðlich fur euenin þertowart; ful of stench unþolelich, for ne mahte in eorðe na cwic þing hit þolien; ful of sorhe untalelich, for ne mei na muð for wrecchedom ne for wa rikenin hit ne tellen. Se þicke is
5 þrinne þe þosternesse þet me hire mei grapin. For þet fur ne ȝeueð na liht, ah blent ham þe ehnen þe þer beoð wið a smorðrinde smoke, smeche forcuðest, ant tah i þet ilke swarte þeosternesse swarte þinges ha iseoð, as deoflen þet ham meallið ant derueð aa ant dreccheð wið alles cunnes pinen, ant iteilede draken grisliche ase deoflen þe forswolheð ham ihal
10 ant speoweð ham eft ut biuoren ant bihinden, oðer-hwile torendeð ham ant tocheoweð ham euch greot, ant heo eft iwurðeð hal to a swuch bale bute bote as ha ear weren. Ant ful wel ha iseoð, ham to grisle ant to grure ant to echen hare pine, þe laðe helle-wurmes, tadden ant froggen, þe freoteð ham ut te ehnen ant te nease-gristles, ant snikeð in ant ut neddren
15 ant eauroskes, nawt ilich þeose her ah hundret siðe grisluker, et muþ ant et earen, ed ehnen ant ed neauele, ant ed te breosteholke as meaðen i forrotet flesch, eauerȝete þickest. Þer is remunge i þe brune ant toðes hechelunge i þe snawi weattres. Ferliche ha flutteð from þe heate into þe chele, ne neauer nuten ha of þeos twa hweðer ham þuncheð wurse, for
20 eiðer is unþolelich. Ant i þis ferliche mong þe leatere þurh þe earre derueð þe mare. Þet fur ham forbearneð al to colen calde, þet pich ham forwalleð aðet ha beon formealte, ant eft acwikieð anan to drehen al þet ilke ant

196

muchedeale wurse a wiðuten ende. Ant tis ilke unhope is ham meast pine, þet nan naueð neauermare hope of nan acouerunge, ah aren sikere of euch uuel to þurhleasten i wa from worlde into worlde aa on echnesse. Euch 25 aþrusmeð oðer, ant euch is oðres pine, ant euchan heateð oðer ant him seoluen as þe blake deouel; ant eauer se ha i þis world luueden ham mare, se ha þer heatieð ham swiðere; ant eiðer curseð oðer ant fret of þe oðres earen, ant te nease alswa.

Translation

Hell is immeasurably wide, and bottomless in depth; it is full of incomparable burning, for no earthly fire can compare with it; it is full of unbearable stench, for no living thing on earth could stand it; it is full of indescribable sorrow, for no mouth can reckon it or describe it, because of its misery and suffering. The darkness in it is so thick that it can be touched, for the fire gives no light but blinds the eyes of those within with a suffocating smoke, the most awful fumes; and yet, in that very black darkness they can see black things, such as devils which beat them and torment them always, and torture them with every kind of torture, and dragons with tails, as terrible as devils, which swallow them whole and then spew them out again both in front and behind, and sometimes tear them apart and chew them up, every bit — but afterwards they become whole again to face the same unredeemable suffering that they had before. They can see quite clearly, to their fear and horror and to increase their torment, the loathsome reptiles of hell, toads and frogs, which eat out their eyes and the gristle of their noses, and adders and frogs creep in and out, — not like those here [on earth] but a hundred times more horrible — at the mouth and at the ears, at the eyes and at the navel, and at the hollow of the chest, like maggots in rotten flesh, thicker than you have ever seen them. In the burning there is wailing, and in the ice-cold waters there is chattering of the teeth; they move quickly from the heat into the cold, and they can never tell which of the two seems worse to them, for they are both intolerable. In this rapid alternation the second [experience] always hurts all the more because of the first. The fire burns them up into cold ashes; the pitch boils them until they melt away, and immediately they revive to suffer all the same pain over again, and far worse, always without end. And this very despair is their worst torment, in that none of them has any hope of ever recovering; they know for certain that every evil will last in sorrow forever through world after world, into eternity. Each person crowds upon the other; each one is the other's torment; each one hates both the other and himself like the black devil: always, the more they loved them in this world, the more intensely they hate them there. Each one curses the other, and bites off his ears and his nose.

NOTES

This passage is skillfully rhetorical: note *uneuenlich . . . euenin, unþolelich . . . þolien,* etc., and the alliterative *smorðrinde smoke, smeche forcuðest.*

2–3 *mei . . . mahte:* although formally present and preterite, the sense of the two forms is present, 'can.'

6   *blent ham þe ehnen: ham* is technically a dative of (dis)advantage, 'blinds to them the eyes'; it may often be translated, as here, by a genitive — 'blinds their eyes' — and is consequently often referred to as a possessive dative.

8   *meallið:* compare *maul, mallet,* to which it is related.

8–9 *alles cunnes pinen:* 'pains of every kind,' but the ME phrase in fact develops directly into MnE *all kinds of, every kind of,* through expressions like XXIX(a) *euerich kynde crafte.* See OED *kind* (and also *sort*).

24   *hope:* here in its modern sense; often it is 'expectation' in general.

XXIX

TREVISA

ぐぐぐぐぐぐぐぐぐ

Three Extracts

These passages are all interpolations made by Trevisa in his translation of Ralph Higden's *Polychronicon* (before 1364, translation 1387: see above, p. 136). The extracts are from Vol. II, 83–85, 159–161, 207; the first follows a poem on the city of Chester, the second is Trevisa's comment on Higden's statement that English children are taught French, and the third is his elucidation of a reference to the Zodiac.

(a) God woot what þis is to mene, but poetes in here manere of speche feyneth as þey euerich kynde crafte and leuynge hadde a dyuerse god, euerich from oþer; and so they feyneþ a god of bataille and of fiȝtynge, and clepeþ hym Mars; also þey feyneþ a god of couetise of richesse and marchaundise, and clepeþ hym Mercurius; and so Bacchus þei clepeþ god   5
of wyn; Venus, god of fairnesse and of loue; Lauerna, god of þefte and of robberie; Proteus, god of falshede and of gyle; and Pluto, god of helle. And so hit semeþ þat þis vers wolde mene þat þese feyned goddes regneþ and beeþ iserued in Chestre; Mars wiþ fiȝting and cokkynge; Mercurius wiþ couetise of richesse and of marchandyse; Bacchus wiþ grete drinkynge;   10
Venus wiþ loue nouȝt ful wys; Lauerna wiþ þefte and robberye; Proteus wiþ falshede and gyle. Þan is Pluto not vnserued, god of helle.

(b) Þis manere was moche ivsed to for firste deth [*var.* to fore þe firste moreyn] and is siþþe sumdel ichaunged; for John Cornwaile, a maister of grammer, chaunged þe lore in gramer scole and construccioun of Frensche   15
in to Englische; and Richard Pencriche lerned þe manere techynge of hym and [*var.* and of] oþere men of Pencrich; so þat now, þe ȝere of oure Lorde a þowsand þre hundred and foure score and fyue, and of þe secounde kyng Richard after þe conquest nyne, in alle þe gramere scoles of Engelond, children leueþ Frensche and construeþ and lerneþ an Englische, and haueþ   20
þerby auauntage in oon side and disauauntage in anoþer side: here auauntage

199

is þat þey lerneþ her gramer in lasse tyme þan children were iwoned to doo; disauauntage is þat now children of gramer scole conneþ na more Frensche þan can hir lift heele, and þat is harme for hem and þey schulle
25 passe þe see and trauaille in straunge landes and in many oþer places. Also gentil men haueþ now moche ileft for to teche here children Frensche.

(c) Here take hed þat þe cercle þat þe sonne holdeþ his cours ynne by the ȝere is ideled in twelue parties, and eueriche partie þerof is icleped a signe, and euerich signe haþ his owne name. Þese beeþ þe names of þe signes:
30 þe Wether, þe Boole, þe Twynnes, þe Crabbe, þe Leon, þe Mayde, þe Balaunce, þe Scorpion, þe Archer, þe Goot, þe Sceen [*read* Scenc], þe Fisshe. Also twelue monþes ben in þe ȝere, and eueriche monþe þe sonne entreþ in to a signe, as it falleþ for þe monþe. And so in Marche þey entreþ into þe Weþer; in Averel in to the Boole; in May in to þe Twynnes; in
35 Juyn into þe Crabbe; and so forþ arewe by monþes and signes, so þat in Decembre þe sonne is in þe Goot. Þanne Marcianus wil mene whan he seiþ þat þe Goot makeþ somer to Antipodes, þat whanne þe sonne is in þe Goot þan hit is somer wiþ hem. But in Decembre it is mydwynter monþe; and whanne he seiþ þat þe Crabbe makeþ hem wynter, he meneþ þat
40 whanne þe sonne is in þe Crabbe þan it is wynter wiþ ham, þat is in Juyn, þat is mydsomer monþe: and so hit is iclared what it is to mene, 'þe Goot makeþ hem somer, and þe Crabbe wynter.'

Translation

(a) God knows what this means, but poets in their way of speaking pretend that every kind of skill and way of life [? belief] has a god, each different from the other. Thus they invent a god of battle and fighting, and call him Mars; also, they invent a god of greed for riches and trade, and call him Mercury; they call the god of wine Bacchus, the god of beauty and love Venus, the god of theft and robbery Laverna, the god of falsehood and trickery Proteus, and the god of hell Pluto. And so it seems that this verse intends to say that these fictitious gods reign and are honored in Chester, Mars by their brawling and cockfighting, Mercury by their greed for riches and trade, Bacchus by their great drinking, Venus by foolish love, Laverna by their thieving and robbery, and Proteus by their falsehood and trickery. In this case, Pluto, the god of hell, does not go without service, either.

(b) This practice was in general use before the first plague, and has since been somewhat altered. For John Cornwall, a doctor of grammar, changed

the teaching in grammar school, and substituted English composition for
French; Richard Penkridge and other men of Penkridge learned this
method of teaching from him, so that now, A.D. 1385, the ninth year of
the reign of King Richard II [*lit.* the second Richard since the Conquest],
children in all the grammar schools throughout England abandon French
and compose and learn in English. In this they have on the one hand an
advantage, and on the other a disadvantage: the advantage is that they
learn their grammar in less time than children used to do; the disadvantage
is that nowadays children at grammar school know no more French than
their left heel, which is to their disadvantage if they are to go abroad and
travel in foreign countries and other places. Also, noblemen have to a
great extent given up teaching their children French.

(c) At this point, note that the circle in which the sun holds its annual
course is divided into twelve parts; each part of it is called a "sign," and
each sign has its own name. These are the names of the signs: the Ram,
the Bull, the Twins, the Crab, the Lion, the Virgin, the Scales, the Scorpion,
the Archer, the Goat, the Water-pourer, the Fishes [Trevisa may intend
the singular 'Fish']. Also there are twelve months in the year, and every
month the sun enters into a sign appropriate to the month. Thus in March
they [? it] enter(s) into the Ram, in April into the Bull, in May into the
Twins, in June into the Crab, and so on in order, by months and signs, so
that in December the sun is in the Goat. Thus, when Marcianus says that
the Goat brings summer to the Antipodes, he must mean that when the
sun is in the Goat, then it is summer with them. But December is the mid-
winter month, and when he says that the Crab brings them winter, he
means that when the sun is in the Crab, then it is winter with them — i.e.,
in June, the month of midsummer. Thus the meaning is clarified of the
statement, "the Goat brings their summer, the Crab their winter."

NOTES

2   *euerich kynde crafte:* see XXVIII, 8–9 *n.*
      leuynge: leue is a common form of the verb *live* in ME, but it can also
      be from OE *ge-līefan*, non-WS *-lēfan* 'believe.'
22   *iwoned:* 'accustomed,' the ancestor of *wont* XXXII, 8.
24   *and:* commonly for 'if' in ME.
25   *trauaille:* here with the MnE sense 'travel' rather than 'work.'
30ff.   MnE would use the Latin names for the signs of the Zodiac: Aries,
      Taurus, Gemini, Cancer, Leo, Virgo, Libra, Scorpio, Sagittarius,
      Capricorn, Aquarius, Pisces.

XXX

THE BRUT

Two Passages Concerning Henry V

These two passages are given together because they share the same subject matter, and because they both derive from the fifteenth century chronicle of England known as *The Brut*. However, the first may have been written considerably later than the second. The second is found in the 1419 continuation of the Chronicle, the first in a version that extends to 1475. On the other hand, the account of Henry V's rejection of his former companions may have been written much earlier than the chronicle text in which it is preserved. The pieces are taken from *The Brut or the Chronicles of England*, ed. F. W. D. Brie, Part II, EETS o.s. 136 (1908), 593–595, 374–375. The passages describe events central to two Shakespeare plays, *Henry IV Part 2*, IV, v, V, iv, and *Henry V*, I, ii.

(a)   Henry rejects his former companions

Aftyr the dethe of Kyng Herry the Fourthe, regnyd his sone Herry of
Monmothe, whiche was born at Monmothe in Walyes, whiche was Herry
the Fyfte aftyr þe conquest. And he began to regne on þe xxi^{ti} day of
Marche, in þe yer of our lorde M CCCC xii; and in þe same yer he was crownyd
5 Kyng of Englond at Westmenster on the nynthe day of Aprill, and he was
a worthy kyng, and a gracious man, and a worthy conquerour. And before
he was kyng, what tyme he regnyd Prince of Walyes, he fylle and yntendyd
gretly to ryot, and drew to wylde company, and dyuers jentylmen and
jentylwommen folwyd his wylle and his desire at his commaundment,
10 and lykewyse all his meyne of his housolde was attendyng and plesyed with
his gouernaunce, outsept iii men of his howsolde, whiche were ful hevy and
sory of his gouernaunce, and they counseylyd hym euer contrary, and
fayne woolde an had hym to doon wele and forsake ryot. And þerfor he
hatyd them iii most of al men in his house, vnto þe tyme þat his fadyr
15 was dede. And thanne he beganne to regne for kyng, and he remembryd
þe gret charge and wourship þat he shulde take vpon hym.

And anon he comaundyd al his peple þat were attendaunt to his
mysgouernaunce afore tyme, and al his housolde, to come before hym.
And whan they herde þat, they were ful glad, for they subposyd þat he
woolde a promotyd them into gret offices, and þat they shulde a stonde 20
in gret favyr and truste with hym, and neerest of counsel, as they were
afore tyme. And trustyng herevpon, they were þe homlyer and bolder
vnto hym, and nothyng dred hym, ynsomoche þat whan they were come
before hym, some of them wynkyd on hym, and some smylyd, and thus
they made nyse semblaunte vnto hym, meny one of them. But for al þat, 25
þe Prynce kept his countynaunce ful sadly vnto them, and sayde to them:
'Syrys, ye are þe peple þat I haue cherysyd and mayntynyd in ryot and
wylde gouernaunce, and here I geue yow all in commaundment, and
charge yow, þat from this day forward þat ye forsake al mysgouernaunce,
and lyve aftyr þe lawys of Almyhety God and aftyr þe lawys of oure 30
londe. And who þat doyth contrarye, I make feythful promys to God, þat
he shal be trewly ponisid accordyng to þe lawe, withoute eny favour or
grace.' And chargyd them, on payn of deth, þat they shulde neuer geve
hym comforte nor counsel to falle to ryot no more, for he had takyn a
charge on hym þat alle his wittis and power were to lytyl, withoute þe 35
helpe of God and good gouernaunce.

And so he rewardyd them richely with gold and syluer and othyr juelys,
and chargyd them alle to voyde his housolde and lyve as good men and
neuer more to come in his presence, because he woold haue noon occasioun
nor remembraunce wherby he shulde falle to ryot ayen. And thus he 40
voydyd al his housolde, savyng tho iii personys þat he hatyd most, whiche
were ful sory of his gouernaunce, and them he lovyd aftyrward best, for
þere good counsayle and good gouernaunce, and made them aftyrward
gret lordys. And thus was lefte in his housolde nomo but tho iii men.
And menyone of them þat were eydyng and consentyng to his wyldnes 45
fyl aftyrward to gret myschefe and sorw.

(b)　　Henry V and the Dauphin

And þe ii yere of King Harryeʒ regne þe vᵗʰᵉ, he hilde a counsel of alle
þe lordeʒ of the Reme at Westmynstre; and þere he put ham þe demaunde,
and prayed hem of hir godenesse and of her gode counsel to schewe hym,
as touchynge þe titile and ryʒt þat he hadde to Normandy, Gasquoyne 50
and Guyenne, þe which þe King of Fraunce withhilde hym wrongefully
and vnriʒtfully, þe whiche his auncetreʒ before hym hadde holde be trewe
titill of conquest and riʒt heritage. The which Normandye, Gasquoyne
and Guyenne, þe gode King Edward of Wyndesore and his ansetryeʒ

55 before hym hadde holde alle hir lyveȝ tyme. And his lordeȝ ȝaf hym
counsel to sende ambassetours vnto þe King of Fraunce and his counsel,
þat he schulde yelde vp to hym his riȝt heritage, þat is to say, Normandie,
Gasqueyne and Guyenne, þe which his predecessoris had yholde afore
hym, or ellis he wolde it wynne with dunt of swyrde yn schort tyme,
60 with help of Jhesu.

And þanne þe Dolfynne of Fraunce answeryd to our ambassetours and
sayde yn þis manere: þat þe King was ouyr yonge and tendir of age to
make eny warre ayens hym, and was not like yette to be no gede warryor
to make such a conqueste þere vpon hym; and yn scorne and despite he
65 sent to hym a tonne fulle of teneys-ballis, because he schulde haue sumwhat
to play withalle, for hym and for his lordeȝ, and 'þat become hym bettir
þanne to mantayne eny warre', he sayd. And þanne our lordeȝ, þat were
ambassetours, tokyn hir leue and comyn ynto Engelond ayen, and tolde
þe Kinge and his Counsel of the vngodely answere þat þay hadde of the
70 Dolfyn, and of þe present þat he hadde sent vnto the Kinge. And whanne
þe King hadde herde here wordeȝ and the answere of the Dolfyne, he was
wondir sore agrevyd and ryȝt evil payed towarde the Frenschmen and
towarde þe King and þe Dolfyn, and þouȝt to venge hym apon hem as
sone as God wolde sende hym grace and myght. And anon lette make
75 tenys-ballis for the Dolfyn in alle þe haste þat þay myȝte be maad, and
þat þei were harde and grete gune-stonys for þe Dolfyn to play withalle.

(a)   Translation

After the death of King Henry IV, his son Henry of Monmouth reigned;
he was born at Monmouth in Wales and was the fifth King Henry after
the Conquest. His reign began 21 March A.D. 1412, and on 9 April of the
same year he was crowned King of England at Westminster: he was a
fine king, a gracious man, and a worthy conqueror. Before he became
king, during the time he was Prince of Wales, he was greatly inclined and
prone to riotous living, and associated with wild companions: various
gentlemen and noble women fell in with his wishes and desires at his bidding. Similarly, the whole company of his household supported and delighted in his behavior, except for three men of his household who were
very sad and upset at his behavior; they were always advising him to
change his ways, and would have been glad for him to abandon loose living
and to live well. For this reason he hated these three men more than any
others in his household, until his father died. At this moment he began to
reign as king: he remembered the great responsibility and honor that he
was about to undertake.

Immediately he ordered all those who had before complied with his misbehavior and all his household to come before him. When they heard this, they were delighted, imagining that he would promote them to high offices, and that they would stand in great favor and trust with him, and be his closest advisers, as they had been before. Believing this, they were all the more familiar and bold towards him, and showed him no respect, in that when they came before him some of them winked at him, some smiled, and many of them in this way behaved foolishly towards him. But for all that, the Prince preserved a dignified look towards them, and said: 'Sirs, you are the people that I have looked after and kept in riotous living and wild behavior. I here command you all, and charge you, that from this day forth you must give up all loose living, and live according to the laws of almighty God and the laws of our land. If anyone acts contrary to this, I promise God faithfully, that he will be duly punished according to the law without any favor or indulgence.' He charged them on pain of death never to offer him consolation or to suggest to him that he should again slip back into riotous living, for he had undertaken a responsibility for which all his wits and power were inadequate without the help of God and his own good behavior.

Therefore, he rewarded them generously with gold, silver and jewels, and told them all to leave his household and to live as good men; they were never to enter his presence again, for he did not wish ever to have a reason or a reminder through which he might slip back again into his riotous living. Thus he emptied all his household except for those three men whom he had hated most, the ones who had been upset at his behavior; afterwards, he loved them best of all, because of their good advice and proper behavior, and he made them great lords. Thus there was left in his household no one besides those three men. Many of those who had aided and abetted his wild living afterwards came to great misfortune and unhappiness.

(b)   Translation

In the second year of the reign of King Henry V, he held a parliament of all the Lords of the Realm at Westminster; there he put this question to them, asking them out of their goodness and wise counsel to explain to him about the title and claim that he had to Normandy, Gascony, and Guyen, which the King of France wrongly and unjustly withheld from him, and which his ancestors before him had held by true title of conquest and due inheritance. Normandy, Gascony, and Guyen had been held by the good King Edward of Windsor and his ancestors before him all their lives. The Lords advised him to send ambassadors to the King of France and his parliament, to tell him that he should surrender to Henry his rightful inheritance, namely Normandy, Gascony, and Guyen, which his predecessors had held before him, or else he would take it by sword in a short time, with Christ's help.

Then the Dauphin of France replied to our ambassadors, answering in this way, that the king was too young and tender in years to make any war against him; he was unlikely at the moment to be a good enough soldier to effect such a conquest there at his expense. Scornfully and insultingly he sent the king a barrel full of tennis balls for himself and his lords, so that he should have something to play with — that, he said, was more suitable for him than trying to prosecute any war. Then our lords, the ambassadors, took their leave and returned to England; they told the king and his parliament of the disgusting answer they had had from the Dauphin and of the present he had sent the king. When the king had heard their words and the Dauphin's reply he was terribly angry and furious at the French and the King and Dauphin, and decided to avenge himself on them as soon as God sent him grace and power. Immediately he had tennis balls made for the Dauphin, as quickly as they could be made — they were big and solid cannonballs, for the Dauphin to play with.

NOTES

11   *outsept:* in this hybrid word, the prefix of *except* has been translated into English; sometimes the whole word is translated as *outtake(n).* The origin of preposition *except* is in Latin ablative absolute constructions: *excepto Caesare* 'Caesar having been excepted > except Caesar.'

13   *woolde an had:* literally 'would have had' — the reduced form of *have* as *a* or *an* is seen below in *woolde a promotyd, shulde a stonde.* In all these cases "correct" MnE would use the present infinitive (as in the translations) rather than the past.

25–26   Note the ME contrast between *nyse* 'foolish' and *sadly* 'soberly.'

41   *savyng:* this preposition, from OF *sauf,* was given an English present participle ending.

45   *were eydyng and consentyng:* the sense of the participles here is still partially adjectival, but the development of the *be* + *-iṅg* continuous action is easily observed.

50   *as touchynge:* a French idiom.

59   *with dunt of swyrde:* here the literal sense of OE *dynt* 'blow', (compare

MnE *dent* from the same OE word) is preserved, but it can be seen from here how the phrase *by dint of* acquired its transferred sense.

75–76   *and þat þei were . . .:* a loosely attached noun clause after *lette* — understand 'and told them to make them in such a way that . . .'

XXXI

PECOCK

ଗଡଗଡଗଡଗଡଗ

Writing in the Vernacular

Reginald Pecock wrote his theological tract, the *Reule of Crysten Religioun*, in 1443; this passage is from the edition by W. C. Greet, EETS o.s. 171 (1927), 17–18.

If eny man wole aske and wite whi þis present book and þe bookis to hym perteynyng y make in þe commoun peplis langage, herto y answere þat þis present book, and alle oþere bookis to him longing maad in þe comoun peplis langage, ben so maad principali forto adaunte, rebuke, drive doun
5 and conuerte þe fonnednes and þe presumpcioun of ii soortis of peple. Oon is of hem whiche holden hem silf so stifly and so singulerly, foolili and oonli to þe vce of þe bible in her modiris langage, and namely to þerof þe newe testament, þat þei trowen, seien and holden boþe pryueli and as fer openly as þey daren, alle oþere bookis writun or in latyn or in þe
10 comoun peplis langage to be writun into waast, and not oonly into waaste but into marryng and cumbring of cristen mennes wittis fro þe sufficient and necessarie leernyng which þei myȝten and ouȝten haue bi studie aloone in þe bible or oonly in þerof þe new testament; and so al bisynes which men don forto haunte scolis and forto leerne or to teche bi writing, in eny
15 oþer maner þan bi redyng and studiyng in þe bible, þei holden remelyng aside fro þe riȝt wey and a deceit into which men ben led bi þe feend. For þei seien þus, þat what euer man or woman wole be meke in spirit and wole preie god helpe him, schal wiþoute faile vndirstonde ech partie of holy scripture, namelich of þe newe testament, and þat treuly and verily
25 in þe dewe vndirstonding, as weel þorouȝ out al þe apocalips as eny oþer party of þe newe testament, and þe meker þat þe reder be to god, þe sooner he schal come to þe seid trewe and dew vndirstonding where euer he schal rede in þe newe testament.
An oþer soort is of hem which ouer and bisidis and wiþ the reding and
30 studiyng in þe bible, and namelich in þe newe testament translatid into

her modiris langage, þei admitten, receyuen and allowen þe reding, studiyng
and vse of oþere bookis had in her modiris langage; but þei apprisen so
myche þo vnsauery bokis whiche þei han in her modiris langage among
hem in vse wiþ þe vce of þe bible in her modiris langage, þat þei trowen
and holden and seien, as fer as þei dare for drede of her prelatis, þat þo   35
now seid bookis had among hym in her modiris langage bisidis þe bible,
ben noble and worþi and profitable bookis to alle cristen mennes leernyng
and rewling, and ben as riche jewelis to be derþeworþly biclippid, loued
and multiplied abrood of alle cristen peple.

Translation

If anyone wishes to ask and find out why I am writing this present book
and the books associated with it in the vernacular, my answer is as follows:
this present book and all the other books which belong to it written in the
vernacular are written in this way mainly in order to quell, rebuke, sup-
press, and convert the foolishness and presumption of two kinds of people.
First, those who restrict themselves in such a rigid and uniform way so
foolishly and uniquely to the use of the Bible in the vernacular, and particularly to its New Testament — [so much so] that they believe, say and
consider both privately and as openly as they dare, that all other books
written either in Latin or in the vernacular are written in vain — and not
only in vain, but to the detriment and confusion of the minds of Christians,
[keeping them] from the sufficient and necessary learning which they could
have and ought to have by studying only in the Bible, or only in its New
Testament. Therefore all the trouble which men take to attend universities
and to learn or teach by writing in any other way than by reading and
studying in the Bible, — all this they consider to be wandering aside from
the true way, a deception into which men are led by the Devil. For they
say that any man or woman who will be humble in spirit and pray for
God's help will not fail to understand every part of the Holy Scripture,
particularly the New Testament, truly and accurately with a proper understanding, throughout the whole of the Book of Revelations as well as any
other part of the New Testament: the humbler the reader is before God,
the sooner he will come to this true and proper understanding, wherever
he reads in the New Testament.

The second kind is those who, over and above and in addition to the
reading and studying in the Bible (particularly the New Testament translated into the vernacular), also accept, admit and allow the reading, studying and use of other books translated into English. So highly do they value
these distasteful books in English which they keep in addition to [or for]

the use of the Bible, that they believe, consider and say (as much as they dare for fear of their bishops) that these said vernacular books, which they have in addition to the Bible, are fine, worthy, and profitable books for the learning and guidance of all Christians, and that they are like fine jewels, to be honorably embraced and loved, and to be spread everywhere by all Christians.

NOTES

The "heaviness" of Pecock's style consists partly in the length and complexity of the sentences, and partly in the frequent repetitions, e.g., *adaunte, rebuke, drive doun and conuerte.*

  5 *ii soortis of peple:* the development of the word *sort* should be compared with that of *kind* — see XXVIII, 8-9 *n.*, and compare also *manner.*

  7 *her modiris langage:* compare Caxton, XXXIV, 74-75, *maternal tongue.*

7-8 *to þerof þe newe testament:* 'to its New Testament.' In this passage Pecock uses *þerof* several times as a substitute for the genitive singular of *it:* compare I, 15 *n.*

 15 *remelyng:* for the MnE form *rambling*, compare XXIV, 20 *n.*

XXXII

PASTON LETTERS

ᏽᏽᏽᏽᏽᏽᏽᏽᏽᏽᏽᏽᏽᏽ

Margaret Paston to her husband John (19 May 1448)

This text is from the famous collection of "Paston Letters" written to and by the Norfolk family of Paston during the fifteenth century. [Norman Davis, *Paston Letters* (Oxford: Clarendon Press 1958), pp. 7–9.]

Ryght worshipfull husbond, I recomaund me to yow, and prey yow to wete that on Friday last passed before noon, the parson of Oxened beyng at messe in oure parossh chirche, evyn atte levacion of the sakeryng, Jamys Gloys hadde ben in the toune and come homward by Wymondams gate. And Wymondam stod in his gate, and John Norwode his man stod   5
by hym, and Thomas Hawys his othir man stod in the strete by the canell side. And Jamys Gloys come wyth his hatte on his hede betwen bothe his men, as he was wont of custome to do. And whanne Gloys was ayenst Wymondham, he seid thus: 'Covere thy heed!' And Gloys seid ageyn, 'So I shall for the.' And whanne Gloys was forther passed by the space of iii   10
or iiii strede, Wymondham drew owt his dagger and seid, 'Shalt thow so, knave?' And therwith Gloys turned hym, and drewe owt his dagger and defendet hym, fleyng into my moderis place; and Wymondham and his man Hawys kest stonys and dreve Gloys into my moderis place, and Hawys folwyd into my moderis place and kest a ston as meche as a forthyng lof   15
into the halle after Gloys, and than ran owt of the place ageyn. And Gloys folwyd owt and stod wythowt the gate, and thanne Wymondham called Gloys thef and seid he shuld dye, and Gloys seid he lyed and called hym charl, and bad hym come hym self or ell the best man he hadde, and Gloys wold answere hym on for on. And thanne Haweys ran into Wymondhams   20
place and feched a spere and a swerd, and toke his maister his swerd. And wyth the noise of this asaut and affray my modir and I come owt of the chirche from the sakeryng, and I bad Gloys go into my moderis place ageyn, and so he dede. And thanne Wymondham called my moder and me strong hores, and seid the Pastons and alle her kyn were [. . . *hole in paper:*   25

211

room for about ten letters] seid he lyed, knave and charl as he was. And he had meche large langage, as ye shall knowe herafter by mowthe.

After non my modir and I yede to the priour of Norwich and told hym al this cas, and the prioure sent for Wymondham, and therwhyle we yede
30 hom ageyn, and Pagrave come wyth us hom. And whil Wymondham was wyth the prioure, and we were at hom in oure places, Gloys stod in the strete at my moderis gate, and Hawys aspyed hym there as he stod on the Lady Hastyngis chambre. Anon he come doun wyth a tohand swerd and assauted ageyn the seid Gloys and Thomas my moderis man, and lete flye
35 a strok at Thomas wyth the sword and rippled his hand wyth his sword. And as for the latter assaut, the parson of Oxened sygh it and wole avowe it. And moche more thyng was do, as Gloys can telle yow by mouthe.

And for the perilx of that myght happe by these premysses and the circumstances therof to be eschewed, by th'advyse of my modir and other
40 I send yow Gloys to attend upon yow for a seson for ease of myn owen hert, for in good feyth I wolde not for xl *li*. have suyche another trouble . . .

The Lord Moleyns man gaderyth up the rent at Gresham a gret pace, and Jamys Gresham shall telle yow more pleynly therof at his comyng.

No more at this tyme, but Almyghty God have yow in his kepyng.
45 Wretyn in hast on Trynyte Sunday at evyn.

Yours, MARGARETE PASTON

Qwhan Wymdham seyd that Jamys xuld dy, I seyd to hym that I soposyd that he xuld repent hym if he schlow hym or dede to hym any bodyly harm; and he seyd nay, he xuld never repent hym ner have a ferdyng wurth of harm thow he kelyd yow and hym bothe. And I seyd yys, and he sclow
50 the lest chylde that longyth to yowr kechyn, and if he dede, he were lyke, I sopose, to dy for hym. It is told me that he xall kom to London in hast. I pray yow be ware hw ye walkyn if he be there, for he is ful cursyd hertyd and lwmysch. I wot wel he wyl not set upon yow manly, but I beleve he wyl styrt upon yow or on sum of yowr men leke a thef.

Translation

My dear husband, I commend myself to you. I want you to know that last Friday before noon, when the parson of Oxned was at Mass in our parish church, at the very moment of the elevation of the Host, James Gloys, who had been in town, was coming home past Wyndham's gate. Wyndham was standing in his gateway with his man John Norwood at his side, and his other man, Thomas Hawes, was standing in the street by the gutter. James

Gloys came along with his hat on his head between both his men, as was his usual habit. When Gloys was opposite Wyndham, Wyndham said, 'Cover your head!' Gloys retorted, 'I'll do so for you!' When Gloys had gone three or four strides further on, Wyndham drew his dagger and said, 'Will you indeed?' At this Gloys turned round, drew out his dagger and defended himself, fleeing into my mother's place. Wyndham and his man Hawes threw stones and drove Gloys into my mother's house; Hawes followed after him into my mother's and threw a stone as big as a farthing-loaf at Gloys, and then ran out of the place again. Gloys followed him out and stood outside the gate, and then Wyndham called Gloys a thief and said he'd die; Gloys said he was lying, and called him scum; he told him to come himself, or else the best man he had, and Gloys would give him an answer, one against one. Then Hawes ran into Wyndham's house and fetched a spear and a sword, and gave his master his sword. At the noise of this attack and uproar my mother and I came out of the church from the sacrament, and I told Gloys to go back into my mother's place, and he did so. And then Wyndham called my mother and me raging whores, and said the Pastons and all their kin were [. . . *words missing*], said he was a liar, fool and scum that he was. The language he used was very broad, as you'll hear later by word of mouth.

After noon my mother and I went to the Prior of Norwich and told him the whole affair; the Prior sent for Wyndham, and meanwhile we went back home, and Pagrave came home with us. While Wyndham was with the Prior, and we were at home at our places, Gloys was standing in the street at my mother's gateway, and Hawes spotted him from where he was standing in Lady Hastings' room. Immediately he came down with a two-handled sword and again attacked the said Gloys and my mother's man Thomas, and let fly a blow at Thomas, and tore his hand with his sword. As for the second attack, it was seen by the parson of Oxned who will testify to it. And a lot more happened, as Gloys can tell you by word of mouth.

Now because of the need to avoid the dangers that might happen as a result of these affairs I have mentioned and these circumstances, on the advice of my mother and other people I am sending Gloys to be at your side for a while, in order to put my mind at ease, for in all honesty I wouldn't have such another disturbance happen for forty pounds.

Lord Molyn's men are collecting the rent at Gresham at a great pace, and James Gresham will tell you about it more clearly when he arrives. No more for the present, but may almighty God keep you safe. Written in a hurry, evening, Trinity Sunday,

Yours, MARGARET PASTON

P.S. When Wyndham said James was going to die, I told him that if he killed him or did him any bodily harm, it was my opinion that he would have cause to regret it; he said he'd never regret it, nor would he suffer a farthing's worth of damage even if he killed both you and James. I said he certainly would, if he killed the most lowly child of your kitchen — if he did, in my opinion he was likely to die for it. I have heard that he is planning to come to London without delay: please be careful how you walk if he's there, for he's very evil-hearted and malicious. I know he won't set on you like a man — I think he'll surprise you or one of your men like a thief.

NOTES

12   *knave*: MnE is surprisingly deficient in nouns which can be used alone, in the vocative, as terms of abuse. The MnE tendency is to reinforce them, first by the addition of the pronoun *you*, and usually by some additional abusive adjective or present participle.

13   *my moderis place:* this use of *place* to mean 'home' is still current in MnE, which also abbreviates such phrases even further to 'my mother's,' etc.

21   *toke:* the common ME sense of *take*, 'give', ambiguous at least to modern readers, probably comes from *betake*, OE *bitæcan*.

27   *large:* for the semantics, compare also *broad*, e.g., Chaucer *Canterbury Tales* A 739 'Crist spak hymself ful brode in hooly writ.'

38   *And for the perilx* . . .: Professor Davis remarks on the legalistic language of this sentence.

47   The postscript is written in a different hand from that of the main letter (written, of course, by a scribe, not by Margaret Paston herself).

XXXIII

A COURTESY BOOK

ઉજ્ઉજ્ઉજ્ઉજ્ઉજ્ઉજ્ઉજ્ઉજ્ઉજ્ઉજ્ઉજ્ઉજ્ઉજ્ઉજ્

Instructions

Midfifteenth century. Taken from *A Fifteenth-Century Courtesy Book*, ed. R. W. Chambers, EETS o.s. 148 (1914), 11.

The marshall in the mornyng ought to come into þe hall and se þat it be clene of all maner thyng þat may be fond vnhoneste þer-in: þe stolis, trestelles, or elles formys, yef ony be, þat þey be set in ther owne places at melis at þe bordes, and afore and aftur melis in corners farthest from encombraunce; and all þe hallynges and costers dressed in þer kynde 5
places and shaken or betyn wyth roddes yef nede be; and þat none houndes be abydyng in þe halle from morne to evyn. And to parforme þese thynges seyd afore he shall charge þe vsshere and þe grome of the hall þer wyth.

Also in wynter tyme þe seyd grome by þe ouersight of þe vssher shall bryng into þe hall as moche wode and colis as shall be spent dayle in the 10
hall, and bere oute þe ashes and all oþer fylthe of þe hall. The seyd grome shall also kepe þe kay of þe woode and cole, and delyuer it oute dayle by taill to þe kechyn, halle and leuereys, and bryng the seyd taill to þe sty-warde at þe wokes ende; þe seyd grome shall also contenually be in þe halle at þe firste mete or souper to bere away dysshes and kepe oute houndes 15
and feche sawces, and to obey all oþer commondmentes of þe hede offycers, þat is to sey, of stywarde, marshall and vssher.

Also halfe an oure or þe lorde go to mete or souper þe marshall shall take þe rodde in his hande and commonde þe panter and ewer to couer and make redy for þe lorde and for þe housold; and assone as it is made 20
redy, þe marshall shall commond the sewer to awayte when þe cokes be redye; and þen shall þe sewer go to þe ewry and take a towell vppon his shulder, and þe marshall and he to go togeder and shewe afore the lorde, so þat he may knowe þer-by when his mete is redy.

215

Translation

In the morning the marshall should come into the hall, and make sure that anything he finds offensive in it is cleaned away; the chairs, trestles or benches (if there are any) should be put in their proper places — at the tables at mealtimes, and before and after meals in the corners as far out of the way as possible; all the hangings and tapestries should be arranged in their appropriate places, and shaken or beaten with sticks if necessary; no dogs should be allowed to stay in the hall from morning till evening. The carrying out of all these duties should be made the responsibility of the usher and the hallboy.

In the wintertime this hallboy, under the supervision of the usher, should bring into the hall as much wood and coal as is consumed in the hall during the day, and take out of the hall the ashes and all the other dirt. This boy must also keep the key to the wood and coal; every day he must bring it [? wood and coal] out to the kitchen, the hall and the livery servants, keeping a reckoning, and at the weekend he should bring this reckoning to the steward. This boy should also remain in the hall the whole time at the first meal or at supper, in order to carry out the dishes, keep out dogs, fetch sauces and obey all the other orders of the chief servants, i.e., the steward, the marshall, and the usher.

Also, half an hour before the lord goes to his meal or to supper, the marshall should take the rod in his hand, and tell the pantryboy and ewerer [servant who brought the water for washing] to lay the table and make it ready for the lord and the household. As soon as the table is prepared, the marshall should tell the waiter to see when the cooks are ready; then the waiter should go to the ewery [recess where the water pitchers, etc., were kept], take a towel on his shoulder, and together with the marshall go and stand in front of the lord, so the lord will know by this when his meal is ready.

NOTES

13 *leuereys:* servants in general. The word ultimately refers to the provision of clothes, etc., OF *livrée*, Medieval Latin *liberacio* 'allowance,' from which it was applied to the uniform itself, and thence to the servant who wore the uniform.

19 *ewer:* the servant who was stationed by the *ewry*, a small recess for the towels and water pitchers.

23 *to go togeder:* the infinitive is loosely joined to the list of instructions. *shewe:* the verb is both transitive and intransitive in OE and ME (as it still is in some American English and in phrases such as *show up*).

XXXIV

CAXTON

ᖇᖇᖇᖇᖇᖇᖇᖇᖇᖇ

Preface to his Edition of Malory

Sir Thomas Malory completed the books known as *Le Morte Darthur* in 1469; Caxton's printing was made in 1485. The passage is taken from E. Vinaver, *Works of Sir Thomas Malory* (London: Oxford University Press, 1954), pp. xv-xvii.

After that I had accomplysshed and fynysshed dyvers hystoryes as wel of contemplacyon as of other hystoryal and worldly actes of grete conquerours and prynces, and also certeyn bookes of ensaumples and doctryne, many noble and dyvers gentylmen of thys royame of Englond camen and de-maunded me many and oftymes wherfore that I have not do made and 5 enprynte the noble hystorye of the Saynt Greal and of the moost renomed Crysten kyng, fyrst and chyef of the thre best Crysten, and worthy, Kyng Arthur, whyche ought moost to be remembred emonge us Englysshemen tofore al other Crysten kynges.

For it is notoyrly knowen thorugh the unyversal world that there been 10 nine worthy and the best that ever were, that is to wete, thre Paynyms, thre Jewes, and thre Crysten men. As for the Paynyms, they were tofore the Incarnacyon of Cryst, whiche were named, the fyrst Hector of Troye, of whome th'ystorye is comen bothe in balade and in prose, the second Alysaunder the Grete, and the thyrd Julyus Cezar, Emperour of Rome, of 15 whome th'ystoryes ben wel knowen and had. And as for the thre Jewes whyche also were tofore th'Yncarnacyon of our Lord, of whome the fyrst was Duc Josue whyche brought the chyldren of Israhel into the londe of byheste, the second Davyd, kyng of Jerusalem, and the thyrd Judas Machabeus, of these thre the Byble reherceth al theyr noble hystoryes 20 and actes. And sythe the sayd Incarnacyon have ben thre noble Crysten men stalled and admytted thorugh the unyversal world into the nombre of the nine beste and worthy, of whome was fyrst the noble Arthur, whos noble actes I purpose to wryte in thys present book here folowyng. The second was Charlemayn, or Charles the Grete, of whome th'ystorye is 25 had in many places, bothe in Frensshe and Englysshe; and the thyrd and last was Godefray of Boloyn, of whos actes and lyf I made a book unto th'excellent prynce and kyng of noble memorye, Kyng Edward the Fourth.

The sayd noble jentylmen instantly requyred me t'emprynte th'ystorye
30 of the sayd noble kyng and conquerour Kyng Arthur and of his knyghtes, wyth th'ystorye of the Saynt Greal and of the deth and endyng of the sayd Arthur, affermyng that I ought rather t'enprynte his actes and noble feates than of Godefroye of Boloyne or ony of the other eyght, consyderyng that he was a man borne wythin this royame and kyng and emperour of
35 the same, and that there ben in Frensshe dyvers and many noble volumes of his actes, and also of his knyghtes.

To whome I answerd that dyvers men holde oppynyon that there was no suche Arthur and that alle suche bookes as been maad of hym ben but fayned and fables, bycause that somme cronycles make of hym no mencyon
40 ne remembre hym noothynge, ne of his knyghtes.

Wherto they answerd, and one in specyal sayd, that in hym that shold say or thynke that there was never suche a kyng callyd Arthur myght wel be aretted grete folye and blyndenesse, for he sayd that there were many evydences of the contrarye. Fyrst, ye may see his sepulture in the
45 monasterye of Glastyngburye; and also in Polycronycon, in the fifth book, the syxte chappytre, and in the seventh book, the twenty-thyrd chappytre, where his body was buryed, and after founden and translated into the sayd monasterye. Ye shal se also in th'ystorye of Bochas, in his book *De Casu Principum*, parte of his noble actes, and also of his falle. Also Galfrydus,
50 in his Brutysshe book, recounteth his lyf. And in dyvers places of Englond many remembraunces ben yet of hym and shall remayne perpetuelly, and also of his knyghtes: fyrst, in the abbey of Westmestre, at Saynt Edwardes shryne, remayneth the prynte of his seal in reed waxe, closed in beryll, in whych is wryton "Patricius Arthurus Britannie Gallie Germanie Dacie
55 Imperator"; item, in the castel of Dover ye may see Gauwayns skulle and Cradoks mantel; at Wynchester, the Rounde Table; in other places Launcelottes swerde and many other thynges.

Thenne, al these thynges consydered, there can no man resonably gaynsaye but there was a kyng of thys lande named Arthur. For in al places,
60 Crysten and hethen, he is reputed and taken for one of the nine worthy, and the fyrst of the thre Crysten men. And also he is more spoken of beyonde the see, moo bookes made of his noble actes, than there be in Englond, as wel in Duche, Ytalyen, Spaynysshe, and Grekysshe, as in Frensshe. And yet of record remayne in wytnesse of hym in Wales, in the
65 toune of Camelot, the grete stones and mervayllous werkys of yron lyeng under the grounde, and ryal vautes, which dyvers now lyvyng hath seen. Wherfor it is a mervayl why he is no more renomed in his owne contreye, sauf onelye it accordeth to the word of God, whyche sayth that no man is accept for a prophete in his owne contreye.

Thenne, al these thynges forsayd aledged, I coude not wel denye but 70
that there was suche a noble kyng named Arthur, and reputed one of the
nine worthy, and fyrst and chyef of the Cristen men. And many noble
volumes be made of hym and of his noble knyghtes in Frensshe, which I
have seen and redde beyonde the see, which been not had in our maternal
tongue. But in Walsshe ben many, and also in Frensshe, and somme in 75
Englysshe, but nowher nygh alle. Wherfore, suche as have late ben drawen
oute bryefly into Englysshe, I have, after the symple connynge that God
hath sente to me, under the favour and correctyon of al noble lordes and
gentylmen, enprysed to enprynte a book of the noble hystoryes of the sayd
Kynge Arthur and of certeyn of his knyghtes, after a copye unto me 80
delyverd, whyche copye Syr Thomas Malorye dyd take oute of certeyn
bookes of Frensshe and reduced it into Englysshe.

Translation

After I had finally completed several works of contemplation, as well as
other stories of historical and worldly deeds performed by great conquerors
and princes, and also certain books of moral examples and doctrine, many
various noble gentlemen of this kingdom of England came and asked me
many times for the reason why I have never had composed and printed
the noble story of the Holy Grail and of the most famous Christian King —
first and chief of the Three Best Christian Worthies, King Arthur, who
ought to be remembered most of all among us Englishmen before all other
Christian kings.

For it is a well known fact throughout the whole world that there are
Nine Worthies, the best men that ever lived, viz. three pagans, three
Jews, and three Christians. Now the pagans lived before the Incarnation
of Christ; their names were, first, Hector of Troy, whose story has come
down to us in both song and prose; second, Alexander the Great; third,
Julius Caesar, the Roman Emperor, stories of whom are well known and
readily available. The three Jews also lived before the Incarnation; the
first was the general Joshua who brought the children of Israel into the
promised land; the second was David, king of Jerusalem; the third was
Judas Macchabeus. The Bible narrates the noble histories and deeds of
all three of them. Since the Incarnation there have been three noble Christians, who have been accepted and admitted throughout the whole world
into the number of the Nine Best Worthies; the first of them was the noble
Arthur, of whose fine deeds I intend to write in this following book; the
second was Charlemagne (or, Charles the Great), whose story is available
in many places in both English and French; the third and last was Godfrey

of Bouloigne, whose life and acts I put into a book for that excellent prince, the late King Edward IV.

The said noble gentlemen urgently pressed me to print the story of this noble king and conqueror, King Arthur, and of his knights, together with the story of the Holy Grail, and the death and end of King Arthur. They maintained that I should print his acts and noble deeds in preference to those of Godfrey of Bouloigne or any of the other eight, in view of the fact that he was a man born within this kingdom, and was its king and emperor, and that in French there are several fine volumes concerning his deeds and also concerning his knights.

I replied that there are various men who believe that no such Arthur existed, and that all such books written about him are no more than fictitious fables, on the grounds that some chronicles make no mention of him, and do not record him or his knights at all.

They answered this point, and one in particular said that anyone who said or thought that there never was such a king called Arthur could well be charged with great stupidity and blindness, for he said that there were many pieces of evidence to the contrary. Firstly, you can see his tomb at Glastonbury Abbey, and also in the *Polychronicon*, Book V, ch. 6 and VII, ch. 23, [you can see] where his body was buried, and later discovered and transferred to the Abbey. Moreover, you can find part of his noble deeds and of his fall in the history of Boccaccio, the book *De casu principum* [*On the fall of princes*]. Also, Geoffrey [of Monmouth] gives an account of his life in his book on Britain [or *The Brut*]. And in several places in England there are still many memorials of him which will remain for ever, and also of his knights: first, at Westminster Abbey, in the shrine of St. Edward, there is extant the print of his seal, enclosed in beryl, on which is written "Patricius Arthurus Britannie Gallie Germanie Dacie Imperator" ['Noble Arthur, Emperor of Britain, France, Germany and Scandinavia']; also, in Dover Castle you can see Gawain's skull and Cradoc's cloak; at Winchester, the Round Table; in other places, Lancelot's sword, and lots of other things.

Therefore, in view of all these things, there is no one who can reasonably deny that there was a king of this country called Arthur. For in all places, both Christian and heathen, he is reckoned and counted as one of the Nine Worthies, and as the first of the Three Christians. Also he is more spoken of abroad, and more books are written about his noble deeds there, than in England, not only in French, but also in German, Italian, Spanish and Greek. And still in his memory there survive in Wales, at the town of Camelot, as witnesses to his existence, the huge stones and marvellous works of iron lying under the ground, and the royal vaults which many people still alive have seen. It is, therefore, remarkable that he is no longer honored in his own country — except that it is in accordance with the word of God which states that no man is accepted as a prophet in his own country.

Thus, when all these arguments had been made, I could hardly deny that there had been such a noble king called Arthur, reckoned as one of the Nine Worthies and as the first and chief of the three Christians. There are many fine volumes written about him and his noble knights in French, which I have seen and read abroad, but which are not available in our language. But there are many in Welsh and in French, and some in English (but nowhere near all). Therefore, for such material as has recently been translated briefly into English, I have undertaken, with the simple ability that God has given me, and under the favor and correction of all noble lords and gentlemen, to print a book of the noble stories of the said King Arthur and some of his knights, in accordance with a copy which I have been sent, which Sir Thomas Malory took out of certain French books and translated into English.

NOTES

5-6   *do made and enprynte:* I have translated *do* as a causative verb, but it may equally be the pleonastic, colorless *do* often used in ME and early MnE. On *do* + past participle instead of infinitive, see Mustanoja, pp. 605–606, where he gives examples from Chaucer, Gower, etc.; this particular usage is interesting in that it has both past participle and infinitive.

11   *to wete:* this survives as *to wit,* literally 'to know'; I have translated it by *viz.,* the MnE printing of *viꝫ,* an abbreviation for Latin *videlicet.*

39-40   *ne . . . noothynge:* multiple negatives are common in the best English, even in early MnE.

50   *Brutysshe:* probably 'concerning Britain,' but many ME Chronicles were known as *The Brut* because they began with the legendary founder of Britain, Brutus.

82   *it:* on the repeated pronoun, compare XXVI, 23-24 *n.*

OLD ENGLISH WORD LIST

This list includes only very common words; the meaning given is the most common or most generally useful. It does not include words whose meanings could easily be grasped by an application of the principles outlined on pp. 34-35; variant inflexional forms are not given unless the 'root' form of the word changes. The prefix *ge-* is ignored; note that *i* and *y* are interchangeable.

ac *but*
æghwilc *each, every*
ægðer *either; ... ge ... both ... and*
ælc *each*
ǣr *before*
ān *a(n), one*
āscian, āxian *ask*
bēgen *both*
bēon *be*
būton, -an *without, unless, except*
cann *know(s)*
clypian *call*
cōm(on) *came*
cuman *come*
cūðon *knew, could*
cwæð, cwǣdon *said*
cweðan *say*
dæg, dagas *day(s)*
dēð *does*
dōn *do(ne)*
dyde *did*
ēac *also*
ēalā *oh, alas, lo*
eall *all*
eart *are (pr. 2 sg.)*
eft *later, afterwards*
ēode *went*
eom *am*
ēow(re) *you(r)*
for ðām (ðon) *because, therefore*
gān *go*

gē *ye*
ge ... ge *both ... and*
geond *throughout*
gēt, gīet(a) *yet, still*
gif *if*
habban *(infin.) have*
hæfde *had*
hæfð *has*
hwā *who*
hwylc *which*
ge-hwylc *every*
hwȳ *why*
ilca *same*
ge-līc *like*
lȳtel *little*
mā(ra) *more, bigger*
mæg, magon *may, can*
meaht *may, can (pr. 2 sg.)*
meahte, mihte *could, was able*
mid *with*
mycel *much, great*
nā *never, not*
nabban *have not (see habban)*
nǣnig *not any, none*
næs *was not*
nān *no, none*
nāt *does not know (see wāt, etc.)*
ne *not; ... ne ... neither ... nor*
nis *is not*
ond *and*
ongēan *against, back*

223

oð *until*
ōðer *other, second*
oððe *or*
sægde, sǣde *said*
sāwon *saw*
sceal *must, shall*
sceolde *had to, should*
sculon *must, shall*
secgan *say*
segð *says*
sēon *see*
seah *saw*
sī(e), sȳ *pr. subj. of* bēon
sindon, sint *are*
siððan *afterwards, since*
sōðlīce *truly*
sprǣc, sprǣcon *said, spoke*
sum *some, (a) certain*
swā *so, thus, as*
swilce *likewise, as if*

swīðe *very*
twēgen *two*
þā *when, then (also = the)*
þæs *to this extent*
þās *these*
þē *thee*
þe *that (relative pron., often after a conjunction)*
þēah *though, however*
þonne *than, when, then*
þurh *through, by*
wāt *knows*
wearð *became*
wiste *knew*
witodlīce *truly, indeed*
witon *know*
wolde *was willing, would, wished*
worhte *made*
wurdon *became*
ymbe *about, after*